THE
BUSINESS
OF
BROADWAY

An Insider's Guide to Working, Producing, and Investing in the World's Greatest Theatre Community

Mitch Weiss
and Perri Gaffney

ALLWORTH PRESS
NEW YORK

792. 0293
WEI

Allworth Press books may be purchased in bulk at special discounts for sales promotion, corporate gifts, fund-raising, or educational purposes. Special editions can also be created to specifications. For details, contact the Special Sales Department, Allworth Press, 307 West 36th Street, 11th Floor, New York, NY 10018 or info@skyhorsepublishing.com.

19 18 17 16 15   5 4 3 2 1

Published by Allworth Press, an imprint of Skyhorse Publishing, Inc.
307 West 36th Street, 11th Floor, New York, NY 10018.

Allworth Press® is a registered trademark of Skyhorse Publishing, Inc.®, a Delaware corporation.

www.allworth.com

Cover design by Chris Ritchie.

Library of Congress Cataloging-in-Publication Data is available on file.

Print ISBN: 978-1-62153-465-5

Ebook ISBN: 978-1-62153-476-1

Printed in the United States of America.

TABLE OF CONTENTS

ACKNOWLEDGMENTS

Special thanks for their support and knowledge (in no particular order): Harrison Lee, Nancy Gibbs, Nina Skriloff, Marcia Goldberg, Peter Bogyo, Bob Reilly, Susan Sampliner, Richard Backer, Susan L. Schulman, George Forbes, Tina Fabrique, Nick Kaledin, all ATPAM staff, David M. Conte, Jason Laks, Darnelle Radford, Gail West, Syra and Marty Weiss, and all of the professional interviewees in Chapter 25. We would like to thank the staffs of NYC's Signature Theatre (W. 42nd St./10th Ave.), Starbucks (8th Ave./W. 43 St.), Astor Row Cafe (W. 130th St./Lenox Ave.), Lenox Saphire (W. 127th St./Lenox Ave.), and Corner Social (W. 126th St./Lenox Ave.) for their hospitality during the writing of this book. Apologies to the excellent, talented people, friends, and colleagues who contribute so much to the Broadway theatre but were not mentioned in this book.

Charts designed by Rachel W. Gozhansky: "Who's in Charge?" (Chapter 3) and investors pie chart (Chapter 10).

Photo Credits
Choclattjared by Kimneak Arnold Photography
Christopher Recker by Greg Joskin
Chuck Cooper by Deborah Brevoort
David Henry Hwang by Lia Chang Photography
Deidre Goodwin by Bran Amundson
Harrison Lee by Dorothy Shi
Karen Mason by Stephen Mosher
Mitch Weiss by Carol Rosegg
Nancy Piccione by Michele Piccione

Paul Libin by MDT Photo

Perri Gaffney by Fredric Michaels

Peter Bogyo by Nan Melville

Ron Raines by Carol Rosegg

Stephen Tyrone Williams by Courtney B. Vance

Thomas Grasso by Carmen Milagro

Tina Fabrique by James E. Alexander

Arthur French, Count Stovall, Islah Abdul-Rahim, Lawrence Darden, and Woodie King, Jr. by Perri Gaffney

Adrian Bryan-Brown, Bob Reilly, Christopher Nass, David Calhoun, Janice Rodriguez, and Richard Frankel by Mitch Weiss

INTRODUCTION: Footnotes before Footlights

Unless you already work on Broadway, there are few ways to learn how it operates. This book shares information not readily available to the general public. This information is derived from current 2014 and 2015 industry rulebooks, union websites, the authors' firsthand knowledge, Broadway professionals, and common practice. The experiential advice and opinions, unless otherwise designated, belong solely to the authors.

Spelling "theatre" vs. "theater": "Theater" is the common American spelling and "theatre" is the traditional British spelling. All Broadway houses use the British "re" ending and since this book explores Broadway theatre, that's the spelling that applies throughout this text. The only exceptions are the names of theatrical institutions, such as Joseph Papp's Public Theater in New York, that have transferred productions from their "theater" companies to a Broadway "theatre."

All salaries, fees, and expenses in this book are 2014/2015 numbers and will undoubtedly increase each year.

If the reader wishes to suggest a correction, please join our community discussion at www.JustLearnSomething.us. Each show has its own story, and union regulations change with each negotiation. The authors will be updating material on this website as well.

PART 1
WHAT MAKES BROADWAY TICK

Chapter 1
The Danger Is Thinking You Know More Than You Do

There is great danger in thinking you know more about Broadway than you do. Broadway theatre can provide one of the most exhilarating of experiences, whether you are in the audience, or one of the two hundred people who help to create each fabulous musical or riveting play.

Most of us fall in love with theatre working in our first school production. It's the teamwork, everyone working individually and collectively toward one goal, the results of which are actually attained in a short period of time and enjoyed together. It creates goodwill and camaraderie, a sense of major achievement, and a pride in self and others. In many ways, it's similar to a school sports team. No matter how depressing the team scores, or how mediocre the school production, the pride we garner in that joint accomplishment often lasts a lifetime.

The business aspects of Broadway are as impressive as the production values and technology that are unquestionably second to none. The quality and standards of a Broadway production are beyond the scope of theatre most anywhere else because the pool of talent vying for the Broadway stage has no comparison.

Yes, London, England, can boast that the West End in Piccadilly is the breeding ground for transfers to Broadway. Chicago's nonprofit Steppenwolf Theatre Company, or Seattle's Seattle Rep, or Washington DC's Kennedy Center can prove a long history of superior productions, many of which have moved to Broadway and have deservedly received Tony Awards. But only New York City's

Broadway district has forty live theatres that earn over a billion dollars annually, entertaining diverse audiences of almost 13 million people from every corner of the globe for all fifty-two weeks of the year.

This is where a playwright knows that his or her work has the best chance to reach the largest audience and receive the best production in the hands of caring and skilled talent. And this is where regional and community theatres, high schools, colleges, and touring venues will find their next production to entertain, educate, and stimulate their audiences.

Only Broadway productions have enough money behind them to sink the Titanic on stage, or fly a helicopter into Saigon, or burn down a house, or fly Spiderman and his nemesis in an aerial chase around the theatre, every night. Only Broadway can afford to bring celebrity film and television stars up close, live, and personal for an extended period of time.

Broadway remains the goal of every new play or musical. Once you've played Broadway, you are suddenly a part of theatre history. That's why thousands continue to flock to New York in the hope of being a "Broadway baby." And after film and television personalities perform on Broadway, they are regarded as serious actors.

Broadway is the Holy Grail for producers around the world. Without inhabiting an official Broadway theatre, no show can call itself a Broadway show. The Tony Award–eligible Broadway district runs north from West 40th Street to West 54th Street between Sixth and Ninth Avenues with only one exception, the Vivian Beaumont Theatre at Lincoln Center for the Performing Arts at West 66th Street. The smallest Broadway theatre has 597 seats (Helen Hayes Theatre) and the largest has 1933 (Gershwin Theatre). In past decades there were Broadway theatres with as few as five hundred seats but it is difficult to pay Broadway wages and expenses with so few seats today. Theatres in Manhattan with less than five hundred seats are considered Off Broadway (99–499 seats) or Off-Off Broadway (generally under 99 seats).

Mentoring is the backbone of the Broadway community. You can bring book-learning and the love of theatre to the job, but you will never know all you need to know about putting on a Broadway show before you study and work under someone else.

This is especially problematic for new investors who, due to success and experience in other businesses, want to contribute to a show and add the title "producer" to their credits. They may be the sole decision-maker for their own businesses, and not used to conferring with people who know as much or more than they do. It's hard to step back, listen, and follow when it's your money being spent and you are accustomed to leading.

While studying Broadway management at NYU, two adult students introduced themselves as having been Broadway producers. They explained, "This time, before investing in a second production, we would like to know what a General Manager is supposed to do." This book is written to offer an opportunity for would-be-producers and investors to learn about all of the people their money will hire, and what these people do.

The famous Harold Prince won a record twenty-one Tony Awards for *West Side Story, Company, Cabaret, Sweeney Todd*, and dozens more. The infamous David Merrick won more than ten Tony Awards for the hit musicals and plays *42nd Street, Mame, Travesties*, and *Hello, Dolly* among others. They were "lead producers," the sole decision-maker for their shows. Every producer is not a lead producer. Your producing title may not entitle you to make any decisions at all. As a producing novice, you might want to first learn from the successes and mistakes of others.

A Broadway investment is riskier than Wall Street or a Las Vegas gamble. Almost 80 percent of all Broadway shows lose every penny of their investment. Some of the other 20 percent of shows pay only a slight profit, and an even smaller percentage hit the jackpot. A major hit can pay a whopping 250 percent annual profit on its original investment for decades. No stock future or derivative can match that. But before you leap, the rule of thumb for Broadway investors is that you need to be able to lose your entire gamble without flinching, or you should not invest at all.

Most Broadway investors admit that they want to be involved in the excitement. They want to go to an opening night party, meet the stars while they are in rehearsal, brag to their friends that they are part of a hit Broadway show, and have the connections to buy "house seats" (the best seats in the theatre) at a moment's notice. That's a very expensive piece of excitement in most cases.

Some Broadway shows are produced by nonprofit theatre organizations or a combination of investors and nonprofit producers. The monster hit musical *A Chorus Line* was produced on Broadway by creator Michael Bennett and Joseph Papp's nonprofit New York Shakespeare Festival. It was funded by a single donation from the Chair of the Board, LuEsther Mertz, heir to the Reader's Digest fortune and beloved philanthropist.

Costing $500,000 to transfer from the New York Shakespeare Festival's Off Broadway Public Theater venue to Broadway's Shubert Theatre in 1975, *A Chorus Line* became Broadway's longest-running musical by 1983 and ran until

1990. At that time no show had earned as much money—hundreds of millions of dollars. The Supreme Court had recently declared that as long as the profit did not benefit anyone's personal pocketbook, but instead returned to the stated purpose of the nonprofit institution (in this case, the production of theatre, education, and the arts), profit was a glorious result of nonprofit work.

The largest loss in Broadway history began in 2010. The musical *Spider-Man: Turn Off the Dark* raised a reported $75 million to open its production on Broadway. Most of its investment was lost by the time it shuttered in early 2014. The production needed to credit more than twenty investors, including major corporations, as producers in order to fund the massive production.

Over the decades, the stakes have gotten higher and the number of investor virgins has had to increase due to the cost of producing on Broadway. Corporations like Disney and Paramount have changed the "mom and pop" nature of Broadway into a corporate world of bureaucratic committees.

Dramas, comedies, and small musicals are less costly because fewer performers are needed. Actors are not by themselves expensive, but more actors mean additional salaries and costumes to design and maintain. Smaller productions usually involve less complicated sets and lights. Fewer stagehands are needed to run and maintain these shows. Wireless microphones may not be needed for amplification in smaller theatres, and both rent and utility bills are reduced. Writers and directors are paid less up-front fees and advances. All of this has been predetermined by nineteen unions and associations, and their rules negotiated and developed over time.

While an average big musical in 2014 might cost around $12 to $16 million, an average nonmusical can cost around $3 to $6 million. Smaller costs sometimes allow lower ticket prices, but the lower prices translate into less profit potential. Nothing is easy.

An experienced general manager, the most important advisor to a lead producer, will know how to balance potential income with probable costs as determined by the artistic needs of the script.

Let's not forget that the entire project hinges on the quality and success of what has been written and/or composed. Often we read how film actors and film directors use improvisation in scenes, rewriting lines and sometimes entire scenes. A film script is often just a well-designed guidepost at best, or a vague suggestion at worst. That is almost never true on Broadway.

The script is the primary reason why a lead producer decides to raise funds. She or he believes that the script has the potential to become art and change the world, or at least make a lot of money. Hopefully both. Raising funds for a gamble like a Broadway show is very difficult. It takes major talent to be a lead producer and raise millions of dollars when there is about a 20 percent chance that the money will be returned.

New York State and its Attorney General's office regulate the raising of these funds. These laws are found nowhere else in the world. The rules are strict. The rules protect the investor, not the producer. These laws change depending on how many investors you have, and in what states or countries they reside. These laws dictate how and when funds must be paid back and the conditions under which the lead producer must also apply to the Federal government for approval. Specialized entertainment lawyers prepare the required prospectus given to every investor. It is detailed and brutal in some cases, listing the success rate of the lead producer and sharply warning against the risk.

Being a lead producer does not mean that you know what you are doing. It's about finding the script, falling in love with the script, and raising funds. It's the general manager who turns the lead producer's wishes into reality. General managers are hired for their personal contacts, knowledge of union rules, budget expertise, personality, and negotiating experience. The lead producer and general manager should feel comfortable with each other and respect each other. This does not always happen, so big problems often start here.

General managers are best friends for hire. Even an alcoholic, obnoxious lead producer can find a general manager to work with, as long as the checks don't bounce. Right or wrong, it's a tough business to make a living and every project has the potential to provide long-term employment for the general manager and many others. If the project is interesting and seemingly worthwhile, a problematic boss may have to be tolerated, like any other business.

At this point, the new show has a great script, a lead producer, an entertainment law firm, and a general manager. We are now at least six months to two years away from opening the show on Broadway and we've already paid up-front fees to the playwright, composer, and lyricist, the law firm, and general manager, perhaps exceeding $150,000. The lead producer needs deep pockets, and there's no income stream in sight at this point.

Welcome to Broadway.

Next will come a director, technical supervisor, and designers, each with up-front fees, negotiations, and contracts. Perhaps another $150,000 will be needed. Lead producers spend their own money up front, unless they can raise "front money." Investors who are willing to provide front money take a big risk by allowing the lead producer to spend their investments without waiting for full capitalization of the project. If the project never happens, front money is lost. In return, these risk-friendly investors receive extra percentages of the profit, if there are any profits (see Chapter 10: Producing and Investing).

Every show has its own story and so no one path is the same. By the end of this book, we will have strolled through the preproduction, production, opening, and postproduction stages that hopefully lead to long-running profitable shows.

It's not really a stroll. It's a high-energy sprint during which every penny of a multimillion dollar show will have been spent, most of it within an eight-week window.

Some of the invested cash will rent a theatre. Broadway theatres do not provide lights, sound, or other equipment. This is known as a four-wall deal, meaning that rent pays for nothing but the four walls. The theatre hires its own personnel: box office treasurers, house manager, ushers, doormen, porters, and security, and their salaries are charged back to the show.

Management will also use the money to hire stars, supporting cast, understudies, stage managers, a company manager, press agent, marketing and advertising companies, musical director, stage crew, wardrobe crew, photographer, and on and on. Rehearsal studios, lighting and sound equipment, costumes, props, scenery, and union bonds must also be covered. Once a marketing plan has been developed, the cost of promoting the show will eat up considerable funds as well.

The general manager and company manager are there because they know what these things are supposed to cost and keep these expenses within budget. The goal is the creation of a great show that makes everyone proud to have been a part, with ample ticket sales and profits so that the show can run for a long time and inspire investors to invest in another show.

Of course, most of the time, the show will close quickly and lose all of its investments. Hard work will go unrewarded and hundreds of jobs will be lost. But optimism lives. The next show will be "the hit."

The Broadway community forgets that few outsiders know the facts that we take for granted. So, let's cover some of the basics.

Each Broadway show presents eight performances each week and is required to have one full day off in each week. Simple, it seems, except that many regional and Off-Off Broadway theatres set their calendars around weekends only, and in entertainment cities, like Las Vegas or Branson, Missouri, shows can perform as often as twelve times per week.

Historically, many stages were built on a "rake," a slant rising upwards toward the back of the stage so that audiences could see an actor standing behind another. So "upstage" is a theatre direction meaning farthest away from the audience. "Downstage" means closest to the audience. Stage left and stage right are stage movements from the viewpoint of the actor looking at the audience, the exact opposite of how the audience would move left or right.

Broadway shows in the evening begin at 7:00 PM, 7:30 PM, or 8:00 PM. This is sometimes confusing for audiences because once upon a time, all Broadway shows began at the same hour. Today each show gambles that its target audience will be more likely to buy tickets based on show time. The audience may be comprised of young families (7:00 PM), or wish to have dinner between work and show time (8:00 PM), or prefer that lengthy shows begin earlier (7:00 or 7:30 PM) so they can get home at a decent hour. Some union employees receive extra pay if the show ends after 11:00 PM or runs longer than four hours. Since shows compete for similar audiences, the lead producer and managers will determine what time and days will best attract an audience and whether box office income will outpace extra union costs.

Traditionally, Broadway shows perform on a Tuesday through Sunday schedule with Mondays off. This schedule includes two matinees usually on Wednesdays and Saturdays. Yet there are reasons to choose other schedules.

Sundays cost more. Box office treasurers, stagehands, ushers, and musicians get a "premium" (additional pay) for performances on Sundays. Also, since fewer shows perform on Mondays, some productions prefer presenting on the less competitive Monday night. Beginning in 2014, some shows have experimented with Thursday matinees. Family shows like *The Lion King*, or *Cats*, or *Wicked* may choose to perform matinees and evenings on both Saturday and Sunday and take the less popular Wednesdays or Thursdays off entirely.

Some long-running shows change schedules by the season. New York audiences tend to go out of town on weekends during the summer and so week-day performances may be increased. Due to cold and snowy winters, January and February often suffer during the weekdays when people want to get home after work; therefore the weekend has a better chance of selling tickets. Experienced managers, theatre owners, and box office treasurers understand the many considerations that keep a show afloat. Always, there are financial and union considerations when making changes.

The Broadway community is relatively small and job opportunities are therefore small. Working on Broadway is seldom what you might expect, both in its lack of Hollywood-style glamour and its numerous unexpected surprises. The daily crises waiting for quick solutions require more than an MBA education and are unique to Broadway. Bad decisions can be costly and sometimes catastrophic. Seemingly good marketing ideas may not prevent a show from closing prematurely. There are no guarantees.

There are no financial saviors able to invent an audience if the public doesn't want to buy tickets. Even though this is the world's richest theatre family, some actors net less than $900 in their weekly paycheck after taxes and fees for agent, manager, and union dues are deducted. The Tony Awards can be either a great asset or tremendous trouble (Chapter 6: Tony Awards). Critical reviews, even when they're good, can hurt ticket sales (Chapter 9: How to Sell a Big Flop). The business of Broadway can be the total opposite of what the public and producers expect. Trouble can come from thinking you know more than you do.

Chapter 2
The Jobs

The jobs on Broadway shows are plentiful, an average of one hundred to two hundred per show, and extremely varied. This chapter is an overview of the kinds of work available on a Broadway show. Those Broadway jobs below that require union membership in order to be hired are followed by (UNION). All other jobs in this chapter are available without union membership. Chapter 4 offers additional details about the unions that govern most Broadway workers, along with the union websites that carry information about how to become a member. There are also chapters devoted to many key jobs described below. The skilled applicants looking for work on Broadway far outnumber the positions available. The competition is fierce so whatever you can bring to the job (experience, knowledge, references, etc.) that can set you apart from the others will enhance your chances for being hired.

This chapter is not meant to encourage or discourage anyone from joining the ranks of the unemployed hoping to work on Broadway. Passion, perseverance, and talent are welcome.

Most Broadway actors are a community of "triple threats." They excel in acting, singing, and dancing. The seasoned, consistently employed Broadway performers will tell you that they continue classes with super-talented teachers/coaches as often as possible because excelling in anything takes hard work.

Off stage there are even more jobs. You can always find a detailed list of the support staff for each show in the Playbill program in very small print after the bios. Colleges rarely tell you about these critical support jobs, listed below, that allow theatre lovers to be a part of the Broadway family and make a living wage behind the scenes.

An important note before we continue: Gender diversity in employment is important to many theatre people, yet it is not always the case. In terms of company managers and house managers, the ratio of men to women is about fifty/fifty. For stagehands, box office treasurers, and other key backstage positions, women represent a much smaller percentage. In positive terms, a woman who wants one of these jobs has an excellent chance of being considered across the entire community. Historically, the first team of superstar female producers hit the scene as late as the mid-1970s. Elizabeth McCann and Nelle Nugent became a major force on Broadway (*Morning's at Seven, Dracula, The Elephant Man, Amadeus*) opening doors for many female producers thereafter including but not limited to Fran Weissler (*Chicago*), Lynne Meadow (Manhattan Theatre Club's *Casa Valentino, The Tale of the Allergist's Wife*), Daryl Roth (*Proof, Kinky Boots*), Carol Shorenstein Hayes (*Fences, Doubt*) and many more.

One would think that the liberal theatre community would be ahead of the curve in hiring minorities both onstage and backstage. Not yet true. To be fair, very few older men on Broadway desire early retirement. When jobs open up, the opportunities are definitely there, especially if the applicant brings a variety of skills.

Onstage, there is still a long way to go to convince directors that color and ethnicity should not hinder casting a role. Unless specifically defined by the script, most directors still think white when casting. In the 1970s producing giant Joseph Papp and his casting director Rosemary Tichler opened doors for interracial casting of all Shakespearean plays and the theatre world was forever changed, although not in consistent fashion on Broadway. Now things are much better than they used to be and attitudes are improving.

How much can you earn working on a Broadway show? First, it is essential to understand that unlike most occupations, most theatre jobs are temporary. Shows close regularly, some prematurely, some open as limited-runs. The unions have always concerned themselves with making sure that its members can survive between employments since many of them don't work fifty-two weeks a year. The minimum salaries negotiated for some of these jobs are intended to help with the unemployed weeks between shows.

Except for six-figure theatre owners, millionaire lead producers, investors with hit shows, and celebrities in starring roles, no one should expect to make a fortune on Broadway. Based on union negotiations, salaries rise slightly each year, although they are not tied to the cost of living. More details can be found in appropriate chapters later in this book, but suffice it to say that a nonunion office administrator can earn about $450 per week with, and more often without, benefits, not much more than they did twenty years ago. A Broadway chorus singer/dancer earns $1,861 per week plus benefits. A production stage manager earns $3,058 per week plus benefits while a head carpenter can earn the same or more when overtime and extra duties are added to the minimum weekly salary of $2,321.25. The ushers, who actually do more than their titles suggest, gross about $400 to $500 per week plus benefits, and stage doorpersons earn about $700 weekly, including overtime, plus benefits. Note: these are gross figures, before deductions for taxes, union dues, agent and manager fees.

Worker benefits (healthcare, pension, annuity, vacation pay, and payroll taxes) add between 33 percent and 50 percent in costs to the payroll. Therefore a $2,000 per week union employee actually will cost the production up to $3,000 in the budget. As the new Affordable Care Act system (Obamacare) rolls out over the next few years, this cost may change but no one is budgeting with this in mind.

CREATIVE JOBS

ACTORS, SINGERS, AND DANCERS (UNION)

Without actors, New York City would have a dearth of waiters causing hundreds of restaurants to close. At any one moment, approximately 88 percent of the forty-nine thousand Actors' Equity Association (AEA) union actors are not employed in the theatre. Having a second flexible job is almost a requirement. Add the enormous number of nonunion actors living in New York without an income from theatre and you can begin to appreciate the actor's challenge. Often an actor's height, weight, hairstyle, age, skin color, ethnicity, and gender have more to do with being hired than talent. Perseverance and patience are as important as performance. New York City has the most talented pool of performers available in the world and that helps make Broadway the gold standard.

DIRECTORS AND CHOREOGRAPHERS (UNION)

The director is the force guiding all creative decisions needed to turn a script into a live staged production. Sometimes the director and choreographer are the same person, sometimes not. The Society of Directors and Choreographers (SDC) governs their minimum fees and working conditions. They receive an up-front fee, a guaranteed sum as a royalty advance, and once the show is running, a weekly royalty based on the box office income.

DESIGNERS: COSTUMES, LIGHTS, SET, SOUND (UNION), AND VIDEO

The United Scenic Artists (USA) is the union for Broadway designers. Since each design requires a different process, the minimum fees vary tremendously between art forms. In each case, the designer earns a fee, a guaranteed sum as a royalty advance, and once the show is running, a small flat weekly amount for as long as the show runs.

Many shows now employ video as part of the scenic design and so the scenic designer may collaborate with a nonunion consultant/specialist.

FIGHT DESIGNER/CHOREOGRAPHER

When a play requires a few minutes of punches, sword fighting, martial arts, wrestling, etc., the show will hire a specialist in safe, dramatic fighting to direct and rehearse the players.

MUSICAL JOBS (UNION)

Composers and general managers will consult together about whom to hire in the key positions of orchestrator, musical supervisor, and arranger based on their previous experiences, friendships, and professional recommendations. The jobs are explained below, and there is more about these positions in later chapters (see Chapter 4 and Chapter 21). In general, these jobs are extremely specialized and in some cases a bit political.

MUSICAL DIRECTORS/SUPERVISORS often perform as the show's conductor as well, and establish the feel of the music into a coherent show as conceived by the composer. She or he rehearses the musicians and vocalists. In addition, the musical director/supervisor oversees the consistency of musical interpretation for the show if and when it goes on tour.

ORCHESTRATORS turn the composer's songs into instrumental charts for the musicians to play, and the conductor to interpret.

VOCAL ARRANGERS turn the composer's songs into vocal charts for the soloists and choral performers to sing.

DANCE ARRANGERS work with the choreographer to create musical interludes for dances and musical staging.

MUSICIANS perform the music live. Their numbers vary per the show's orchestrations and budget restrictions, and are subject to union minimums for each Broadway theatre.

VOCAL CAPTAIN is not found on all shows, but is hired to keep the cast's vocals fresh and precise, especially on long-running shows.

MUSIC CONTRACTOR is the casting director for the orchestra's musicians.

SYNTHESIZER PROGRAMMER is the designer of a variety of sounds used on a digital electronic keyboard instrument; this designer can be nonunion.

SUPERVISORY JOBS

GENERAL MANAGER

The GM rises to this senior position having collected professional contacts and developed relationships with people in all departments over an extensive theatre career. She or he is the producer's right hand and advises the producer in all matters. The GM creates an accurate budget, hires the staff to "make things happen," and supervises all financial matters and expenditures including the investors' returns. The GM follows the law, working directly with attorneys, represents the producer with union issues, and makes decisions for the show based on previous experience and/or the producer's directives. The GM usually negotiates for the show's stars and key supervisors.

Unlike the company manager, the nonunionized GM is not exclusive to one producer and often works on multiple shows at the same time. You only get to be a GM if a producer hears about your reputation and decides to hire you. The GM is given a sizeable up-front management fee to cover the preproduction planning and, just before rehearsals begin, receives a weekly salary for the life of the Broadway run.

GENERAL PRESS REPRESENTATIVE AND PRESS AGENTS (UNION)

The press agent is the liaison between the media and the show. Writing skills are important, but so is experience in writing successful press releases, a pleasant professional phone voice, and the ability to think outside the box. The hours are superlong and nonstop, but also exciting at times. The critics, journalists, editors, bloggers, television reporters, and performers must all find the press agent trustworthy, helpful, smart, and personable.

Press offices work on multiple shows and projects. A general manager, with the producer's approval, will decide which agency to hire. The general press rep (the boss) will choose the show or projects to which each agent is assigned. A hopeful press agent must apprentice for a number of years, attend required union seminars, and pass a union test.

TECHNICAL/PRODUCTION SUPERVISOR

There are a small handful of qualified technical supervisors, also called technical directors (TDs) or production managers or supervisors, who can be considered the general manager of all technical elements and technical staff in a Broadway show. There are currently no females in this group. The TD sometimes supervises many shows at the same time, making sure that the designers' visions are carried out at a price that fits the budget, and the show is operated by a trusted and skilled crew. He is hired because he knows everyone and everything technical. He receives a significant up-front production fee to cover a tremendous amount of preshow planning and, once in performance, a weekly fee as a retainer or royalty. If and when the show goes on tour, this is the person who supervises every detail about replicating and adapting the Broadway production to other stages, knowing the financial obligations and union realities outside of New York City.

CASTING DIRECTOR

Before the 1980s, this position did not exist on Broadway. In those days, office staff would send out role descriptions by hand and by fax to agents who would then call the producer's staff directly to schedule an audition. The director and often the producer would attend the auditions and see a limited number of actors over a brief period of time.

As the workload increased and as Equity rules about auditions leveled the playing field, a need grew for a specialized person to oversee the process and to help make decisions based on familiarity with the actor's past work. Casting offices can be as small as two people and as large as forty, handling movies and television along with Broadway. They are paid an up-front production fee of $30–$35,000, depending on the number of roles to be filled, followed by a flat weekly fee to cover the ongoing search for replacements throughout the show's run.

COMPANY MANAGER (UNION)

Often hired only one week prior to the first rehearsal, the company manager is the right hand of the general manager and represents the business concerns of the show on a daily basis. Company managers work at least six days a week. Calculating and determining a wide variety of union payrolls and benefits; overseeing box office income; paying creative royalties, investor returns, and all bills; supervising budget controls; and contracting all employees are just some of the duties. This job deals with all crises, events, projects, marketing, legal, accounting, and insurance concerns while being production central for all questions, approvals, and hires.

A general manager must trust the company manager to understand all union rulebooks as protection against penalties. Union membership for the CM requires two years of apprenticeship under a working manager, eighteen seminars, study groups to learn union rules, and then a six-hour written and oral exam before the union will certify a manager ready to work on Broadway.

New York State right-to-work laws allow a producer to hire nonunion managers without this preparation, but for a limited time and only one show, after which the manager must join the union.

PRODUCTION STAGE MANAGER AND ASSISTANT STAGE MANAGERS (UNION)

As a member of the Actors' Equity Association union, stage managers must have the complete trust of the director, the producer, the crew, and the actors since they are the protectors of the quality of the show on a daily basis, especially in the director's absence. There is a hierarchy among the multiple stage managers with assignments that include cueing onstage changes for the lights, props, set pieces, and sound, policing backstage equipment, monitoring actors entrances, replacing an actor onstage in an emergency, and rehearsing understudies and replacement actors on a weekly basis. The company manager and stage managers must be partners with constant communication between the backstage and business side of running a show. Stage managers earn more than a company manager even though management hires and fires stage managers.

CREATIVE-RELATED JOBS

DESIGNER ASSISTANTS (USUALLY UNION)

All designers for scenery, costumes, lights, and sound need assistants. Hopeful assistants apply directly to the designer of a show. A general manager negotiates with the designer to put an upper limit on the number of union-salaried design assistants, but the designer will often engage an additional assistant or two paid personally by the designer. Broadway's next great designer starts as someone's assistant.

ASSISTANTS TO THE DIRECTOR, CHOREOGRAPHER, PRODUCER, ETC.

Key staff members are under a great deal of stress. They need pleasant, resourceful, diplomatic, and hard-working assistants who can handle mundane errands and, sometimes, difficult situations. These are short-term positions with long hours, usually ending on opening night. Each director, choreographer, star, producer, and manager has their own unique personality, and they will each have their own method of hiring and firing. An assistant can learn a lot through observation and make invaluable contacts when it all works out. A great letter of introduction with a strong recommendation can open doors to working with extraordinary Broadway artists and leaders.

For large corporate producers like Disney Theatricals and Cameron Mackintosh, an assistant director is an important position, taking over or supplementing directing duties from the show's director for touring and international companies when the director is not available. In a sense, the producer has hired someone who will be consistently available to oversee the quality of productions around the world. In some cases, the production stage manager of the original show on Broadway moves up into this position.

PRODUCTION AND BACKSTAGE JOBS

HAIR AND WIGS (UNION AND NONUNION)
Hair and wig designer. Hair stylist.

WARDROBE (UNION)
Wardrobe supervisor. Wardrobe assistants (as many as two dozen in large musicals). A star's dresser.

CARPENTERS (UNION)
Production carpenter and head carpenter. Multiple assistant carpenters including fly-persons, automation, winchmen, riggers, and more.

ELECTRICIANS (UNION)
Production electrician and head electrician. Multiple assistant electricians including spotlight operators and portable board operators. Also automated lighting programmers.

VIDEO OPERATOR/PROJECTIONIST (UNION)
When a production utilizes video design elements, the projectionist/technician is often an electrician with special skills.

SOUND (UNION)
Production sound engineer. Assistant sound engineer(s).

PROPS (UNION)
Production prop master, head prop master, and assistants.

TUTORS

Productions employing child actors are legally required to provide educators. They coordinate with each child's school to keep them current with class work while in rehearsal. Companies like On Location Education provide certified teachers backstage and on tour.

CHILD WRANGLERS (UNION)

All shows with underage actors require backstage adults to guide and train the youngsters on backstage etiquette, and make sure that they are ready for their cues. This is particularly important for shows with very large numbers of young actors like *Annie*, *Matilda*, and *Billy Elliot*. Wranglers have just recently become members of the Wardrobe union (see Chapter 4).

STAR DRESSERS (UNION) AND PERSONAL ASSISTANTS

Sometimes a star comes with a regular assistant to help with their day-to-day needs. If prearranged, this personal assistant will be added to the show's payroll temporarily. On the other hand, a star's costumes may require special handling, especially when there are many changes during a show. In this case, someone from the wardrobe department may be assigned as a personal dresser and often becomes close friends with the celebrity for life.

ANIMAL TRAINER

There are only one or two people who can provide a trained animal that can deliver eight live performances each week. The trainer is also backstage at every performance. The most popular of these Broadway specialists is Bill Berloni.

THEATRE OWNERS AND VENUE-RELATED JOBS

Forty Broadway theatre venues are owned and run by eight companies: Shubert Organization, Nederlander Organization, and Jujamcyn Theaters are the largest and most powerful, owning more than three quarters of all Broadway theatres. Other Broadway venues are controlled by four nonprofits: Roundabout Theatre Company, Lincoln Center Theater, Second Stage Theatre, and Manhattan Theatre Club. One theatre is owned by Disney Theatrical Group.

These organizations have numerous executives, lawyers, finance, and general staff to oversee some of New York City's most valuable real estate. They supervise repairs, renovations, design, taxes, finances, utilities, and adherence to fire regulations and city codes. The owners also decide what shows rent their theatres and negotiate rental terms that have a weekly guaranteed rent, bolstered with a percentage of the box office income ranging widely between 3 percent and 14 percent based on many factors. The theatre owners hire and pay the following positions:

HOUSE MANAGERS A.K.A. THEATRE MANAGERS (UNION)

The House Manager (HM) is the center of all business at the theatre. Using the weekly box office income, the HM deducts the theatre's payroll, pension payments, real estate taxes, utilities, supplies, and other invoices approved by the theatre owners. The balance of the box office income is then given to the show's managers who will pay the show's weekly expenses. The HM is also responsible for making on-the-spot decisions to resolve audience problems during the performance, yet will wait for the approval of the theatre owners and sometimes the show's GM and CM for larger issues. Each theatre owner defines the financial duties and work hours of the HM differently, depending on how much work they wish their centralized office staff to handle.

THEATRE ENGINEERS (UNION)

Control and maintain heat, water, and air conditioning at theatres.

BOX OFFICE TREASURERS AND ASSISTANT TREASURERS (UNION)

Use and maintain the computerized system of ticketing and sales, generate reports, analyze audience statistics, handle and protect money, credit card receipts, discounts, and seating maps while serving the customers with information and patience.

PHONE AND ONLINE SALES AGENTS (UNION)

An extension of the box office, operating outside the box office space but often in the theatre itself.

STAGE DOORPERSONS (UNION)

Provide basic security for backstage access and communication central for actors and staff.

TICKET TAKERS (UNION)

Collect and validate tickets at theatre entrances.

USHERS (UNION)
Direct the audience to reserved seating and police the audience for decorum and safety.

PORTERS/CUSTODIANS AND CLEANERS (UNION)
Maintain the cleanliness of the theatre before, during, and after performances. Porters sometimes help direct box office traffic.

EXECUTIVE ASSISTANTS
A handful of super-people who handle the communications and business lives of theatre owners.

SECURITY GUARDS
A security force that watches the streets around each theatre, protects the owners' offices, sets up barriers for special events and opening nights, and works closely with the New York Police Department.

RECEPTIONISTS
Field a large number of calls from producers, audience, government officials, etc. Other staff works in accounting, merchandise, and events.

NONPROFIT INSTITUTIONAL JOBS
Nonprofit theatre institutions mostly operate in the Off Broadway arena but also produce shows on Broadway. A very few nonprofits own their own Broadway theatre; others transfer a successful Off Broadway show to Broadway by collaborating with a commercial producer or raising the funds themselves.

The most active nonprofit New York–based companies with a history of Broadway transfers include Roundabout Theatre Company, Manhattan Theatre Club, Lincoln Center Theater, Second Stage Company, and the Public Theater/New York Shakespeare Festival.

These companies hire many nonunion staff workers at lower-than-Broadway salaries who support all of the company's work on and off Broadway. The following jobs are unique to nonprofit organizations:

SUBSCRIPTION DIRECTOR AND STAFF
Nonprofits develop a member-based audience that supports the theatre and its productions, in exchange for extra institutional benefits including discounts.

AUDIENCE DEVELOPMENT DIRECTOR AND STAFF

Online and printed communications, group sales letters to schools, promotional events, merchandise, and the theatre's branding including logo and graphics all fall under this department.

DEVELOPMENT DIRECTOR AND STAFF

Nonprofits earn money from ticket sales but it is never enough to run a year-round staff and production costs. The development department researches and writes grant proposals, designs and produces fund-raising events, and courts theatre-lovers with deep pockets to cover the balance of the annual budget. They become the personal face of the nonprofit providing a one-on-one connection with people of means who support the theatre.

OUTSIDE CONSULTANTS AND RELATED JOBS

ADVERTISING AGENCY REPS

The major ad agencies specializing on Broadway assign each show one or more liaisons to concentrate on the needs of that one show.

ARTIST AND LITERARY AGENTS AND MANAGERS

Creative people, who have reached professional working status (actors, designers, writers), are usually represented by an agent, and sometimes a manager. Agents must apprentice before they can become a licensed agent, subject to the conditions set forth by the unions. These regulations protect artists from rip-offs, and limit the agent's share to 10 percent of their client's work income. Managers, on the other hand, are not licensed nor regulated, and have no required training, but can guide an artist to a successful path through their contacts and business acumen.

INSURANCE BROKER

There are only a few insurance companies that hire and train agents specializing in theatre and entertainment. "Theatrical umbrella" policies are common on Broadway.

BANKING ASSOCIATES

A few key banks have specialists who understand the unique deposit and spending methods employed by general managers to keep a show running smoothly.

PAYROLL SERVICES

Different unions require different dues, benefits, vacation pay, etc. A few Broadway payroll specialists have these calculations built into their payroll system.

SCENIC BUILDING SHOPS (UNION)

On Broadway, all scenery must be built by a union shop and must receive fireproof-certification. Scenery from other theatres cannot be re-used on Broadway for this reason. Stagehands sometimes work at these scene shops when not working on a Broadway production.

LIGHTING RENTAL SHOPS (UNION)

Lighting equipment and cables do not come with a Broadway theatre and must be rented or purchased. These union shops re-use, re-build, upgrade, and re-design the equipment that a lighting designer needs. Electricians can sometimes find temporary employment between shows at lighting rental shops.

SOUND RENTAL SHOPS (UNION)

As with lighting, sound equipment and cables do not come with a Broadway theatre and must be rented or purchased. Sound engineers can find employment here between shows, if available.

ATTORNEYS

Entertainment lawyers are a very small, specialized group. Only New York and California have detailed entertainment laws regulating investments, safety, licensing of agents, and theatre obligations.

PHOTOGRAPHERS

The most famous images of Broadway were photographed by a few trusted photographers: Carol Rosegg (*Victor/Victoria, Grease, La Cage aux Folles*), Joan Marcus (*Wicked, The Lion King, The Book of Mormon*), and Martha Swope (*A Chorus Line, Cats, Into the Woods, The Wiz*) to name a few. They hire their own assistants. While they are not in a union, they must know and follow the rules of the other Broadway unions. Their understanding of the theatre's unique onstage lighting makes this a specialized skill.

TICKET AGENCIES AND GROUP SALES SERVICES

Hotels hire nonunion ticket agents directly. Online and phone sales are handled by companies such as Ticketmaster and Telecharge (owned by the Shubert

Organization) who hire many nonunion personnel to answer the phones and process ticket orders.

Independent group sales offices market discounted tours to schools and community organizations, sometimes hiring actors for part-time work.

TKTS (UNION), the half-price ticket booth on West 47th and Broadway, is manned by union treasurers. Additional TKTS windows operate in lower Manhattan and downtown Brooklyn. These treasurers operate as an extension of the box office with seating locations and availability strictly managed from each theatre's central box office computer. Managers often hire theatre-lovers part-time to promote their shows to those waiting in line to buy tickets.

MERCHANDISING SALES ASSOCIATES
Nonunion people are hired through outside companies such as Theatre Refreshments Inc. to sell drinks and snacks in theatre lobbies. These jobs can be a worthy alternative for actors looking for a flexible part-time job that allows them to attend auditions.

MERCHANDISING DESIGN AND PRODUCTION
The show designs its own merchandise and finds a company to produce the products. In many cases, the licensed refreshment vendor will also sell merchandise in the lobby. In other cases, the producer may be permitted to hire their own people, like Disney Theatrical Group.

WEBSITE DESIGNER
This work is sometimes arranged through a marketing director or ad agency, or is sometimes designed by an individual who shows up at the right moment.

ONLINE MARKETING
Like the website designer, this work is sometimes handled through a marketing director, ad agency, or an individual who shows up at the right moment.

STUDY GUIDE CREATION/PRINTING AND EDUCATIONAL OUTREACH
Special projects for shows that believe they have a significant school audience and educational value.

APPRENTICES, ASSISTANTS, AND INTERNS (NONUNION (UC))

Administrative assistants and interns are often engaged to assist these people: general manager, company manager, press representative, casting director, advertising agency, artist and literary agents, production photographer, legal counsel, accounting, travel services. In 1980, the starting salary for most office assistants was $250–$400 per week. In 2014, these introductory jobs paid from $400–$550 per week. The tremendous competition for entry-level administrative jobs keeps the salaries low.

Every show hires production assistants (PAs) usually for no more than four to eight weeks from first rehearsal through the show's opening night, doing errands, copying, filing, and observing. They are paid a small amount of expense money. The US Supreme Court has recently created employer guidelines for internships to be sure it is more than getting coffee and copying. This is good news for those who can afford to start at the bottom. The real benefit is watching how a professional show is put together and possibly getting a recommendation for your next job.

Chapter 3

Who's in Charge, and What Are They in Charge Of?

The hierarchy of Broadway is both logical and chaotic. It is obvious that an assistant works under a supervisor. On Broadway, there are some assistants by the nature of their expertise who are above some supervisors. Some managers, sharing equal decision-making powers in one area of their jurisdiction, autonomously control decisions in another area, but then must defer to someone else in still other areas.

Power does not flow cleanly between roles. For example, the technical supervisor listens to the designers who listen to the director on creative issues, and the general manager and producer on financial issues. As the budget watchdog, the company manager can also oversee the technical director's decisions. It's a multilevel collaboration that works well when each person is cooperative, friendly, and willing to listen to one another, and more importantly, knows their place in the process of putting a show together.

The producer is responsible for raising the money. In a capitalistic Broadway theatre venture, the producer is the ultimate boss over the show. However, the producer often doesn't know as much as an experienced general manager regarding . . . well, almost everything. Therefore, the staff and crew will respond as much to the general manager as the producer.

The staff, crew, and cast learn that the company manager (CM) represents the voice of the producer and general manager (GM). Since the CM is more visible on a day-to-day basis once the show is in performance, the CM becomes the top boss to most people.

Since the theatre is a separate entity from the show and is occupied on a rental basis, the theatre personnel have a separate hierarchy. The house manager (HM) is most visible on a daily basis and speaks for the theatre owner, so the theatre staff and crew will treat the HM as their boss.

The production stage manager (PSM) runs the show at every performance, and in so many ways is the equal to the company manager and house manager, yet the company manager is the PSM's boss in other ways. The cast will respond to the PSM as though they work directly under him or her. If the PSM wants to go over the CM's head, then the director and general manager will resolve the issue. It's a confusing collaboration that works well after all parties learn the subtleties of each person's responsibilities and jurisdiction, and respect the boundaries.

It should be helpful to frequently reference the chart (on this chapter's final page) while reading this book. This industry is not like corporations with CEOs, presidents, and vice-presidents who oversee managers and workers in linear paths of power. On Broadway, every direct line of supervision has many exceptions and requires a lot of explanation.

At the top: Producers must hire a general manager (before making assumptions about a budget, please!) and an attorney (to get an "option" from the show's author, or authors, and write a government-required investment prospectus). The general manager is usually involved in the legal discussions and writes an initial budget at that point, consulting with the director in creative affairs and with the producer at all times.

The GM will also hire a technical director (TD), a choreographer, designers (set, lights, costumes, sound, video), a press representative, and an advertising agency while opening accounts at a Broadway-affiliated bank. While all principal hires will try to follow the producer's wishes, they will usually treat the general manager as their true boss, since the GM will be the one to approve financial terms and help the producer make decisions that time has proven to be well-advised.

The general manager will then negotiate for a Broadway theatre, always in consultation with producer, director, and tech supervisor, and hire a casting office, pay union bonds, oversee the creation of schedules for design completion, rehearsals, and performances. Finally just before rehearsals, a company manager will be hired to take over unfinished contract negotiations, finish banking arrangements, payroll services, and union paperwork.

At the theatre itself, staff employees are on a year-round contract and are a part of the theatre rental agreement. They are experienced in the ways of that particular theatre. This includes a small house crew to protect the physical plant of the theatre. This crew is definitely not there to run the show, although their union allows them to help run the show in minor roles.

The theatre owners, often a small corporate-minded group of lawyers and businessmen, make the big decisions: how to lease their theatres to the best shows that will run forever and pay lots of rent. If the owners feel strongly enough, they will coproduce a show or invest substantial funds as an enticement to the producer to rent their theatre because they believe the show is worthy, or because they'd like a larger share of the show's likely profits.

The director will discuss his or her vision with the designers in an open forum, but has final approval of designs and casting and sometimes choice of theatre. If the design is too expensive, rest assured the general manager will assert his or her authority over the director on behalf of the producer.

The show's technical supervisor will select the key members of the show's "Pink Contract" crew. One difficult concept to understand is the roles of two different stagehand unions working on the same show. Pink Contract stagehands belong to the International Alliance of Theatrical Stage Employees (IATSE), a union that by its very nature permits these stagehands to work in union venues throughout the world. Each Broadway show has at least one Pink production carpenter, production electrician, and production prop master hired through its technical supervisor. These IATSE stagehands are hired to promote the interests of the show and be loyal to the needs of the show's producers and designers.

The number of IATSE employees who can be hired is limited by the local union jurisdiction even though IATSE is the parent union of all local stagehand unions. In New York City, Stagehands Local One has jurisdiction. In Chicago, the union name is Local Two with different numbered locals throughout the country. These stagehands can only work within their individual city. In order to protect local jobs, touring shows are permitted a very limited number of "outsiders." These few IATSE men and women learn how to run the Broadway show and teach it to stagehands in other cities. That protects the quality of the show wherever it plays.

On Broadway, they will protect the show from financial overruns and quality issues. Yet these same IATSE members are not officially the local stagehands' bosses. They must have an excellent rapport with the Local One's Head Carpenter, Head Electrician, and Head Prop Master who are hired by the theatre owners to protect the integrity of the venue.

This is one of the key complaints of Broadway producers. They are required to pay for two sets of supervisory stagehands, one from IATSE and one from Local One.

To truly understand this, the division between the landlord's authority and personnel, and the tenant's employees, must be clear. The theatre has no vested interest in the show except through the rent it receives from a success. Due to concerns that a tenant may destroy their property, the head carpenter, head electrician, and head prop master are hired year-round to protect the theatre. To this end, no one may work in the theatre unless these three head stagehands are present to observe and approve alterations to the theatre's walls, floors, circuitry, etc.

Producers understand that if a stagehand is on the theatre's payroll, their loyalty will be with the theatre owners. The show's management wants stagehands that will give priority to its creative needs and fight to keep costs as low as possible for the production's budget.

In addition, no audience can attend any activity in the theatre unless the house manager and, if needed, the ushers, porters, and doorperson are there to protect the seating areas and bathrooms. Company managers and house managers authorize crew and staff costs before any money is spent and since they are in the same union with similar training, there is a common understanding of what is possible and hopefully fair.

A general manager will negotiate and sign an actor's contract, and can fire the actor, as restricted by Actors' Equity rules. For this reason, it might seem that the actor works for the general manager. But the director and choreographer tell the actor what to do on stage. The stage managers, representing the director, are the actor's immediate bosses at every performance onstage and backstage for the run of the show. The company manager, representing the producer and GM, can discipline and fire an actor, as well as disapprove requested days off and changes in the actor's contract. Confusing and yet totally logical when one understands union rules.

The general press representative will dole out assignments to their staff and can fire and hire press agents in their office at will. The press office responds to the wishes of the general manager who hires them. While the producer is everyone's boss, a wise producer will work through the GM and CM to avoid sabotaging an important news article through media industry ignorance.

The company manager and press agent work closely as equals and brethren since they share the same union. While not the press agent's boss, the CM pays the press agent, and will also authorize expenses.

The authors have no authority over anyone working on the production except to approve or suggest changes to their script. An author who respects everyone else's work, sending all comments only to the director or stage managers, may have great influence even without official authority over the production.

On the other hand, many respected Broadway producers make their ultimate authority evident in every corner of the production. Producer Kermit Bloomgarden sat in on every rehearsal of the unsuccessful *Poor Murderer* and told the director Herbert Berghof when he wanted a scene fixed and how fast. Producer David Merrick ordered musician "walkers" (Chapter 21: Musicians) to play music in the women's lounge during intermission. In these cases, the GM listens more than decides. In all cases, it's a unique combination of decision-makers who cause the show to succeed or fail.

Theatre is a team sport. Everyone brings their expertise to the table, listens to the needs of each player, and somehow figures out how to build upon the creative concepts and make them practical and affordable. When everyone is working for the same purpose, chances of success improve. Those who fail to understand the goal and bring negativity to the process help ensure a miserable experience.

The financial success of a show has nothing to do with a good or bad working atmosphere. It's about ticket sales. Nevertheless, goodwill among the cast, staff, and crew can save the show a lot of money. Union and nonunion players put in extra effort and are willing to bend rules when they believe the show's bosses appreciate them and, most importantly, pay them on time and as promised. This is most likely true in all businesses.

Like stagehands, musicians have a local union (Local #802) and the national parent union, American Federation of Musicians (AFM). The musical director (MD), a.k.a. musical supervisor, works for the producer, GM, and the composer. The musical director's job is to rehearse and conduct the orchestra and singers.

The MD's national AFM affiliation allows the MD to work anywhere in the United States. Only a few key musicians from the Broadway production are allowed to tour. The remainder of the orchestra must be hired locally, and quality varies tremendously from city to city. For this reason, the MD will often go on tour to be sure that the musical standards set by the original Broadway production are maintained. The MD therefore becomes a very important choice for the show.

The musical contractor, also hired by the show, is responsible for hiring the orchestra and approving subs. Sometimes the contractor will play in the orchestra. As with TDs, there are very few contractors to choose from. Seymour "Red" Press must be named here as the contractor of numerous Broadway shows, loved and respected for decades. While he can hire and fire, he is not anyone's boss. The musical director and contractor are on the show's payroll, and respond to the GM's and CM's authority. House managers pay the orchestra members from the theatre's payroll. There's no easy explanation why this makes sense, but it is what it is.

Ushers work under the theatre's house manager. Yet, the head usher sets the schedule and maintains quality control.

The head treasurer schedules the box office assistants, but only the theatre owners directly hire or fire box office personnel. This is understandable since more than a million dollars per week can be involved.

Administrative staff in a producer's or a GM's office can vary greatly depending on the success of a show and the number of shows and tours being managed by that particular office. A singular producer and company manager have desks in a GM's office to save expense and because more space is just not necessary. There are also offices with up to sixty desks running multiple shows and tours. The jobs of receptionist, assistants, messengers, associate producers, and company manager consider their boss to be the general manager.

None of the lines of authority are written in stone. Strong, creative personalities can completely take over the reins of a show. Mel Brooks was the true boss of every aspect of his mega-hit *The Producers* no matter how many people were credited as producers. Director/choreographer/conceiver Michael Bennett intervened in every aspect of *A Chorus Line*, from musical tempos to firing actors. When someone is responsible for the creative integrity of a show, employees tend to respect their authority in areas not officially theirs to control.

Finally, the ultimate bosses for every employee on a Broadway show are the unions. Their rules and regulations may annoy producers and theatre owners, but there are expensive penalties to pay and emotionally exhausting procedures involved when failing to follow the rules. So it might be said that even the top Broadway honchos must work within the framework of the many unions that govern the largest theatre community on earth.

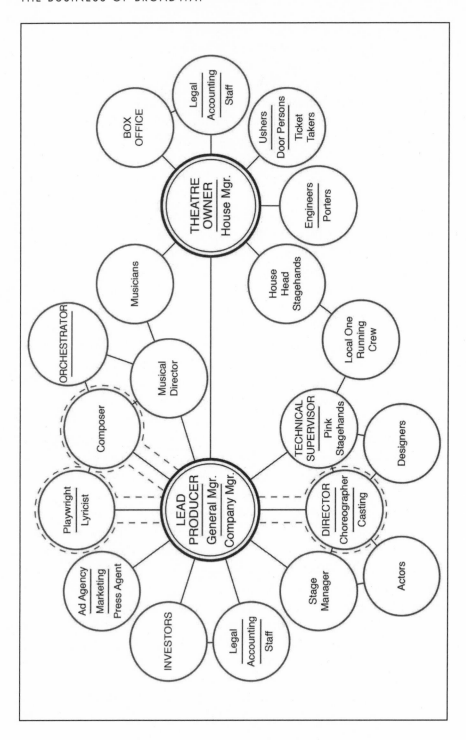

Chapter 4

Eighteen Unions, One Association, and Pensions

There are as many as eighteen unions and one very influential guild overseeing the work rules, minimum salaries, and benefits for every Broadway show. The rules were negotiated over many decades between an association of experienced producers and theatre owners called The Broadway League (formerly The League of American Theatres and Producers), the national unions (i.e. American Federation of Musicians), and the local New York City unions (i.e. Musicians Local #802).

The most important difference between nonunion and union work is that union workers receive vacation pay, sick pay, health insurance, pension, and sometimes annuities (hereafter called "benefits") along with their salaries. Otherwise, it is possible, but extremely rare, that a Broadway salary may be less than that offered in a nonunion regional theatre or touring show. The pensions for Broadway's union workers are paid through an extremely unique and complex system, described at the end of this chapter. Some of the rates used in this book expire in 2015, but it is generally safe to expect a 2 to 3 percent cost-of-living increase from year to year.

Broadway unions require each production to pay "bonds" before the show begins hiring. As a general rule, these bonds are equal to two weeks salary and benefits for every employee. Before the bonding rule, actors and crew were at the mercy of a producer's code of ethics and ability to pay. Broadway producers are still known to skip town without paying final salaries. Today, once a union verifies that everyone has been paid through their final day of work, the union returns the entire bond to the producer who usually uses it to pay for a portion of closing costs.

Once accepted in a union, members are charged initiation dues, from $1,000 to $3,500 depending on the union. Many unions will provide a payment plan if the applicant is not able to pay up front. The purpose is to discourage new applicants who are not serious about making a career in the union's jurisdiction, and to keep the number of workers from overwhelming the number of available jobs. In addition, there are working dues between 2 and 4 percent of income deducted from each paycheck. These dues allow the unions to provide services and maintain an office and staff.

In no particular order, union workers are:

1. PERFORMERS (WWW.ACTORSEQUITY.ORG)

Equity (the Actors' Equity Association or AEA) governs the work rules that protect performers and stage managers who work in theatre, Broadway, and elsewhere. The union's jurisdiction includes most of the major touring theatres across the United States as well as major regional theatre companies. Basically, if you want to use a professional performer in your show, you must abide by the rules that apply to the size and type of theatre that will house your show.

Broadway uses union actors. A nonunion actor may be hired but must then join the union involving an initiation fee of $1,100 and then annual dues of $118 plus 2.25 percent of weekly earnings deducted from each paycheck. As of 2014, Broadway actors can be paid no less than $1,861 plus benefits per week. Actors earn an additional weekly fee of between $15 and $400 for special duties like understudying one or more roles, or having a solo in a musical number, or risky stunts like climbing or flying (called "extraordinary risk"), or rehearsing dancers as a dance captain, or a host of other duties.

Historically there were once two unions, one for chorus performers, and another for featured performers. They combined forces in 1955, similar to the recent merger of Screen Actors Guild (SAG) and American Federation of Television and Radio Artists (AFTRA), but because the negotiated terms of the merger required slightly separate rules for chorus and featured performers, the union still submits different contract paperwork for the two work divisions.

Featured roles and celebrities are paid far above the minimum salary. Non-celebrity actors in important roles may earn $2,500 to $10,000 per week. But film stars may earn $20 million for a single movie so it is not always easy to get a lengthy time commitment to a show without some significant financial enticement. Love of being on stage may not be enough. The general manager will negotiate with a star's agent to determine weekly salary that has sometimes reached over $100,000 per week and/or a percentage of each week's box office income.

Actors' Equity Association has approximately forty-nine thousand members across the United States, most living in New York. Broadway contract rules are described in great detail in the "Production Agreement." The Production Agreement covers the rules of employment for Broadway, "first-class" national tours, and "bus and truck" tours. This multiyear agreement is the result of decades of research, protests, physical threats, strikes, compromises, and unfriendly negotiation meetings. It does not cover work rules for Off Broadway productions, regional theatres, concerts, or anything else. The rulebook is readily accessible online at the Actors' Equity Association website, but these rules are almost never taught in a classroom. Hence, a lot of uninformed young actors move to New York City every day.

As with most unions, there's a "Catch-22" situation. To audition for a union show, you need to be a union member. To become a union member, you need to get into a union show. However, many casting directors, a nonunionized profession, allow nonunion actors to audition under certain circumstances. A nonunion actor can show up for general casting calls and find a slot when an Equity actor has missed an appointment or after all AEA performers have auditioned, if time permits.

There is also an Equity Membership Candidate (EMC) program that allows actors "in training" at stock and regional theatres to accumulate points toward union membership. Call 212-869-8530 or write to Actors' Equity Membership Department, 165 West 46 St., New York, NY 10036.

Agents are licensed through Equity following a required apprenticeship under an existing licensed agency. This protects the performer from unscrupulous and ineffectual people waiting to take advantage of the gullible actor hungry for work. Equity and New York State law forbids an agent from taking more than 10 percent commission on a Broadway show.

Stage managers are the most respected work force on Broadway and they too are members of Actors' Equity. It has often been thought that stage managers and company managers should be in the same union since they work so closely together, but there's also an essential connection between the "manager of everything that touches the stage" and the actors who inhabit the stage.

On Broadway, the supervising stage manager is called the production stage manager (PSM) but sometimes they are just called the stage manager (SM). The first assistant is actually billed with the title stage manager followed by first assistant stage manager, second assistant stage manager, and so on. The size of the cast will determine how many stage managers are needed on a show and Equity must approve this decision. While the assistant stage managers sometimes understudy actors if absolutely necessary, the PSM is never permitted to do so.

The PSM is the director's note taker and memory for staging, light and sound cues, costume decisions, and everything else that affects the show onstage. When the director's initial work is over and the show has opened, the PSM is responsible for keeping the show intact, rehearsing understudies and new cast members, and overseeing the work of the other stage managers at every performance. It's a daunting task that pays a minimum weekly salary of $2,628 for a dramatic play and $3,058 for a musical. That's higher than the company manager who runs the show, approves expenditures, and pays everyone.

2. MANAGEMENT AND PRESS AGENTS (WWW.ATPAM.COM)

ATPAM (Association of Theatrical Press Agents and Managers Local #18032) represents company managers, house managers, and press agents. The union certifies its members who have completed eighteen seminars, studied all of the Broadway union rulebooks, and passed a six-hour written test along with an oral examination.

Being unaware of the rules of even one union could cost a show thousands of dollars. Therefore, the management and press agent's union takes the training of its members seriously. Since most producers do not come from the ranks of management, trained managers are essential. Unfortunately, there are producers who make artistic and financial decisions without first consulting with experienced management.

It must be noted that New York State Right to Work laws allow a producer to hire a nonunion manager for a short period of time, after which the manager must join ATPAM. They will still be uncertified unless they pass the certification qualifying process.

General managers, who are a producer's key advisor and oversee the entire production, are not members of any union. Federal law forbids an executive in charge of hiring from unionizing. Regardless, many general managers began their careers and developed their all-important professional contacts as an ATPAM company manager and remain members of this union.

House managers (a.k.a. theatre managers) go through the same training as company managers. For this reason, company managers and house managers have the option of working in either position.

A house manager is responsible for the payroll of the box office staff, the custodians, the doorpersons, New York Local One stagehands and Local 802 musicians. The company manager pays the cast, stage managers, designers, author, director, choreographer, general manager, press agent, technical supervisor, Pink Contract stagehands, musical director, investors, and others.

A house manager receives an annual contract at a particular Broadway theatre. Each September, the theatre owner has the option of rehiring the house manager or not. If there is no show currently leasing that theatre, the house manager does not work. The HM can sometimes sub at a different theatre during that HM's absence due to vacation or illness.

A company manager is hired by the show's general manager to oversee the daily business of the show, and usually attends every performance. Company managers lose their job when the show closes.

Press agents are hired by the general manager individually, or through a senior press agent's office, to represent the show's brand to newspapers, magazines, television, radio, online and in print, to provide promotional stories and factual information about the show throughout its run on Broadway. As members of ATPAM, they elect their own union board members from their chapter, separate from the managers' chapter.

Press agents are trained through the union's apprenticeship program culminating in a written and oral test. Unlike managers, press agents can work on multiple shows at the same time, and usually do. Managers can work as press agents, and press agents can work as managers under ATPAM jurisdiction but making connections in the media is a full-time occupation, so there is rarely any cross-over.

ATPAM is a member of IATSE (International Alliance of Theatrical Stage Employees).

3. DIRECTORS AND CHOREOGRAPHERS (WWW.SDCWEB.ORG)

Formerly known as SSDC, Society of Stage Directors and Choreographers, the union has changed its name to SDC, Stage Directors and Choreographers Society. Imagine you have won awards for your choreography in *West Side Story* and everyone worldwide is copying your dance steps, often badly. Yet you are not paid a nickel for the use of your talented work. SDC has fought and won victories to grant ownership rights to the original creators of the work that directors and choreographers contribute to the success of a show.

On Broadway, these creative talents are paid in multiple ways: a lump sum to begin, a non-recoupable advance on royalties, a weekly royalty, and benefits. First, there is a fee to be paid covering the work done prior to the beginning of rehearsals, often more than a year in advance, including work with designers, the playwright, casting directors, and producer. At this time, the minimum directorial fee is $26,705 for a musical, $32,270 for a nonmusical, and the required non-recoupable advance royalty payment is $40,050 and $25,205 respectively.

The combined totals of fee and guaranteed royalty are paid one-third when contracted, one-third at the first rehearsal, and the final third at opening night.

If the show closes before the amount paid as a royalty advance has been reached, the director and choreographer keep that money anyway. In a sense, this is a guaranteed minimum for having spent a year or more of your life developing a show, even if it flops.

The choreographer makes less than the director, and when the director and choreographer are the same person, the money lies somewhere in the middle of the two. After a show begins selling tickets, the managers and accountants must keep track of the 2 percent (director), 1 percent (choreographer), 1.5 percent (combined director and choreographer) royalty of box office income. If a show earns $700,000 in a week, the director will receive $14,000 for that week, plus pension payments, healthcare credits, and other benefits.

Like actors, there are star directors and choreographers who earn considerably more.

4. DRAMATIST GUILD OF AMERICA (WWW.DRAMATISTGUILD.COM)

This is not a union, but an association of six thousand playwrights, composers, lyricists, and librettists that has developed a plan for the sharing of wealth between a Broadway producer and the playwright. While no playwright must join, nor follow these rules, it is almost impossible to negotiate so many details and therefore the Dramatists' guidelines are a welcome tool. Without them, a producer would have to wait for negotiations to be complete before raising investment money.

The most important concept is that the playwright is always the owner of their script. A producer licenses the script and shares in the playwright's income, not the other way around. Playwrights are usually represented by literary agents. The agents keep track of the income from multiple sources that result from a Broadway production.

The Dramatist Guild rules govern and limit the producer's rights over the playwright's property, the play. Because the producer and investors are responsible for the Broadway production, they have rights that continue, usually for forty years following the final Broadway performance.

The producer must acquire the rights to a show before legally raising any investment money and so a playwright is the second person a producer contacts. A specialized entertainment attorney is usually the first person to come on board. The attorney will write an agreement called an "option." This "option" gives the producer a number of months to accomplish certain goals, such as raising the needed capital to hire the creative team and lock in the theatre.

There are celebrity playwrights who can command significant option payments, especially when there is competition for the rights to the play, but option payments are never less than $5,000 for a six-month period.

The producer will have the right to extend this six-month option if he thinks the investment money may be forthcoming and if the play remains a priority. This will require a second payment and a third, often higher than the first payment, as negotiated in the agreement. At some point, the producer must reach the goals stated, or give up the option and let the playwright search for another producer.

Once the play is funded, called "full capitalization," the playwright is then paid in a similar manner to directors described above: a royalty advance, a weekly percentage, and benefits.

In terms of royalties, the playwright of a drama or comedy usually receives 5 percent of the weekly box office income. For a musical, the playwright can be three separate entities or any combination; the librettists or book writer receives one-third, the lyricist one-third, and the composer one-third. It's been a standard breakdown for decades and it prevents arguments, long negotiations, and inside fighting that could otherwise kill the creative work needed to make the show succeed.

Once the Broadway show ends, the ownership of the play reverts to the playwright under the watchful eye of the literary agent. At this point, a movie sale based on the play is paid directly to the playwright, whose agent then sends the Broadway producer a share of that income based on the Guild's rules. This is true for original cast recordings, television, merchandise, future regional, stock, and school productions, and many more potential revenue sources. In many cases, there is more money to be made after a show has closed than while it is performing on Broadway. This is why you want a knowledgeable entertainment attorney and general manager working with a smart literary agent.

5. TREASURERS AND TICKET SELLERS LOCAL 751 (WWW.LOCAL751. COM) AND PHONE AND MAIL ORDER CLERKS LOCAL B751

Box office treasurers are a small group of bonded sales people who not only sell tickets at the theatre, but collect and analyze sales information on a daily basis.

They also process all ticket sales from the web, TKTS (a kiosk for left-over tickets), discount offers, house seats (producer priority locations), mail orders, phone orders through TicketMaster and Telecharge, hotel concierge requests, group sales, and other outlets. Like Broadway stagehands and managers, their union is a local member of IATSE.

The size of your show and the demand for tickets determine the number of treasurers needed to work a show. The theatre owners, the union, and general manager decide the minimum of box office employees. These skilled treasurers are employees of the theatre owners, not the show's producer. The theatre owner decides who they want to work with their computers, bank accounts, corporate accountants, and security forces.

Money can be saved by not opening the box office until a few weeks before the show previews. However, it doesn't make sense to begin advertising and not have someplace for the public to purchase tickets.

Treasurers lose their job shortly after a show closes. They must either substitute at another theatre, or find outside work until their theatre brings in another show. Considering how important it is to have skilled, honest, and friendly representatives, this is a precarious employment situation. The union knows this all too well.

Getting hired as a box office treasurer requires personal connections, great recommendations from another theatre box office, and formidable computer skills. It also requires a temperament to diplomatically handle uninformed customers from within a small confined space. Flexibility is fundamental since work schedules change weekly. There are only two to five treasurers in each of the forty Broadway theatres and they are not easy jobs to get. 2014 salaries started at $1,538.05 per week, plus benefits.

An extension of the box office works with mail and phone orders under the rules of Local B751. Telecharge, the sales organization owned by the Shubert Organization, handles credit card sales and pays its staff an hourly rate of between $15.75 and $24.16, depending on hiring date and seniority.

6. UNITED SCENIC ARTISTS LOCAL 829 (WWW.USA829.ORG)

Three different design disciplines are housed under one umbrella, the USA (United Scenic Artists). The complexity of each division—lights, scenery, and costumes— is daunting. Fees change with the number of design elements needed for the show. It is important for a general manager to understand the elements that go into the finished product in order to create the budget. The number of assistants permitted is negotiated based on realistic needs and budgetary constraints.

The director and scenic designer will develop a concept and then share it with the general manager and technical supervisor. Will the show require one living room set? Will scenic elements move on and off within one living room set? Will computers bring in a hundred set pieces from under the stage floor, the wings, and the fly space above? The technical supervisor will estimate the cost. The general manager may have to adjust the budget, or with the producer's approval, tell the director and designer to go back to the drawing board due to financial constraints.

There are basically three categories of scenic design that affect payment to the scenic designer who receives an up-front fee and royalty advance, plus a flat AWC (additional weekly compensation) after the show begins performances. There is a separate list of minimum payments for single sets, multi-sets, and unit sets for musicals vs. dramas. A famous designer can command more.

Under the least expensive style of scenery for a single set drama, the designer will earn $9,081 up front, $2,277 advance on royalties, and $333 per week as additional weekly compensation. For the most expensive style of scenery for a multi-set musical, the designer will earn $31,551 up front, $6,723 advance on royalties, and $406 per week as additional weekly compensation.

At first, lights are always rented for each Broadway show, not knowing if the show will hit or miss after opening night. The technical supervisor and designer know how to best budget for rentals after the design plans are developed between the three designers. The range of minimum payments to lighting designers is $6,808 fee and $1,709 advance with an AWC of $333 for a single set drama, and $23,664 fee and $5,043 advance with an AWC of $406 for a multi-set musical.

Costume designers have unique categories of payment. Most shows require multiple costumes per actor. People do not wear the same clothing two days in a row, and characters in a play are no different. Each character may require multiple costumes to be designed and built. In addition, it is considered more difficult to design a period piece in sixteenth century China or Elizabethan London than it is to design contemporary street clothing. Costume designers are paid either by the number of actors or the number of characters (one actor can play more than one character in a show). Additional payments are required for a show in a noncontemporary period or foreign traditional dress.

Between one and seven characters in a contemporary show earns the costume designer a fee of $6,639 and a royalty advance of $1,400. Over thirty-six characters in a period piece pays a fee of $53,033 and a royalty advance of $11,068. The AWC, as with the other designers, is $333 for a drama, and $406 for a musical.

7. MUSICIANS UNION LOCAL 802 (WWW.LOCAL802AFM.ORG)

Depending on seating capacity, each Broadway theatre has been assigned a minimum number of required musicians that must be employed for any musical show inhabiting the space. The largest required orchestra is now nineteen musicians. There's a long history to this union practice. Of course, with the advent of digital recording and other technological advances, producers have been anxious to replace live musicians with computers and synthesizers. Compromises have been reached and synthesizers are now permitted in an orchestra pit, subject to limitations on their use and additional salary for those who program and play the instrument.

Broadway's Local 802, which is a member of the national union American Federation of Musicians, is comprised of musicians, arrangers, conductors, and copyists, working in New York's opera companies, clubs, theatres, arenas, and on recordings. When a clarinetist performs in a Broadway orchestra, minimum weekly salary through March 2015 is $1,819.38 (including media fee and vacation pay), plus benefits. If the clarinetist alternates between the clarinet and the flute, he is considered to be "doubling," and requires an additional increment of $210.09, with more for each additional double. This can greatly affect the weekly musical budget of a show.

Union minimum for an orchestrator or arranger is literally paid according to the number of lines in the written sheet music and for each instrument playing those lines. Since it is almost impossible to calculate using these union regulations, the general manager negotiates a flat fee and royalty based on past precedents of similarly sized musicals. "Star" orchestrators like Jonathan Tunick can earn significantly higher sums, but the average fee for a big musical pays $150,000 plus benefits and a weekly flat royalty, paid to the singular person who can take a composer's music and make it sound great in the pit.

The orchestrator scribbles his arrangements that must then be transcribed by a copyist into clean musical pages for use by the musicians. A union copyist gets paid by the note, literally! It's all in the union rulebook. Only copyists know how to calculate their own fees, but since most composers change the music right up to opening night, the copyist must work under great pressure and long hours to make sure the orchestra has the most accurate music to play. The general manager, not knowing if the show will go through minor or major rewrites before opening night, will budget between $50,000 and $150,000 for the copyist.

As with actors, there are many small but important duties that may be added to a musician's role, and there are extra payments for each one.

8. ENGINEERS (WWW.IUOELOCAL30.ORG)

When the air conditioning breaks down or a plumber is needed, there is no time to wait for an outside repairman. When the inevitable complaints come in about a cold or warm theatre, someone must respond quickly. Each theatre owner hires a licensed and well-trained engineer from the International Union of Operating Engineers Local 30 to make repairs and adjustments, and is present when the audience arrives, at intermission, and when the audience leaves. Sometimes an engineer must be available for more than one theatre at a time. The house manager has the engineer's cell phone number at easy reach.

The larger theatre chains (Shubert, Jujamcyn, Nederlander) hire a supervisor who oversees the entire system operating multiple theatres and is every engineer's direct boss. The house manager represents the authority of the theatre owners who are the ultimate authorities over engineering decisions. When conflicts arise, compromises must be found.

One example of the issues facing an engineer comes from the Tony-winning drama *The Grapes of Wrath* at the Shubert's Cort Theatre. During that hot and humid August of 1990, a powerful, new air-conditioning system installed in the ceiling was responsible for keeping more than one thousand ticket-buyers, the backstage, and onstage areas cool. During the final twenty-two minutes of the show, director Frank Galati had a rainstorm alternating between drizzles and deluges pour down directly over the cast that kept them wet and cold. For the health of the cast, the a/c was turned off for the final scene, but the audience was comfortable only when the a/c was on. One system, two valid situations. The engineer was able to devise an unusual on/off system from a location blocks away from the theatre to balance the comfort of both.

An engineer's minimum weekly salary is about $1,200 plus benefits.

9. USHERS, DOORPERSONS, TICKET TAKERS (WWW.LOCAL306.ORG)

The ushers, backstage doorpersons, and the people who scan your tickets as you enter the theatre are members of the union Local 306, operating under the international union IATSE along with treasurers, managers, and stagehands. Some ushers have worked in the same theatre since they were in their twenties and are the children of former ushers. They are also true lovers of theatre. An usher is not only there to direct the audience to their assigned seats, and hand out Playbills (free programs), but to watch the audience for illegal use of cameras, recording devices, and to respond to sudden health crises, disturbances, and more. Their schedule changes weekly as coordinated by the head usher and they are paid per performances worked. In 2014, a head usher earned approximately $553 per eight-performance week, plus some benefits. The director, the second in command, earns about $429 each week. General ushers earn less, either $50.48 per performance, or $403.86 for an entire week. They are given a small cleaning reimbursement if they are required to wear a white collar or other identifying uniform.

Last minute cast substitutions and other notices are printed on little slips of paper and inserted in each Playbill. The ushers come in a bit early and stuff the programs with the inserts, earning an extra $10.61 per week for a musical, and $5.68 per week for all other presentations. They arrive at the theatre for an 8:00 PM show between 6:30 and 7:00 PM. The usher's shifts alternate between "short" (meaning they leave the theatre as soon as the show begins, after directing everyone to their seats), and "long" (staying to act as customer service for complaints and information during intermission, then re-seating, and whatever might happen at the end of the show). Although the head usher directs her staff, the house manager is the formal boss with the power to discipline and fire.

Ticket takers now use electronic scanners to check both home-printed and box office ticket barcodes when admitting patrons into the theatre. They earn $569.39 per week where more than one ticket taker is working, or $612.63 when they work alone. At least one remains to supervise the re-admission of ticket holders after intermission.

Backstage doorpersons deliver messages to cast and crew, and protect the backstage area from unexpected visitors. Every day brings a new group of guests and even stalkers wishing to come backstage. Because work hours start early and remain until the last person has left, there are two built-in overtime hours above the regular weekly paycheck of $696.18, raising the salary by $52.20.

10. PORTERS AND CUSTODIANS (WWW.SEIU.ORG)

Theatre custodians, known as porters, are seen in the lobby before each show, sweeping and looking for potential issues like a torn lobby mat on a rainy day that may cause an insurance claim or an overflowing toilet. They also steer people to the box office or to the ticket takers to avoid traffic jams just before a show. Before and during the show, porters will clean and restock the restrooms. Most importantly, they unlock all exit doors before a show, and padlock them before they leave the theatre, following strict fire code requirements.

During the non-show hours, a couple of cleaners work their way through the seats picking up garbage and Playbills, vacuuming, and preparing the theatre for the next audience.

The Service Employees International Union (SEIU) Local 32BJ District 4-Theatre Division is the overseeing union for these workers. Salaries for porters begin at $475 and rise to $778 per week plus overtime and benefits.

11. COSTUME MAINTENANCE AND WARDROBE (IA764.COM)

The Theatrical Wardrobe Union Local 764, another member of the IATSE, provides a wardrobe supervisor, assistants, and dressers for each show. Since many theatrical costumes are made of unique materials specifically designed to work under theatrical lighting or add flow to a dancer's moves, special care may be needed in the cleaning and maintenance of very expensive garments. Big costume shows like *The Phantom of the Opera*, *Wicked*, and Disney's *The Lion King* require over two dozen wardrobe people to grab the costumes as soon as they get offstage to prevent damage, highly specialized dry cleaning establishments to pick up and return the costumes within twelve hours, and high-capacity washers and dryers backstage.

When an understudy goes onstage, often with only thirty minutes notice, "wardrobe" will alter each costume to fit the temporary performer, unless the show has been running long enough to afford making a second expensive costume collection for the cast replacements. The wardrobe department helps the actors into and out of their costumes during the show, again to protect these valuable assets. Sometimes they bring the costumes to the actors' dressing rooms and sometimes they have makeshift quick-change rooms a few feet offstage to be sure that the actor can get back onstage for the next scene.

The wardrobe supervisor in consultation with the technical director and costume designers will calculate how many assistants are needed to operate the show and will propose who should be hired full-time, part-time, and as a sub. While there are often many hours of overtime, the base weekly salary in 2014 for a supervisor is $1,551.87 and the base weekly salary for an assistant is $1,448.18 plus benefits.

Child guardians, known as wranglers, have recently organized under Local 764. There just isn't enough room backstage to welcome the underage actors' parents.

12. AMERICAN FEDERATION OF MUSICIANS (WWW.AFM.ORG)

Musical supervisors and conductors (a.k.a. musical directors) belong to the musician's national union American Federation of Musicians. They are not hired under the New York City musician's union Local 802 contract that covers

Broadway orchestra musicians. This is because the job also supervises national touring companies of the Broadway show. To this end, the musical conductor is the only musician on the production's payroll at a minimum of $2,975 per week, plus benefits. In addition, there is an up-front fee, ranging widely between $20,000 and $35,000, depending on experience and reputation. The rest of the orchestra is on the theatre's payroll (see above).

13. MAKE-UP ARTISTS & HAIRSTYLISTS (WWW.798MAKEUPANDHAIR.COM)

Local 798 has a membership that gives both regular and specialized haircuts for actors, styles and maintains wigs, and creates character-inspired, non-toxic make-up designs. Most contemporary shows require the actors do their own make-up, sometimes after receiving a lesson or two from a stylist, but in the cases of a green witch in *Wicked*, or a giraffe in Disney's *The Lion King*, or a role requiring an actor to age from adolescent to grandparent, these professionals are hired on a full- or part-time basis and paid a wide range of salaries (at a minimum of $1,183.86 per week plus vacation and benefits, or $35.19 hourly) subject to their workload.

14. LOCAL STAGEHANDS (IATSELOCALONE.ORG)

Stagehands represent the wide range of crew who load in and install the show, do repairs week by week, and run the show from backstage at every performance. Sometimes they work from 8:00 AM repainting parts of the scenery and stage floor, changing light bulbs, reprogramming computers, fixing broken seats in the audience, changing photos in a glass case outside the theatre, purchasing props like food used in each performance, and safeguarding the theatre from fire. Then they come back after a break to mop the stage floor and prepare backstage before the actors arrive and run the hundreds of cues for lights, scenery, and props, designed to make the show exciting.

Job titles include electricians, carpenters, fly persons, automation, property persons, and fireguards. They have to know New York's strict fire codes, environmental protection codes, computer programming, and so much more. The old days when a stagehand basically moved a chair and a table are long gone. When the script calls for sinking a three-story Titanic on stage, stagehands have to make sure it works at every performance.

As late as the 1980s, load-ins, the time it takes to move the lights, scenery, and props into the theatre and put all the pieces together would require a week or two. By the 2000s, load-ins required five weeks or more. Considering that a big musical has needed over two hundred stagehands to load in a show, you can imagine the effect this has had on budgets. Many load-ins now cost over a million dollars by themselves, and the show hasn't even opened. The technological advances, as well as the audience's desire for spectacle, have changed Broadway forever.

The technical supervisor, a few key supervisory stagehands, the company manager, and house manager are all entrusted with overseeing the costs of load-ins. So much money is involved that no one takes this tech period for granted.

Each theatre has three department heads to oversee and protect the interests of the physical space. They are the head carpenter, head electrician, and head property master, hired on an annual basis to work every event in their venue. They often have work to do in the theatre between shows but they may have unpaid down time if the theatre is empty for an extended period of time. No one is allowed to work in the theatre space unless these department heads are present and paid, even if it's a non-show-related event like a benefit, a memorial, a party, or a one-night concert.

A small percentage of the load-in stagehands will stay to operate the show itself. The minimum wage for each stagehand is dependent on their job responsibilities, ranging from $1,810.14 per week for a prop assistant to $2,321.25 per week for a head carpenter, plus benefits and additional duties and work calls, such as repairs and mopping, all of which can add up to $1,000 extra to weekly pay.

15. IATSE PINK CONTRACT STAGEHANDS (IATSE.NET)

The International Alliance of Theatrical Stage Employees (IATSE) is an international parental organization of local unions as well as a union itself for people whose work runs across city, state, national, and international boundaries. As a parent union, the strength of millions of employees helps give the smaller unions more clout to negotiate with producers and theatre owners with less fear of recrimination. ATPAM, USA, Local One, Wardrobe, and the Treasurer's unions are all members of IATSE and pay hefty dues for their membership and protection.

The IATSE Pink Contract stagehands are the eyes and ears of the show's managers and technical supervisor. They ensure that everyone hired is needed and working to help keep costs at a minimum. If the show can operate safely with one less prop person, it can save the show up to $100,000 per year. These Pink Contract men and women work every performance and supervise the technical operation of the Broadway show. They also then direct the re-creation of the production in other cities when a show goes on tour.

Their name comes from the pink-colored contracts used to hire them. Union rules limit the number of Pink Contract stagehands to usually between four and ten per show. Their salaries and benefits are usually equal to the theatre's head stagehands, even though the IATSE minimums are less than the Local One stagehand minimums.

16. CAST RECORDINGS AND TELEVISION APPEARANCES (WWW.SAGAFTRA.ORG)

In 2012, two Hollywood-based unions merged. One was called the Screen Actors Guild (SAG), and the other was the American Federation of Television and Radio Artists (AFTRA). Broadway does not follow SAG/AFTRA rules except when an original cast recording of a musical is made or a television special or commercial is produced, because they are special events that are not covered under the Equity production contract. A second group of qualified producers and staff are hired in these events, but the show's general and company manager create the hybrid budget and therefore must understand the very different union rules for payment and work hours.

17 & 18. AGMA AND AGVA (WWW.MUSICALARTISTS.ORG AND WWW.AGVAUSA.COM)

As with SAG/AFTRA, the rules of the American Guild of Musical Artists (AGMA) and the American Guild of Variety Artists (AGVA) are relevant in special cases only. If an opera comes to the Broadway stage, as when a contemporary remake of *La Bohème* played the Broadway Theatre in 2002, then the show's producers can apply to Actors' Equity Association to replace the usual production contract with an AGMA contract which offers different rehearsals benefits and a slightly lower pay scale for big choruses. If a solo artist does a concert in a Broadway theatre, the show's producer can likewise apply to be placed on an AGVA contract, especially in cases where the artist is not already a member of Equity.

19. TRUCKERS (TEAMSTERS.ORG)

The world-famous Teamsters union, that bills itself as "North America's strongest union," touches only one area of Broadway: the trucking of lights and scenery from union shops to the Broadway theatres. Once the manager gets clearance from the police department for trucks to park in the theatre district, the Teamsters will deliver equipment to the sidewalks in front of the theatre, no farther. The Local One union stagehands will then move the equipment from the sidewalk to the inside of the theatre in the appropriate order necessary to put the show together. The coordination is masterful and designed by the tech supervisor and Pink Contract stagehands. The Teamsters require payment from management before they depart the sidewalk. That will be the last time the show and Teamsters interact until the show closes.

UNION PENSIONS: THE TURKUS AWARD

There used to be an admissions tax to all shows in New York City. No longer. Following a 1960 strike by Actors' Equity Association demanding a pension plan for actors, the city allowed the producers to use that city tax percentage to create a pension fund for the actors instead of paying it to the city. This meant that the producers would not have to pay extra, the city would not lose the tourism revenue that shows generate, and the Broadway workers would get their pension plan and end the strike.

The 4.5 percent (soon to be known as "The .045" pronounced as either "point oh-4-5" or "the oh-4-5") evolved into a system that paid into the pension plans for all unions on Broadway. In 1963, an arbitrator named Burton Turkus came up with the official formula of sharing the .045 among the unions, now known as the Turkus Award.

Turkus based his formula on the percentage of workers from each union working in 1963. Those numbers have changed significantly, but there is a fear that if the unions go back to the table and revamp the percentages, the fighting between unions will be too much to handle. And so the formula has never been changed.

Most unions now require from 6 to 8 percent of each worker's salary to be put into a pension plan. So each week the house manager at each theatre calculates the pension based on each union's current percentage, and then compares it to the 1963 Turkus formula. Whichever calculation is higher determines if and how much extra the theatre contributes to a union's pension fund.

So the .045 is now the minimum guarantee for union pensions. If the .045 is based on salaries for ten musicians, but the show has twelve musicians, then the theatre owes additional pension for two musicians. If the show has eight musicians, then no additional pension is due but none is refunded either. In this case, the extra pension is called an overage. A producer can use this overage to make pension payments for a national tour of the same show, thereby reducing payments for the tour. If the show does not go on tour, the pension plan still keeps the overage.

Box office treasurers deduct the .045 after each performance from the gross receipts on the box office statement. The house managers make pension payments each week.

Health plans and annuities are also paid weekly, as negotiated by each union. Some unions have negotiated that vacation pay be added in increments to weekly salaries. This means that when an employee takes a vacation, they receive no salary for that week since it was already paid. Other unions accumulate vacation credits for each week of work, so paychecks continue during vacation.

Broadway works with specialized payroll companies that have these distinctive union payments included automatically.

PART 2
SELLING TICKETS/ IT'S NOT WHAT IT SEEMS

Chapter 5

Marketing vs. Press vs. Promotion
vs. Advertising

Promotion is generally divided into three budgetary categories: marketing, press, and advertising. They must all work together. Marketing consultants invent *minimal-cost*, outside-the-box events to help brand the show. They find audiences beyond theatre-loving folk. Press agents (also known as press representatives) invent reasons for the media to promote the show free of charge through news articles, commentary, and gossip items. A press rep will also handle personal appearances on television, radio, and Internet.

Advertising agencies design the branding image for posters, flyers, magazine and newspaper ads, television commercials, Internet ads, and more. They adapt that image to various sizes, shapes, and formats, then advise the producer of the best placement choices that stay within the budget. In some cases, the ad agency and/or the press rep will also act as a marketing consultant.

MARKETING

Disney has a corporate division called "Synergy" that ensures the right hand knows what the left hand is doing. For example, as the musical *Aladdin* opened on Broadway in 2014, Synergy contacted the merchandising department, the Imagineering division that creates the rides in the global theme parks, and a dozen other divisions to discuss how to maximize income in each of these separate divisions. Disney counts on the sale of merchandise, film, and music to reinforce the public's interest in buying a Broadway ticket.

Most shows don't have a corporate giant in their pocket, so shows hire a marketing consultant. Up-front fees for a marketing director on a big musical generally average $25,000 up front as part of the production budget, plus a weekly stipend of at least $1,000 as part of the operating budget. Producers face a huge decision here. Does the show need someone like that at all? Traditionally, the position of marketing consultant was something that the press rep handled. Less than forty years ago, separate consultants didn't exist.

On the one hand, especially when reaching broader audiences, there is value in having a knowledgeable and connected person reaching out to specialized communities. On the other hand, just because someone is clever and has done good work for one show doesn't guarantee results for the next show. The costs of special marketing ideas may far outshine the potential ticket sales.

The following example might be considered a clever idea at first glance, but let's analyze what can go wrong and how much time and money can be wasted when marketing tries to validate its own fees. In this case, a struggling show gets the idea to place its unique costumes in an ethnically specific store window. It seems like a simple idea until you consider that the costumes are expensive and one-of-a-kind. Are you going to make copies? The show's wardrobe staff needs to carefully pack up and install the costumes in the window at the store to protect the show's property. (Would you trust your expensive raw silk gown to the local store manager?) You will also need to add posters and enlarged, framed photos, not to mention insurance, transportation, and cleaning when the property is returned. Your team is working hard on this, spending money, and clocking untold hours. When it's all over, the biggest question is: How many tickets did it sell?

John Leguizamo's *Freak* sent staff to hand out coupons at clubs frequented by young Latinos and garnered a uniquely young demographic, earning a profit during its limited twenty-week run. Innovative distribution of discounted coupons can succeed if you know your targeted audience.

Big hits like *Wicked* and *Jersey Boys* can afford marketing outreach. Marketing can strengthen the show's branding throughout New York City and the nation, and in the long run help to make your show run long. Recently, hit shows are experimenting with selling tickets at street fairs in New York City.

Social media outreach, with a well-designed and interactive website, plus Facebook, Instagram, and Twitter pages can engage a youthful audience, but is extremely time consuming and is almost impossible to quantify in box office ticket sales.

The Broadway Green Alliance (BroadwayGreen.com) has worked since 2008 to raise environmental consciousness on and off Broadway, as well as in touring, regional, and college theatres around the country. *Wicked* producer David Stone launched the project with an industry-wide town hall at the Gershwin Theatre, enlisting environmental experts and theatre owners, and representatives from casts, crews, and unions from almost every Broadway theatre. After that, the Alliance was formed, chaired by *Wicked* company manager Susan Sampliner and Charlie Deull, who are still fighting the good fight. Simply by changing the light bulbs outside Broadway houses, the first year saw an 85 percent drop in electricity costs. Backstage batteries are now recharged. Electronics, Playbills, and wardrobe materials are now recycled, and cleaning supplies are environmentally friendly. BroadwayGreen.com saves all Broadway theatre owners and producers significant money and brands them green as the witch of the west.

Unfortunately, it is usually the producer of a struggling show that expects miracles from a marketing consultant and social media. This is sometimes just throwing money away.

Marketing consultants are not unionized, nor are they required to have any particular training. Often their experience comes from working in ad agencies, press offices, film, other entertainment fields, and their unique craftiness.

PRESS REPRESENTATION

Every producer's dream is a press frenzy costing nothing and resulting in a sell-out production running for years. This kind of monster hit show brings never-ending phone calls requesting interviews, photos, and information from literally thousands of journalists, gossip columnists, and bloggers, all with stressful deadlines. And of course you will hear from the real fans and the crazy ones too. Someone needs to filter out the less worthy requests from the serious ones and respond quickly.

Someone also needs to make sure that the correct information—your theatre's name, prices, performance dates, synopsis, credits, and approved photos with correctly spelled and billed names—arrives by deadlines.

And when your star is scheduled for an interview, someone has to make sure all details are covered, and that the celebrity can relay the needed information to sell tickets. For this reason, a press rep usually accompanies everyone being interviewed, including a producer.

This nonstop work is done by a union press agent, a member of Association of Theatrical Press Agents and Managers (ATPAM). Press releases are circulated announcing casting, previews, opening nights, special events, awards, and human-interest angles. They include the press agent's contact information. Press releases don't guarantee that the media is interested sufficiently to print this information. Almost any political or world event story can bump any entertainment story off the pages of even the smallest newspaper.

The press agent has a continually updated list of over a thousand major and minor media representatives, editors, and writers not available to the general public. And the media protects itself by not responding to releases from nonprofessionals, which is by itself worth the price of hiring a press agent.

The press agent contacts the critics, handles their free seating at one of three or four "frozen" performances. Frozen means that the script, songs, and staging is locked in place so that the critic attending the first press performance sees the same show as the critic attending the official opening night show.

The number of critics, their schedules, and the computer age forced the industry to change the traditional concept of an opening night where previously all critics attended and then ran to their typewriters to meet the midnight deadline. When critics arrive, they do not go to the box office, but instead meet a press representative in the lobby. The press rep will bear witness that the real critic has arrived.

ATPAM press agents have gone through serious seminars, a multiyear apprenticeship, and passed a written test and oral interview. They are paid a minimum of $2,162.08 a week beginning well before the show's first rehearsal and continuing until the show closes. This salary must also cover the office rent and utilities. A press rep also expects reimbursement for office expenses such as monthly copying, phones, and Internet, similar to the way that attorneys do.

Since press reps frequently handle more than one show at a time, they often have associates, assistants, and interns in their office. Each show only pays one weekly salary and the press rep must cover additional office salaries needed to work on multiple shows. It should be noted that an assistant is often the primary contact on your show.

There is a great deal of contention among producers that the value of a press agent decreases the longer a show runs. Press agents naturally feel that they are always needed and sometimes work even harder as a show continues, stating that it is more difficult to get free promotion from the media after the show is no longer new. Recent contract negotiations have given a producer the right to reduce the weekly fee to the press agent by 25 percent after three years of service, and 50 percent after seven years. The press agent then has the right to quit the show, of course. But the PA cannot be fired without cause. Since ATPAM requires all Broadway theatres to have a union press agent, the producer would then have to find a new press agent willing to handle the show at the reduced rate. To date, no producer has used this new rule.

The marketing consultant and press agent are always proving themselves in terms of new media positioning and box office surges. Producers want results, and no matter how dedicated or how much work has been performed, producers complain . . . a lot. The problem for press agents of long-running shows (and marketing consultants too) is that there's always a new show ready to open, and the media sells more papers, and the Internet gets more "hits," by covering new events.

The largest press agent's office at this writing is Boneau Bryan-Brown. They handle many of Broadway's biggest hits and have a large staff of experienced press reps, union apprentices, and interns. One advantage for big offices is their ability to make quiet deals with the media. "If you want the first interview with Denzel Washington, you need to promise me that you'll include my other show's author prominently in a different article." This makes both show's producers and one author very happy that they are receiving attention.

The union's "multiplicity rules" restricts press agents from handling more than three shows without hiring union associates, who are paid less than the senior press rep but work just as hard. This protects the producer by keeping a press agent from being spread too thin, and probably protects the press agent from having more stress attacks than they already have.

The smallest press offices consist of independent press reps like the ones portrayed in old Hollywood movies, sometimes with an assistant, sometimes not. They personally cater to the wishes of producers and stars alike. One example is the one-woman office of Susan L. Schulman who, after forty years in the business working in larger offices, has decided she prefers to work on her own. Sometimes she's able to wield the same influence as the larger offices, and sometimes not. A dedicated press agent can focus on one show's interest. But a dedicated press agent has no additional shows to bargain with. Each producer and general manager makes a judgment call about the ideal press representation.

In common, all press agents are eventually blamed when the producer doesn't get the desired media coverage. The effort might have been great, but it's only the results that matter.

ADVERTISING

There doesn't seem to be a way to avoid the costs of advertising. There is no independent consultant to hire. There are only a few giant specialized theatre agencies.

Serino-Coyne, SpotCo, Pekoe Group, and AKA NYC are major ad agencies focused on Broadway theatre. Each show gets individualized treatment, and comes with years of experience knowing what makes a show flop or hit big. The size and reputation of these giants can help your show find appreciable advertising discounts, special offers, and ideas with impact.

Advertising agencies do a lot and charge a lot. A big musical can spend over $2 million in advertising before the show reaches opening night. A small drama might spend $350,000 before opening. While it may be costly to have them design the artwork, these agencies understand the formats needed to fit into the multiple platforms used, making it advantageous.

An ad agency's job is to put your show in its best light. A print ad, and a radio or television commercial are the only times when the media doesn't get to tell you what they like or don't like about your show. You have total control because you're paying for it. Unfortunately many producers want it all and don't want to listen to the realities of a Broadway budget. Spending too much can close a show very quickly. It's the ad agency's rep, along with the general manager, who must teach novice producers how to make effective choices and not overspend.

Weekly meetings are held at the agency's offices, where producers are presented with options for magazines, newspapers, online blogs, websites, television, radio, billboards, tourist brochures, banner ads, and much more. When possible, ad reps will use their influence to get radio and ad space in exchange for "trade" (barter in exchange for complimentary tickets). Suggestions for logo artwork, size of ads, catch phrases, use of critic's reviews, billboards, and other creative choices will be presented and debated. Except for the major logo choices, there is no time to ponder these decisions outside of this meeting. The media has real deadlines, and special deals and discounts must be accepted quickly or lost. Think of this as buying the house you love when there are multiple offers on the table. You must act fast.

These weekly ad meetings are attended by the show's lead producer, the press agent, the general manager, the agency's chief, and assigned agency representative. The company manager rarely attends this meeting, but is notified about the final decisions to plan for the budgetary impact of that day's choices.

It is the production itself that ultimately decides if a show will survive, but until you can visually brand your show through art and graphics in well-chosen locations, you may not be able to convince total strangers from other states and countries to pay exorbitant ticket prices. Obviously, the public already knows the comic book superhero Spiderman, but they may have no idea what an *Equus* might be. Yet the original production of *Equus* was a hit and *Spider-Man: Turn Off the Dark* was Broadway's biggest financial flop to date.

Posters in store windows, on billboards, in subway stations, on taxi cabs, on the backs of buses, and in ticketing offices have traditionally put a face on each show. In the days when ticket brokers littered the theatre district with small storefronts, they covered their walls and windows with window cards.

Only seventeen inches wide and twenty-two inches tall, these posters mounted on inflexible card stock took up less room than a traditional movie or concert poster. They are still used today, even though only a few ticket brokers remain in the lobbies of hotels with digital displays instead of posters.

The large vertical theatre poster, known as a "three-sheet," is wallpapered in subway stations, printed in two unequal sizes: the bottom part is one-third of the total poster and the top portion is two-thirds of the three-sheet. The other subway poster size is horizontal and fits specific wall shapes in certain areas of subway stations.

The producer and general manager must decide if the budget should pay for a television commercial requiring writers, a director, designers, actors, graphic artists, camera operators, sound engineers, and a commercial producer. There are many types of commercials and none of their costs are small. After the commercial is made, your show must buy time on television, another expensive chunk of change from your already taxed budget. The ad agency will add commissions to all costs. That's how they make their money.

The least expensive television commercial production is known as a "testimonial" where the camera captures audiences testifying how much they loved the show as they exit the theatre. Truth be told, most of these audience members work for the ad agencies or other related companies. It doesn't mean that their opinion is to be rejected. The excitement in the voice of one lady as she left Harvey Fierstein's Tony-winning hit play *Torch Song Trilogy* declaring that "it is the only Broadway show I have seen recently that I would gladly pay more for" seemed to match the word-of-mouth buzz from others who had seen the show. Some people bought tickets to this show because of that ad alone and kept the groundbreaking comedy running for three years. It is sometimes thought that a television commercial can save a struggling show. Producers ask investors for "overcall" money (see Chapter 11: Unique Broadway Financials) or find new angles to cover the cost of production and airtime.

Some producers do not recognize that it takes at least three weeks for an effective television commercial to translate into ticket sales at the box office. Therefore it is not a quick fix for sagging income. Broadway theatre is just not a priority and the public won't jump into action just because a commercial has sparked some new interest.

Broadway shows cannot afford to buy national airtime on major network shows, and the predominant television audience is not going to buy a Broadway seat no matter what you show them. Historically less than 20 percent of the public in the tri-state area (New York, New Jersey, and Connecticut) have ever seen even one theatrical presentation anywhere. The audience has expanded thanks to Disney's outreach and thanks to the draw of monster hits like *The Book of Mormon*, *Cats*, and *Mamma Mia*, but it is still limited.

Ad agencies will suggest a graphic artist or provide someone in-house. *Equus*, first produced on Broadway in 1974 by the successful producer Kermit Bloomgarden, who also brought us *The Diary of Anne Frank* and *The Miracle Worker*, created a buzz with three weeks of small ads in the *New York Times* that had no writing, no title, or anything else. The graphic artist Gilbert Lesser designed a provocative and haunting logo making us ask the question, "What is this?" People began talking about the ad. This was an expensive gamble, but it sold tickets. Luckily the show was wonderful, a financial hit, and won the Tony Award for Best Play.

Few poster artists gain fame for their body of work like Paul Davis. His work helped brand and sell Broadway shows originating at the New York Shakespeare Festival and Lincoln Center theatres from *For Colored Girls . . .* to *Caroline or Change*, for decades.

After all is said and done, the audience must easily find your show's information. The *New York Times* is noted for its ABCs, an alphabetical listing of every Broadway and Off Broadway show currently selling tickets. They charge each show by the line, so every quote from a critic, every descriptive line, every credit for an actor, author, or producer costs more money, and it adds up quickly. Your ad agency will suggest how much value you get for your buck. Sometimes it will be worth the extra cost to include a rave review; sometimes it will use up ad money you may need to pay for television time or magazine ads.

There are so many important decisions to make for the health and wealth of a show. In any one week, your ad budget can be divided among outdoor (phone kiosks, parking garages, billboards, tourist centers), local, national and international print (weekly, monthly, quarterly magazines, and daily and weekly newspapers), online (ads on Facebook, Twitter, Google, theatre websites, online Broadway magazines), direct response sales websites (TDF, Theatremania, Broadway Box, BroadwayWorld, Groupon, Living Social, Broadway.com), special promotions (American Express, Visa, and other business partnerships), television and radio commercials (local and national), and special events. There is never enough money to go around, and the *New York Times* is no longer the sole domain of theatre audiences.

It is the producer and general manager who decide what they can afford and where they get the biggest bang for the buck. They must know the audience that will buy tickets and reach them with decisions made sometimes months in advance. A New Jersey suburban middle-age couple will buy seats differently than their twenty-something children. Church-going groups from Maryland will organize a trip to New York City on a limited budget, and make their selection based on different criteria than a high school group from the Bronx or Connecticut or Manhattan.

The producer can spend most of every day analyzing box office data and deciding about future ad expenditures, making it all the more important to have a trusted management team to rely on for everything else. The ad agency will offer suggestions, discounted deals, and insight, but the producer will ultimately decide.

BILLING

Advertising space costs money and every line needs to make an impact. Celebrities sell tickets. There are celebrity performers, playwrights, directors, and plays. Agents will argue the power of their clients and why their client's name should be BIGGER, **bolder**, highlighted, or written in a fancy font.

Contract negotiations can get very specific about where and when special billing is given. Management may already plan to give someone special billing, but not want to be contractually obligated. Poster credits become obsolete when the cast changes and posters need to be reprinted and redistributed, which is costly. The size of an ad varies; in order to permit a small ad, management will need to be free to omit as many credits as possible. Marquee changes require new artwork, reprinting, an outside contractor, and union labor to take down the old and put up the new. Every time a billing credit changes, money is spent.

Billing is not only for stars. Sometimes agents will accept a slightly lower salary for their client in exchange for special billing, because a special billing can make a star. If an unknown artist is given a standout billing, the implication will be, "Need we say more?"

To avoid these issues and costs, nonprofit producing organizations tend to offer alphabetical billing for all actors including stars, even on Broadway.

Billing an actor above or below the show's title can affect the eligible category for a Tony Award. The Tony Award committee can also be petitioned to move a performer from Best Actor to Best Featured Actor category and vice versa. Agents, managers, ad executives, and press reps are all aware that billing can make a difference during award season.

PROMOTIONAL GAME PLANS

Most Broadway budgets put aside a minimum of 20 percent of their total production and weekly operating budgets for advertising, press, and marketing. Often 20 percent will not be enough if the producer wants to blitz all media.

How much to spend is a critical decision. If the sets and salaries eat up most of the budget, then there is little money for promotion and the decision is already made, although perhaps deadly.

There are two basic avenues of thought when it comes to promotion.

If you have the money, you can use a myriad of media outlets available to you worldwide. This game plan says: If enough tickets are sold and a lot of money is made before opening, the show can survive almost any critical reviews. Selling advance tickets means flooding the media with advance advertising and can be costly. Many big musicals follow this game plan. *Evita* and *Cats* are examples of shows that used this philosophy successfully. *Cats* arrived in New York with the largest box office advance in history at that time, and ignored mediocre reviews.

There are limits to this concept of media spending. *Ragtime* producer Garth Drabinsky spent infinitely too much money on ads in the *New York Times* for more than six months to sell advance tickets. *Ragtime* was a major critical success but never paid back its investors. His many critical hits on Broadway produced under his company Livent (*Kiss of the Spider Woman, Ragtime, Fosse*) never paid any profits to his investors. Note: Mr. Drabinsky was eventually convicted of fraud and forgery, and disbarred in his native Canada.

The other producing style believes that a show should spend as little as possible up front, since a show is a major gamble and has a very small chance of being a hit. We've said this before in this book, but it bears repeating: Only about 20 percent of all Broadway shows will return the original costs to its investors.

The idea behind this game plan is to wait until the audience and critics say it's a hit. With good word-of-mouth and great reviews, it now makes sense to spend box office earnings on advertising. Most nonmusicals practice this philosophy. This way, if the show closes quickly, at least investors lose the smallest amount absolutely necessary to mount the show before the critics arrive on opening night. Examples of successful plays that waited for the reviews to come out before investing in advertising include *Freak, The Motherf**cker with the Hat*, and *I Am My Own Wife*.

These wait-and-see producers may not be guided by a business plan, but rather by the limited money available to spend. A show that has a large cast or expensive scenery needs the money for necessary production costs, and there just isn't enough to also saturate the media.

A variation of this wait-for-the-reviews game plan has a bit less risk to it. If a show has received rave reviews Off Broadway or abroad, the play comes to Broadway with a reputation that can sell tickets without using a big ad budget. These successes sometimes have a celebrity in the cast to boost ticket sales. But the New York reviews can still dampen enthusiasm and stop the momentum cold.

Either way, experienced producers usually know why they are spending a little or a lot of money for promotion. Inexperienced producers must rely on their general managers and ad agencies, and as long as they are prepared to make quick and informed decisions, they too can turn an unknown theatrical event into a bona fide Broadway hit.

Chapter 6

Opening Nights and the Tony Awards

Abbreviations used in this chapter and in the theatre world at large:

ON = opening night(s)
GM = general manager
CM = company manager
PR = press representative/agent
AEA = Actors' Equity Association

OPENING NIGHT

Company managers (CM), the people who run the show's operations and represent the producers and general manager (GM) on a day-to-day basis, will tell you that every official opening night (ON) is a new production unto itself. That this important event must be planned at the same time as rehearsing and previewing the new show makes it especially exhausting.

To qualify as a Broadway theatre, audience capacity must be at least five hundred seats. Currently the two largest theatres, the Gershwin and Lyric Theatres, have just under two thousand seats. The smallest Broadway house is the Helen Hayes Theatre with five hundred ninety-seven seats. These seats are filled on opening night with critics, media, and family and friends of the producers, cast, crew, staff, and industry folk, as well as some of the general public. They can't all sit on an aisle in the orchestra section of the theatre.

Opening nights are disasters waiting to happen, and yet there are relatively few problems because the people in charge are experienced professionals. The general manager, company manager, and press representative consider it their solemn duty to make the night a positive experience. If the show closes soon after it is reviewed, it may be the last time the show has something to celebrate.

Some producers and managers see little reason to spend a lot of money on an opening night party, restricting the event's budget to under $35,000. Other producers, a la Cameron Mackintosh (*The Phantom of the Opera, Cats*), want to use the party as a marketing tool and have spent over $300,000 for the one-night gala and party. This is a discussion and a decision between producer and general manager, and of course is determined by the amount of money raised by the producer and needed to get the show to opening night and beyond.

There are producers who are extravagant spenders and, like any bad business partner, their spending habits must be reined in. There are also producers who are tight with their money and/or hate unions and believe everything should cost less than it does. The general manager's job is to advise, teach, control, and ultimately help make the production a success by keeping it all within practical standards.

The GM will have negotiated away some seats to the production's stars for their family, agents, and friends. Seating locations will have been promised to certain producers, designers, agents, and others. Investors will expect special seating as well, although it is a common practice to charge investors full price for their ON seats. Those working on the show, a restricted number of guests, and VIPs are usually offered complimentary tickets. The critics and their one guest get in for free.

The CM usually organizes the assignment of seats with the box office treasurers making sure that the seats assigned actually exist (yes, it's happened where the seating chart isn't the same as the physical seats in the theatre).

The CM will likely count every seat in the theatre before tickets go on sale. Sound equipment and lighting grids can change the shape of some rows of seats and the use of boxes (small, separate balconies extending from the side walls, usually with 4 or 5 seats). Once the director has staged the show, it might be determined that some seats have partial views or no view at all. This can greatly affect where you seat VIPs and friends. Critics get the preferred seats, unless the ceiling starts to leak over the prime section during a massive rainstorm, like it did on one opening night. Of course the show went on. In 1995's *On the Waterfront*, a featured actor had a heart attack on stage during the third scene and had to be replaced by his understudy after a short hold. The actor survived and the show got a lot of press coverage, but terrible reviews. It closed a week later.

There are so many critics nowadays that the rules of engagement for ON have changed. Bloggers and other self-anointed Internet critics can affect the show's word-of-mouth and therefore cannot be dismissed as unimportant.

The rules and lists of approved critics are rewritten annually by the press community and the Broadway League (association of producers and theatre owners). In general, critics are invited to any one of four performances, known as press performances. The fourth and final of these shows is considered the official opening night. The mainstream press has long ago agreed not to publish a review of a show until after the official opening night. Many bloggers follow no such rules. However, disobeying these rules can result in being dropped from the critics list.

The producer applies early to the Broadway League to reserve an official opening date. This avoids conflicting and overlapping opening nights so that mainstream critics and their editors can more easily schedule the publication of reviews. As the Tony Award nomination deadline approaches in late April, getting the first choice ON date can be problematic. The Tony Awards air in early June and producers want their show to be an eligible nominee.

In previous decades, the newspaper deadlines required scheduling the official opening night performance at 6:15 PM or 6:45 PM rather than the usual 8:00 PM curtain time. This was to accommodate the reviewer's writing deadline and to allow the company to arrive at the party at a reasonable hour. The Internet has eased deadline requirements, and adding three more press performances for critics has eliminated the requirement for an early curtain.

Of course, there are many famous stories of critics who wrote 75 percent of their reviews before they saw the production. Major critics request written versions of scripts in advance, or read the book, or see the film upon which the play is based. They can fill in an actor's name or a comment about the set after they see the show.

Getting correct and complete information to critics and editors is essential, so Playbill, the official free program given to all ticket-holders as they are seated, must be accurate and up to date at every press performance and ON. The press agent (PR) is in charge of correcting and collecting data for Playbill. Playbill cannot make changes overnight. In fact, it usually takes two weeks to make changes in the program. Considering that the cast may change during rehearsals and previews, that musical numbers may be omitted or added, and that names are sometimes printed incorrectly, watching over the primary source of information is not easy and the actors' union is strict about immediate corrections, especially for ON. Ushers are paid to insert an extra correction page printed by Playbill or by the press office itself.

Playbill has a monopoly at all Broadway theatres dating back to an agreement between past theatre executives and the owners of Playbill. This agreement had no termination clause and therefore exists to this very day. Attempts to privately print programs in order to have effortless control over its content have been tried and squelched. Playbill provides a wonderful free program with articles, biographies, history, and lots of ads, but producers are shackled to it.

During a production meeting, the press agent will request specific seating locations to be used exclusively for reporters and critics at all press performances. The producer and managers will compile a list of all other contractual seating commitments and wishes. The box office will take all seats off-line so they cannot be sold to the general public. For the box office, ON is mostly a give-away with a little bit of full-price sales.

Sometimes the manager and press agent will release blocked tickets last minute to be sold to the general public. These seats are usually in the very back or extreme side of the theatre. Management's job is to earn as much money for the producer and investors as possible, and therefore ticket availability is scrutinized carefully and constantly.

The CM acts as the keeper of these seats and no one else talks directly with the box office, unless they are willing to accept a potential mess on ON. When done well, ON can be free of trouble, but it is never without stress. Tickets are handed out by the box office on the day of the show after all last-minute changes have been made. This means potential bottlenecking at the will-call window that evening. Therefore, everyone is asked to make the special trip on the afternoon of ON to pick up tickets. Critics' tickets are held by the press agents and handed out personally outside the theatre just before the show.

There will of course be additional changes immediately before the show and a smart CM will carry a few emergency tickets. The CM will also have a few people prepared to fill seats when a critic or celebrity has failed to show up.

Some critics will only attend the official ON because they want to be invited to the party.

Some parties are bland and others can be exciting. This is New York City and costs per head quickly add up. Finding a large party space at 10:30 PM on a weeknight can also be a challenge, especially in the theatre district.

The producer must decide who is invited to the party. If there are seventeen hundred seats in the theatre, it will be prohibitive to invite everyone. Yet how do you tell a celebrity that she can't bring her entire family, or an investor that there is only room for two of his guests? Producers are not always in contact with many of the people in their employ, and therefore forget to include them, or in some cases, refuse to include them. Such omissions can backfire when staff or crew are asked for a favor later on.

Party guests will rush to the party location, but cast members need to get out of costume and dress for the occasion, and they have friends or family to escort. This may take an extra hour. It is just polite etiquette to keep the food unavailable until the cast arrives. It has been known for a waiting crowd to gobble up the entire buffet before a single cast member enters the room.

Some managers warn against penny-wise and pound-foolish. There is no excuse for telling your crew that they are not invited. Crew may understand if their spouses cannot be accommodated, but chances are that most spouses will not come anyway due to the late hour. Ushers do not necessarily expect to be invited to an expensive party, but if you do invite them, you win their hearts and appreciation for the entire run of the show. Forgetting your box office, your entire cast and understudies, your insurance broker, attorney, theatre executives and their staff (as per the theatre rental agreement), merchandise supplier, group sales brokers, critics, important family members, and possibly everyone's guests, can be detrimental to the work favors you may need as your show struggles for a footing with the public.

Some producers and theatre owners could care less about making everyone happy. Either way, a producer will count on a GM or CM to make sure that costs are carefully controlled while avoiding insulting omissions—very tricky and time consuming.

ON gifts should not be overlooked and may be one of the first things discussed in early production meetings. If your show closes quickly, it may be the only nice thing you have to compensate for your grief and debt. Gifts range from framed posters to engraved coffee mugs to personalized thank-you notes. Celebrities in the cast will often get a significant item worth hundreds of dollars. Managers must make a list of everyone receiving a gift and then arrange for delivery at the ON event, or directly to an office or home sometime after ON.

Long distance travel to an ON party is not the best idea. Broadway theatres are not available for parties. Remember that every time you enter the theatre, you involve substantial union costs. When Public Theater's Off Broadway show *Runaways* transferred to Broadway, they rented buses with waiters and champagne to bring the audience to the theatre's home base in Greenwich Village. In most cases, partygoers walk or taxi from the theatre to party site. One show at the American Airlines Theatre rented Madame Tussauds Wax Museum in the theatre district and catered the event among statues of Barbra

Streisand and Michael Jackson. Creativity abounds when selecting a Broadway party site.

Party tickets must be coordinated with the ON tickets and a staff member guards the door to be sure that only invited guests get into the party. Party crashers are not uncommon. In olden days, there was a ceremonial read of the *New York Times* review around midnight and was an additional reason for guests to stay. That's a rarity nowadays but it's nice when someone takes the initiative to introduce key players. If there is a presentation during the party, someone must arrange for microphones, sound system, lighting, piano, etc. The ceremony of ON has changed, but the potential excitement has not.

The morning after ON has not changed. The lead producer, managers, ad agency, marketing consultants, and PR meet early in the morning at the ad agency's conference room to read the reviews and discuss how to sell tickets to the show. It can be as simple as choosing a few quotes from the reviews and putting them together in an ad. In some cases, the reviews will be ignored completely in favor of branding the show through audience opinions rather than those of the critics.

The box office will open at 10:00 AM the day after ON. The number of people standing in line to buy tickets, and data from overnight online sales, will let everyone know if they have a major hit, a possible hit, a fight on their hands, or a turkey.

The performance schedule is often adjusted for the week of the press performances and ON. It is not deemed a good idea to have a day off just prior to inviting critics. Actors' Equity Association (AEA) has given special concessions to permit a scheduling change leading up to ON. To compensate, the day after the official ON is often a day off.

Of course, the number of performances allowed is still limited to eight in a seven-day week. Rehearsal time is extended to allow for the last minute rush to ON. Such days are called "10 out of 12" allowing performers to rehearse any ten hours over a period of twelve consecutive hours. The crew will often work from 8:00 AM to midnight on these days, and receive overtime pay for the work. Sleep time and meal breaks for crew are regulated as well. Management has no such protections and often works their longest hours during this period.

While union rules allow musicians to use approved substitutes (subs) as much as 50 percent of each work week, this rule is not valid during the weeks leading up to an opening night. Consistency of cast, musicians, crew, and staff is required and guaranteed so that the critics see the best version of the show possible.

Some opening nights have dress codes, because most theatregoers are now a mixture of formal, informal, and downright relaxed. Rarely is the outside of the theatre spruced up with red carpet and rented klieg lights but now and then it happens. ON audiences clog the sidewalks and street waiting to see who is arriving and chatting with theatre associates, right up until the last minute. Staff must announce that the curtain is about to go up (even if there is no curtain) just to get them seated.

Onstage just before the audience enters, cast members get together for the Gypsy Robe ceremony. It occurs at every Broadway musical that has a chorus. Thirty minutes before the curtain rises, a robe decorated with patches from all previous musicals is given to a chorus member in that show with the most Broadway credits. The bearer of the robe circles the stage three times allowing cast members to touch it for good luck, and then visits each dressing room. The robe is then delivered to the next musical on its opening night. The ceremony started in 1950 with *Gentlemen Prefer Blondes* and has been a tradition ever since.

Opening Night can be an amazing event, or just an excuse to let the critics write their reviews, but it still carries the anticipation of success or failure, of financial gain or complete loss, of being a part of the Broadway family and history, or pending unemployment. Hundreds of people are affected by the events of this one night and it is a memory that can last an entire life.

TONY AWARDS

The Tony Awards are not what they seem. While there are many other theatre awards, the Tony Awards offer the most prestige and bragging rights on Broadway. One reason is that it is televised on CBS-TV, a major national television network.

The quiet secret behind the Tony Awards telecast is that it can close the doors on one show as often as keep the doors open on another. It is extremely expensive to perform on the award telecast and productions that have small budgets or are struggling at the box office wrestle with the risk of losing its last dime versus losing a national audience.

The Tonys are a mixed blessing, at best. The CBS broadcast has the lowest viewership of any television special on the major networks in any given year. The program does well in New York City and Los Angeles, but garners little interest elsewhere except theatre fans. Less viewership means less income from commercials. Less income for CBS means a smaller programming budget and higher costs to the nominated shows.

Each Broadway musical trying to make an impression on television wants the biggest splash, as does CBS. An average musical may have twenty performers but they don't show up alone. Wardrobe people are needed to handle the costumes. The scenery and lights are not moved from the theatre to the broadcast stage, but redesigned and built from scratch in a union scene shop, as are any large props. The show's musical supervisor preserves the quality of the music performed. When the Tonys are broadcast from a Broadway theatre, there aren't enough dressing rooms for all the cast and backstage staff from so many shows, so each show's theatre must be opened on a usually dark (closed) night. This requires a doorman, security, house management, theatre crews, and additional utility charges such as air conditioning.

Each Broadway show's managers and press representatives are also working additional hours on a night off, coordinating the event from start to finish. The director and choreographer usually have to adapt and restage the musical number to fit the television time frame and format and that requires rehearsal time, studios, and other costs. And everyone must be transported from the show's theatre to and from the CBS-TV venue.

The entire event has its own budget created by each show's managers. Even the cost of backstage refreshments at the Tony Awards are charged back to the Broadway show. Total cost for a Broadway musical to perform on the Tony Awards can reach over a quarter of a million dollars. It is sometimes suggested that it would be cheaper and more effective to use that money to broadcast a new TV commercial instead.

There's more to report. While in the past, nominees were required to pay for their own seats at the award show, they are now given two free tickets per nominee. In the past, only one, two, or three producing names appeared over the title of the show. In the contemporary theatre world, there can be more than twenty-five producers who will want to walk onstage if their show wins the big award, Best Play or Best Musical. The cost of seating all of the producers is outrageous; so additional producers, beyond the general partner (lead producer), must purchase their own tickets.

In recent years, the Tony Awards have broadcast from Radio City Music Hall with over five thousand seats, ensuring that there is enough room to sell tickets to the public in addition to the theatre participants and their families. The controversy is that some of the traditional Broadway union jobs at Radio City are staffed by nonunion people. Some argue that an event that celebrates Broadway should utilize the union community that gave the nominated shows their life.

On the other hand, when the Tony Awards were held in a Broadway theatre, seating large numbers was difficult and the production numbers had to work around the scenery from the current production in that theatre. Rehearsal time and space were also limited by the theatre's performance schedule. Ultimately, the American Theatre Wing's Tony Award administration, CBS Television, and the management/production office that oversees the entire operation, decide where to produce the telecast on a year-by-year basis.

The Tony Award administration invites a select group of experienced Broadway veterans to serve as nominators for three years. These thirty-three nominators are a combination of playwright, director, producer, manager, designer, composer, etc. Their personal tastes can greatly affect whether a rock musical or a Rodgers and Hammerstein revival receives more nominations, and determine which actors are nominated. They meet to vote the night before the nominations are announced; each nominator submits their personal choices and it is tallied and televised early in the morning on nomination day, similar to the Oscars.

Once nominated, each show must promote the awards, adding to the show's advertising costs. Currently there are eight hundred six Tony Award voters comprised of: Broadway producers, theatre owners (from across America), board members from all theatre unions, and theatre professionals in acting, writing, and design categories. The Tony administration no longer allows critics or the press to vote with the exception of the members of the New York Drama Critics Circle. Each show immediately sends out invitations to voters who have approximately one month to see all nominated shows. These voters are allowed to bring one guest with them and, of course, sit in great seats, translating to 1,612 free high-priced seats that must be given away in the month of May. At approximately $175 per ticket (up to $450 per seat if the show has premium locations!), each show is losing about $350,000 or more in ticket sales. This is very expensive for a show that has just recently opened, not to mention a show that may end up winning one award or no award at all when the contest is over.

Careful ticketing records are kept about which Tony voters RSVP and how many times they change their reservations. IDs are usually required at the box office to be sure that the actual voter is attending the show. The company manager supervises this process. The press agent will still add press-worthy celebrities and critics during this time, but the "house seats" usually reserved for producers' associates will be reduced to almost nothing while Tony voter month is active.

The Tony Awards are not the only game in town. Deadlines and award categories vary. Some organizations choose to include all New York shows, not just Broadway. The list of award ceremonies in alphabetical order include:

CLARENCE DERWENT AWARDS

Best individual male and female supporting role performances on Broadway ($2000 each given by AEA in honor of the union's past president).

DRAMA DESK AWARDS

All professional productions are considered for an award, not just Broadway. Presented in May by a committee of theatre writers, critics, and editors.

DRAMA LEAGUE AWARDS

Distinguished musical, play, revivals, and performers with special honorary awards as well. No design awards. Presented by the Drama League of NY around May of each year at a luncheon.

FRED AND ADELE ASTAIRE AWARDS

Awards are presented each June to a Broadway choreographer and dancers recognizing outstanding achievement in dance.

GLAAD MEDIA AWARDS

A national award that honors performers and media people with remarkable contributions to the LGBT community.

HENRY HEWES DESIGN AWARDS

The American Theatre Wing (Tony Award presenters) also present an award for theatre design originating in the United States.

NEW YORK DRAMA CRITICS CIRCLE AWARDS

Twenty-six New York drama critics bestow an award for Best Play and Best Musical in New York City. Playwrights receive a cash award. A separate award is sometimes granted for a show originating outside the USA.

NAACP THEATRE AWARDS

A national award that honors theatre performers and media people of color in a televised Los Angeles ceremony.

OUTER CRITICS CIRCLE AWARDS

Twenty-four categories receive awards from a group of critics, reporters, academics, and others from outside the New York area. Broadway, Off Broadway, and Off-Off Broadway are eligible.

PULITZER PRIZE FOR DRAMA

Awarded by a jury of one academic and four critics for American dramas or musicals staged in the United States during the previous January 1 through December 31. The committee sometimes chooses not to grant the award to anyone. The winning playwright receives a cash award.

THEATRE WORLD AWARD

Many American performers making their debut on Broadway are honored each year for their first distinguished appearance. Recently, new awards have been added for acting ensemble work and lifetime achievement. Awards are presented by a small committee of theatre writers sponsored by Theatre World books.

Additionally, the Broadway League, the Dramatist Guild, and many unions honor their own each year. For example, the Horton Foote Prize is given to playwrights for excellence in American theatre through the Dramatist Guild. Please visit each union's websites to discover the slew of supportive awards offered (see Chapter 4: Unions).

Three other New York theatre awards target non-Broadway productions, but help to promote Broadway transfers:

AUDELCO "VIV" AWARDS (AUDIENCE DEVELOPMENT COMMITTEE, INC.)

Awards directors, performers, writers, designers, and producers from the African American community working with nonprofit theatres that have produced for at least two years anywhere in New York City, including community theatre, Off Broadway, and Broadway.

LUCILLE LORTEL AWARDS

The League of Off Broadway Theatres presents these awards in May for Off Broadway theatre only. If a show transfers from Off Broadway to a Broadway venue, it takes the kudos with it for marketing purposes.

OBIE AWARDS

Obie stands for Off Broadway. Some shows originate in Off Broadway and Off-Off Broadway venues, then move to the larger marketplace of Broadway and take the award status with them for marketing purposes. Obies are presented by the *Village Voice*, a free newspaper available on the streets of Manhattan every Wednesday.

New York has a different sensibility than other cities across the United States. New York critics and audiences appreciate a bit of cynicism, blue humor, nudity, serious intellectual challenge, and more liberal subject matter. New York audiences have already "seen everything" and may not be impressed with the same material as other American regions.

As with all entertainment awards, politics play a role. But there is a high level of integrity involved too.

Chapter 7

Merchandising, Original Cast Recordings, and Holiday Scheduling

There are two moneymaking enterprises that operate like stepchildren in a close-knit family: merchandise and original cast recordings. Until these business opportunities are in the producer's face, they remain off the grid. Considering that money must be advanced to produce these materials, and how much money can be earned, it is surprising that budgets are created without any dedicated budget line, often burying costs in promotion or contingency expenditures.

Following Disney Theatrical's expertise and success, managers have learned more and more about this side business. Until Disney scored big with merchandising for *Beauty and the Beast* on Broadway, souvenir sales had not been a primary focus for Broadway producers. Disney Theatricals reportedly earned more weekly profit from merchandise than ticket sales during some weeks in its early years on Broadway. That raised many eyebrows among older producing organizations that had previously set up one booth in the lobby and hoped for the best. Now Disney showed them that this secondary business could be extremely lucrative.

Of course, if the show flops, then the merchandise takes up storage space and nothing more. If the show doesn't lend itself to souvenirs, such as some dramas, then souvenirs may not make sense at all. This is a judgment call and a big gamble. Even major concerts can lose money on merchandise because of high costs and lack of audience interest.

Obviously, Broadway has always been a tiny marketplace in comparison to major distributors of tourism t-shirts, mugs, key chains, posters, and recordings. The shopping public is limited to the size of each show's audience, which has only thirty minutes before the show, fifteen minutes during intermission, and another fifteen to thirty minutes after the show.

The initial outlay of cash to produce the souvenir items along with the operating costs of salaries, souvenir stands, signage, sales tax, accounting, and storage can mean a significant loss for an unpopular show or failed design choices.

The quality, color, and design of a t-shirt affect prices, but the size of the order and the company behind it matter more. A show jacket with an intricate logo on its back costs $200 each from a New York company but less than $100 each from a Los Angeles company whose clients are movie studios with super large orders. Advertising firms can help find the best company, but managers often rely on recommendations from other managers.

The other option is to hire an outside firm to run concessions including souvenirs. Again, recommendations from other managers makes more sense than hiring your uncle who is promising you a family deal, that will most likely backfire and create ill will among family and friends.

The original cast album for musicals, discussed in more detail below, is both a desired product and a great tool for marketing the show. It is also commonly a losing proposition for the record labels. Only a handful of Broadway cast albums have turned a profit for their labels, and therefore producers have found resistance in finding a label until a show has shown some evidence of success.

T-shirts and coffee mugs are a staple in the souvenir world but unless the color, design, and quality are popular, they may just end up in a producer's basement. Professional t-shirt makers know what colors sell best and it is wise to follow their advice. Surprisingly, t-shirt manufacturers report that more black or white t-shirts are sold than any other color.

In each theatre, there is at least one refreshment stand. These stands are not equipped to sell anything but drinks and snacks at inflated prices. In the newer and larger venues, merchandise can also be sold at the counter, except that the audience may not be able to get past the line for a cocktail in the short intermission time. Merchandise stands are therefore added at the producer's cost and only where there is sufficient room without affecting fire exit access. This is particularly difficult in the older, smaller theatres.

Each show in one of the older and smaller theatres must therefore find a hot spot to sell its wares. During *Beauty and the Beast*, Disney Theatricals opened merchandise booths on every level of the theatre and had a dozen booths available in the main lobby as everyone entered and exited. Disney also sold items outside the theatre on a mobile cart during the day when the theatre was closed.

A $1 bottle of water on the New York streets will cost $4 in the theatre. Hard drinks and large noisy bags of candy cost the public more than their street value. The attendants and the supervising refreshment company take their costs off the top, often 35 percent or more. In some theatres, the theatre owner owns the concessions. This will be clearly stated in the theatre rental agreement.

In all cases, the theatre owner monitors and audits the daily and weekly receipts through its central financial staff. The tenant (the show) receives its share after the theatre takes its own share. This is exactly the same system of payment used to distribute box office income.

Concessionaires, whether hired by the theatre or the contracted refreshment company, also provide staff for infrared hearing headsets that are free of charge to patrons, whether they are hard of hearing or more significantly impaired. As technology improves, some theatre owners are now installing hearing loops, allowing those with certain hearing aids to access the show's sound frequencies directly without wearing another device. For the deaf, I-Caption devices, about the size of a tablet, display captions in sync with the action on stage.

While not widely used, the theatre has experimented with language translation headsets, also free of charge to the patron, for shows that welcome large numbers of international tourists. While not translating each spoken line, the recorded voice in the headset is cued to a signal from backstage to follow the action scene by scene. Sound Associates Inc., which rents much of the sound equipment for the show, provides this technology as well.

The employees of the merchandise and refreshment companies have expanded from the days of t-shirts and CDs. They are now customer service for headsets that don't work, or ticket-holders who don't know how to use the equipment correctly. They are security for the ID that patrons exchange to guarantee the return of the equipment. There is little pay, few tips, and a lot of downtime while the show is in progress. Yet this is an important service to many in the audience. The headset hutches are portable and usually placed in a corner of the lobby, away from the money-making souvenirs. All costs are billed to the theatre and passed on to the show's company manager for reimbursement each week as part of the house settlement.

One of Broadway's traditional souvenirs is a poster called the "window card." It has no equal in other industries. The size of seventeen inches wide by twenty-two inches high was created to fit in the windows of ticket broker storefronts that used to litter the streets of Times Square. With the advent of Internet sales, there are no broker storefronts remaining. Yet the window card survives as a staple of Broadway souvenirs.

The souvenir book, packed with colorful photos, stories, and biographies not found in the free Playbill magazine is also a staple. Not all shows lend themselves to an eight to sixteen page booklet. The photographer and the copywriter (often someone on staff who knows the show well) get a very small percentage of the sales. Hopefully the show's stars have approved their likeness for any use related to the show, or the managers may need to pay them a small percentage as well. Quality control, accuracy, and print charges need to be carefully monitored and the audience must be willing to pay the price. Of course, now that photos are available for free on the show's website, and industry sites as well, it will be interesting to see if these souvenirs continue to sell.

Until the show is a bona fide hit, merchandising remains a gamble for the producer and investors. When the show hits big, the merchandise becomes a profit-making machine all to itself. The general manager will discuss with the lead producer the pros and cons of moving quickly or slowly to produce a wealth of branding souvenirs or to schedule the recording of a cast album.

The show's press agent will send out press releases announcing the CD's release. With the loss of record stores, CD sales may be limited to the lobby of the theatre, a few specialty stores, and digital downloads through iTunes or elsewhere online. In the pre-digital world, the music of *The Sound of Music* and other Rodgers and Hammerstein classics were popular because these cast albums on vinyl provided society with its jukebox and radio hits. Cast albums sold well in record stores.

The digital music world has changed expectations of royalties and, in most cases, a CD is now considered a promotional tool only. Beyoncé and Justin Beiber may be top sellers, but nowadays fans share or listen to music online rather than purchase hardcopies. This is true of Broadway cast albums too. While major hits like *Wicked, Rent,* and *Spring Awakening* make money for their record labels, a large percentage of today's sales are on iTunes, which pays tiny royalties compared to the days of *A Chorus Line, Cats,* and *West Side Story.* The primary market for cast albums is in the theatre lobby at a souvenir stand.

The digital world offers the best chance to reach the entire world quickly and to that extent, it makes show music a very effective marketing tool, building audiences who will visit Broadway to see the show with music they already love. However, only a small percentage of the world's music buyers care about Broadway musicals at all.

A cast recording can cost the record label between $400,000 and $900,000. First of all, there are additional union salaries to be paid to the singers and musicians used on these recordings. Featured soloists receive one week's salary for their performance on the CD. Orchestrators receive 100 percent of their initial production fee for the show that can equal $100,000 and more. These union standards were created at a time when cast recordings were on vinyl and were recorded in one day, on the day off following the official opening night. The cast was exhausted and sometimes voices were shot. Original cast recordings are still recorded in one or two days, but are scheduled at various times.

A professional record producer is employed by the label to oversee the entire production that includes engineers, artwork, original cast members, and live orchestra, sometimes supplemented with additional musicians. The recordings may spill into the wee hours of the morning. Scheduling, studio time, cast and musician overtime, and all union rules are watched carefully from a completely unique set of SAG/AFTRA and AFM rules. The show's company manager is paid to work with the label producer to keep costs under control and manage everyone involved.

Very few theatre producers choose to produce their own recording. The negative is funding the recording in the show's production budget (perhaps 10 percent of the total budget) with no experience in distribution; the positive is the ability to own all of the rights to the recording with no middleman. This is a gamble for sure. If a show doesn't believe any known recording label will produce its recording, this may be the only option. Producer Joseph Papp did it in 1984 with *The Human Comedy* with music by *Hair* composer Galt MacDermot. He recorded the show live in one of the New York Shakespeare Festival's Off Broadway theatres. The show went to Broadway but lost its investment. However, the recording assures the show will have a permanent history that could help market future productions of the show.

The musical *13* by Jason Robert Brown was recorded before it opened on Broadway in 2008, in order to have a product to sell in the lobby by opening night. During previews, the composer dropped two songs and added one new one. The cast recording is not an accurate depiction of the show, and yet it has a loyal fan base to this day despite a short life on Broadway.

Historically, Columbia and RCA (both now owned by Sony), Decca Broadway (owned by Universal Music Group and retitled under Verve Records), and more recently Sh-K-Boom/Ghostlight Records produce Broadway cast albums. Considering that there are only four major record labels remaining worldwide, finding a record producer/executive like Goddard Lieberson and Thomas K.

Shepard, whose names appear on many of the greatest cast recordings of the past, is very difficult.

For a good lesson on what goes into a major Broadway recording session, watch the documentary about *Company*, 1970's Tony Award–winning Best Musical. It was the first such recording session ever filmed for public television.

Record labels acquire the rights to record a show and pay a nonrecoupable advance if they feel assured that the show will have a long and popular life. For unknown works, a Broadway producer may be considered lucky to find any willing label, even without receiving an advance.

Some Broadway shows, like Sondheim's 1971 *Follies*, had to edit the musical numbers to fit on one vinyl album. Other shows in the digital era, like *Hairspray*, have added surprise bonus tracks at the end of the CD.

The recording world has gone through a revolution and continues to evolve with iTunes and retail distribution deals that make live touring look like child's play. Cast recordings are primarily sold in the theatre to fans who have just seen the show. In 2015, cast recordings are promotional tools for touring and future ticket sales.

The artwork and liner notes so prevalent on vinyl cast albums in the past were miniaturized when CDs were in vogue, and are now almost missing from digital downloads. Digital sales pay very small royalties and yet digital sales are on the rise while CD sales are diminishing rapidly.

Unlike merchandising, scheduling the performance week is totally in the producer's control. Analyzing the nights and afternoons that attract the most audience is a big part of the discussion between box office treasurers and management.

Every scheduling move by management has a connecting cost. Holidays and Sundays often increase the box office income but also payroll costs since many unions require time and a half pay, or double time, for these performances. Advance planning is needed to notify the unions, the cast, staff, crew . . . and the public. The public is not quick to respond to anything, ever. As previously noted, a television commercial will most likely not improve box office income for at least three weeks following the first broadcast, and it may take much longer than that to see a significant uptick.

Regularly scheduled holidays are a mixed bag. A family show may see a big family audience on Easter Sunday, or not. Additional Sunday pay is a holdover from a time when states had blue laws prohibiting most stores and businesses from operating. Broadway has never been able to lose this Sunday bonus or penalty depending on how you view it. Some shows perform on Mondays and since most federal holidays are now on Monday, these holiday performances also require pay increases. The company and house managers will make sure that payroll follows each union's rulebook. A producer should expect changing payroll totals every time a holiday rolls around.

The unions require and expect eight performances in a week. This is traditional and allows the show to earn maximum income within the guidelines of the standard American workweek. Now and then, a leading actor is only willing or able to perform six or seven shows per week. This is true of Dustin Hoffman in *Death of a Salesman*, and Audra McDonald in *Billie Holiday at Emerson's Bar and Grill*, but the payroll does not change. Most staff and crew are paid union weekly minimums, and minimums do not decrease because of a shortened performance schedule.

There are many considerations when scheduling a show. For a show with a primarily local New York audience, summers mean weekends at the beach, not in the theatre. The usually strong Saturday evening performance may drop suddenly after Memorial Day, and weeknights may do better. Out-of-towners may flock to matinees in good tourism months, but during beautiful weather opt for Central Park during the day and a 7:00 PM early curtain for their youngsters. Most shows take Mondays off but others see Mondays as a golden opportunity due to reduced competition.

The traditionally slow months of January and September should be anticipated in cash flow projections. Slow months are not absolute. Nor are strong months. Each show has its own personality and its own audience. Ad agencies and press agents will explain how to promote the show during particular months to maximize box office income.

Christmas week, spring break, holiday weekends such as President's Day, Martin Luther King Day, and Columbus Day can bring in extra income, while Memorial Day and Labor Day may do the exact opposite. In fact, Christmas week is so strong that the unions allow management to add a ninth performance that week, provided that the following week has only seven shows. It's a compromise between management and unions, and it acknowledges that the theatre's ability to earn more is good for all.

For a long time, all Broadway shows operated six evenings at 8:00 PM and two matinees at 2:00 PM. Before that, most Broadway shows began at 7:00 PM in the evening. Recently, different Broadway shows vary their start times from day to day. Weeknights may be one time and weekends another. Evenings begin at 7:00 PM, 7:30 PM, or 8:00 PM and matinees begin at 2:00 PM or 3:00 PM. Audiences need to read their tickets carefully.

In 2014, a few shows experimented with Thursday and Friday matinees. The jury is out, but one thing is for sure: Broadway schedules will continue to change, seeking the Holy Grail, otherwise known as eight sold-out shows per week.

The unions wish producers to be thoughtful before changing work schedules that affect all of the show's employees.

Chapter 8

The Media, the Critics, the *New York Times*, and Macy's Thanksgiving Parade

Abbreviations used in this chapter and in the theatre world at large:
NYT or the *Times* = the *New York Times*
A&L = Sunday Arts and Leisure section of the *NYT*

TOOLS OF THE TRADE

One of the important tools of the trade is called "B-Roll." While unions restrict videotaping of rehearsals and performances in the theatre, each show is videotaped with one to three cameras only by a small handful of trusted videographers for future promotional use on television talk shows and news programs. No more than a few minutes of footage may be shown behind a local critic's television review or when a cast member visits *Ellen DeGeneres*, or *Oprah*, or *Good Morning America*, and the like. The main subject of any interview is the "A-Roll," and the B-Roll is the supportive video material.

Actors' Equity takes video abuse very seriously. An actor in rehearsal should not have to worry about his or her image and experimentation showing up on YouTube at a later date or being sold to TMZ. For this reason, filming in the theatre has been verboten, except when all unions receive payment for commercial and professional use. The multi-camera, commercial filming of the musical *Memphis* in 2011 was shown in movie theatres throughout the country. 2014's *Of Mice and Men*, starring James Franco and Chris O'Dowd, was shown on over 1400 theatre screens after a limited Broadway run. 1990's *The Grapes of Wrath*, starring Gary Sinise and Terry Kinney, 2009's *Passing Strange*, directed by Spike Lee, and 2013's *The Nance*, starring Nathan Lane, were all shown on public television.

These tapings are governed by SAG/AFTRA payments for performers, rather than Actors' Equity. All other participating union workers are paid according to their union rules. It is not inexpensive to produce a Broadway show on video or film.

In 1970, the unions agreed that Broadway productions could be archived for posterity. Through the New York Public Library's Theatre on Film and Tape (TOFT) archives at Lincoln Center Performing Arts Library, every show has the option of being videotaped live with one camera only. Rules state that these tapes can only be viewed in house, by theatre professionals, students, and researchers with a valid reason and a library access card. There are many amazing productions that have been saved for posterity, although the film quality varies widely. These full production videos are not for promotional use.

All unions also understand the value of promotional video. Rules include giving the cast and crew no less than twenty-four hours notice on the backstage bulletin board. No cast member wants to look out in the audience and be surprised by a red camera light. As of around 2008, a negotiated payment with Actors' Equity called a media fee gives performers an extra 2 percent of salary per week ($36.14 for a minimum wage contract) in recognition that video is now an essential tool to promote the show online, on television, and elsewhere, and that an actor's captured image has monetary value beyond their onstage performance. One restriction still in place is that video footage cannot be used for disciplining or rehearsing. Other unions have also added media fees for their necessary participation in promotion.

Television and Internet commercials came of age with the original production of *Pippin* in 1976, arguably the most effective edited television commercial ever used to promote a Broadway show. Both show and commercial became popular hits. Commercials require their own producers, writers, union workers, and voiceover artists. Creating one can cost anywhere from $100,000 to $350,000 plus airtime (and the ad agency commission on that airtime).

Commercials do not pay off immediately. A commercial will begin affecting sales three weeks or more after it airs. The box office will track increases in sales. If the show needs immediate money to stay afloat, this promotion idea is a waste. And a boring commercial can have little or even a negative effect on ticket sales.

The right production photo can mean a decade of coordinated ads, posters, and front-of-house imagery. In the case of *A Chorus Line*, Martha Swope combined multiple photographs to create the iconic line of seventeen actors forever used by theatres around the world to promote one of the longest running shows in history. Patti LuPone's image with outstretched arms became the symbol of *Evita* after she became the superstar attraction for the musical.

Photograph sessions are rushed in after a late night dress rehearsal or after a preview. Obviously the costumes need to be finished and the scenery installed before a show is complete. Photo sessions are usually directed by a combination of the director, the stage managers, and the press agent, with a carefully orchestrated list of scenes and scenarios throughout the show.

A show's photographic history can help sell the show to regional and amateur theatres. Google *West Side Story* and see the many photographs from the original Broadway production and subsequent revivals. These images keep the show alive and fresh, and the media gobbles them up when writing about the show. Online, these visual images are essential to encourage readers to pay attention to the written word.

Actors' Equity allows initial photographic sessions without payment to the actors if management follows the rules. Sometimes the first group of photographs must be supplemented or discarded due to the replacement of a star, redesigned costumes, or an added musical number during previews. Photos that were taken during out-of-town pre-Broadway runs may not represent the current version of the show. After a couple of photo sessions or extra-long sessions following a preview, the producer must pay the actors for their time. Of course, stagehands get paid every time, since they are moving scenery, costumes, and lights for each scene. If the director isn't reined in with a reasonable number of scheduled photos, or if the scene changes aren't coordinated correctly, photo sessions can become unnecessarily expensive.

Successful branding can come from artwork such as the green witch drawn for *Wicked* or the red sequined boots of *Kinky Boots*. *Phantom of the Opera*'s floating white mask is sometimes displayed with no words at all.

Whether the show finds branding from creative artwork, B-roll video, a photograph of its star, or a large musical number, visuals are powerful tools to encourage the media to pay attention to your show. Your show needs to be sold to the media, not just presented.

Producers may want promotion to be free or cheap, but it is an unrealistic expectation.

THE *NEW YORK TIMES*

Let's get right to the point. A single full-page color advertisement in the Sunday Arts and Leisure section of the *New York Times* costs around $65,000. This expense should not be taken lightly. Of course, fifteen years ago, the same ad would cost $120,000, but as the media has moved online and publications have lost marketing ground, the prices have dropped.

Managers and press agents roll their eyes at the number of times cast members and novice producers suggest that the solution to diminishing ticket sales is a Sunday ad in the Arts and Leisure section of the *Times*. When a show is struggling, this is not a financial option. Just being listed in the alphabetical theatre listings can cost hundreds of dollars each day depending on the number of lines and space used. Considering that the ABCs, as they are known, give the public the address, phone, and schedule for those wishing to buy tickets, it's a very expensive way to spend advertising dollars, as much as $100,000 per year if used daily.

Is it worth the price? Even though the Internet revolution almost destroyed the newspaper business, *NYT* has remained a major source of Broadway articles and advertising online and in print. New York readers still rely on *NYT* critics for the final word on what shows are worth seeing, a fact that has existed for many decades to the woe of most industry insiders.

Sometimes even entertaining shows have closed solely because of the influence of the *NYT* critics. It still amazes the theatrical community that hundreds of bloggers coupled with primary newspapers like the *New York Daily News*, *New York Post*, *Bergen Record*, *Wall Street Journal*, *Newsday*, *Village Voice*, and dozens more hold less influence than a single review in the *New York Times*.

2015's successful opening for the musical *Something Rotten* was overshadowed by the community's discussion of the singularly negative *NYT* review. While other critics raved, critic Ben Brantley wrote: ". . . *Something Rotten* flails like a parachutist in a windstorm . . . Sometimes you wonder if the show isn't made up of scenes culled from the wastebaskets of the *Saturday Night Live* staff." How detrimental this review will be has yet to be seen, but it is feared that it could cut into the initially strong ticket sales.

NYT charges more for theatre ads than it does for major store and fashion ads. Bloomingdales and Macy's pay less for advertising space than a show. In the late 1980s, there was an attempt to break the influence of the *NYT* and its high costs by moving all ads to other New York newspapers. However, no individual show wanted to be the first one to lose the audience reach provided by this one newspaper. So producers and theatre owners collectively decided to work together. *NYT* quickly stopped that effort in its tracks with the threat of an anti-boycott lawsuit and it has never been tried again.

Broadway is not the only fish in the sea and the competition for free coverage is fierce, so the *New York Times* has established unspoken rules. While producers complain that press agents should work harder to get more *NYT* articles about their show, the *NYT* offers only one non-review article that usually runs on the Sunday prior to the show's official opening night. That's it. The press agent will make suggestions to the editors about the topic for the article, but it's the editor who makes the ultimate decision. This is not a democracy or a benevolent dictator.

The days of major gossip columns about celebrity events and sightings are long gone and mostly appear in other New York newspapers, magazines, and online blogs. There is very little investigative reporting in the Broadway world so the *Times'* Sunday Arts & Leisure section has increased its coverage of the other arts including films, museums, and music. Broadway still pays more and gets less from this most powerful source.

Another missing piece from the glory-days of the *New York Times* is the weekly Al Hirschfeld line drawings of cast members and stars. These collectors' items are a source of pride for those who were his subjects and always included "Nina," his daughter's name, cleverly hidden within the intricate lines. He lived to be ninety-eight years old and brought great joy to the Broadway community. Mr. Hirschfeld is now honored with the naming of his own theatre. No one has replaced him at the *New York Times*.

THE MACY'S THANKSGIVING DAY PARADE

Wherever large television viewing audiences exist, there is a potential audience for the Broadway theatre. Since ESPN viewers are not typically Broadway theatregoers, and since Broadway promotion budgets have less to spend than beer and car companies, the theatre relies on less expensive special events with national coverage: Macy's July 4th fireworks concert and Macy's Thanksgiving parade.

While almost every musical would love the publicity, Macy's is very selective in approving the shows that participate each year.

Managers, press reps, stage managers, wardrobe supervisors, and cast members are all involved on their one off day that week. Broadway performances happen on the street at the beginning of the program early in the morning, filling airtime before the floats and balloons have made their way closer to Macy's. The performers dance on the uncushioned street to their taped vocals prerecorded at a studio a few weeks ahead of the parade. There are no microphones and no live singing at the parade. Macy's approves all musical choices and strictly limits the show's time on stage and on air. Rehearsals are necessary to teach the cast a shorter and often different version of the number. Sometimes it rains and often the temperatures outside are below freezing, but the show must go on.

Each show pays its participating actors, crew, and press agents for their time working on the parade.

After the short performance, the cast must walk to a holding room a block or two away where all costumes and equipment are collected and taken back to the theatre. Despite the cold weather, most show people are excited at the opportunity to work the parade.

THE CRITICS

Theatres have been named after critics, such as Walter Kerr and Brooks Atkinson.

Critics are human and few of them have any experience working in the theatre. They are hired, it seems, for their journalistic talents, sometimes witty, sometimes bitter. Newspapers after all are trying to sell papers so a bit of controversy in the theatre pages helps. For the most part, critics are sincere and fair, but within the confines of their personal taste and their moods. After seeing up to five shows a week in the month of May, Tony Award season, it may be difficult to enter a theatre with a fresh perspective.

Producers generally distrust critics completely, even after receiving a positive review. A critic's job is to be objective and therefore there is little camaraderie, except between critics and press agents who rely on each other to share information and arrange seating at the theatre.

There is an important distinction between a good review and a bankable review. Many a show has been killed with faint praise; it's about what is *not* said in the review. Broadway theatre tickets can sell for as much as $400, so reading that the scenery is fantastic or that one of the featured actors gives a stellar performance may not be enough to convince anyone to buy seats for an entire family.

A bankable review will result in a line at the box office and major overnight sales online. A good review may have no effect at all. The 1978 reviews for David Hare's *Plenty* were not perfect, but were filled with extraordinary comments about the play's emotional impact and its star Kate Nelligan. This translated into ticket sales. Sometimes a few choice comments are enough to put money in the bank.

Bad reviews hurt. Producers and investors have faith in their productions and are often blindsided by the viciousness in a review. The cast, crew, and ushers often know in their guts that a show is not up to par but producers and creative staff do not ask them. Unless there is sufficient time to make changes while out of town or in previews, a show's fate may be set to close well before opening night. Ultimately, bad reviews will lead to the show's untimely death and up to two hundred people on unemployment.

Editors give critics their assignments. Editors make the decision to review a show starring Hugh Jackman over a show without stars. Editors also rewrite the critic's work, sometimes because of available space on the page. This leads to full paragraphs, often about the designers or an unknown actor, being cut. Thanks to the Internet, the full review can be available online without cuts.

The vast majority of the public could care less about a Broadway review, especially if the show doesn't have a Disney character in it. Even in New York City and environs, less than 25 percent of the public has ever seen a theatrical production. Broadway still attracts a specialized audience, although it is increasing little by little. Editors are well aware of this, which is why theatre reviews are not a priority.

There are three lists of critics categorized by the Broadway League with the input of press reps. "First nighters" include the major news and media outlets like television critics and popular talk show producers, newspapers and their editors, radio stations and their program directors, and a few influential bloggers. They are invited with a guest to any of the three to four press performances leading up to opening night. "Second nighters" include major media outlets outside the New York area from Boston, Philadelphia, San Francisco, etc. They are invited within the first weeks after the show has had its opening night. The third category includes local reporters from small towns, colleges, high schools, the Internet community, and foreign countries. These reporters are expected to provide examples of past reviews and a letter of introduction from their editors, if possible, to prove that there will actually be a review or article. Since all reviews can bring attention to a New York show, legitimate out-of-town media are encouraged.

In the past, one critic's style was to insult the physical attributes of a leading actress rather than discuss the plot. Another critic was fired for regularly falling asleep during a show, allegedly from too much alcohol. He was caught by friends of the leading actor who purchased surrounding seats. Ironically, he was hired by a rival newspaper soon after. One theatre critic from a local television news program admitted in an interview to having no background in the theatre at all, but came from a television family. Everyone's opinion can be considered valid, including a construction worker or a college professor. Each critic brings his or her own taste that may not be the same as the readers. That's why there are so many critics. They cancel each other's extremes, or when they agree, they have a strong influence on ticket sales. Of course, the *New York Times* wields its own power and no one really knows how and why.

Chapter 9

How to Sell a Big Flop, a Big Hit, or a Lukewarm Show

Obviously, if there was a foolproof method of overcoming the odds at the Broadway roulette table, everyone would invest in a Broadway show. The industry has nonetheless discovered ways to extend a hit's success beyond ten years, and prevent a struggling show from closing overnight. The most time-consuming and exhausting task is to take a show with mixed

reviews (some good and some bad), and convince an audience that the show is worthwhile.

A standing ovation is now common on Broadway. It is usually recognition that the cast is superb (and they usually are) but may have little to do with the public's opinion of the book, music, or direction. Sometimes people stand just to see over the heads of the people who are standing in front of them. A show's future cannot be determined by the existence or lack of a "standing o." And so, producers must be prepared to use all the tools at their disposal.

These tools include B-roll video, free press, targeted marketing, and an all-out blitz of paid advertising (see Chapter 5: Promotion). The missing dynamic is word-of-mouth, that elusive collection of audience opinion that travels quickly and effectively. Critics, editors, New York theatre buffs, cabbies, and waiters are influenced by what they hear and it's what they'll talk about. The hardest job for

Broadway management is to find a path to theatre-loving people and convince them to talk about a show, a lot, and in good terms.

Management knows that if there are no bodies in the seats, then nobody can walk out of the theatre singing its praises. After all, the critics may not have written glowing words about the 2013 production of *Rock of Ages*, but the audience left the theatre telling friends and family about the great rock songs and nostalgic excitement. A case of mixed reviews, but a full house for years.

Every production needs to find an audience early in previews. Early reactions can be instrumental for the creative staff, who along with management, will hang out at intermission and after the play to listen to the public's comments. If the comments are bad, or if the only comments are about dinner, an alarm is sounded.

Theatre Development Fund (TDF) can help provide early audiences by offering massive discounts to their large subscriber base. TDF successfully fills hundreds of seats for an extended period of time, until word-of-mouth, or the critics, have kicked in.

Management will offer "comps" (free tickets, also known as "papering the house") to fill in large blocks of empty seats, carefully distributed to known charity and theatrical organizations that can bring in enthusiastic theatre-lovers. Staffs at nonprofits and other management offices may also be comp'd. There are quite a few theatre ticket clubs that, for an annual fee, will distribute free tickets to its members, but this is not a favorite path since the only one who makes money is the club management. It is important not to let the word spread too far about these comps, lest it discourage ticket buying completely. The cast and crew are rarely offered free tickets for their guests, even when most of the theatre is filled with "paper" (comps). Perhaps it is assumed that friends would not react as "normal" people, and that they will probably buy a ticket anyway.

In extreme cases, when general managers and producers demand a full house at every performance, the company manager and box office go a bit crazy dealing with lists of invitees. Since a sparse audience kills laughs, and a full house heightens audience reaction, comp'ing is a common practice for shows that have no star or title recognition to fill seats in early previews. Almost all management teams fill unsold seats during critics' performances.

This all happens before the critics rave, trash, or kill a show with faint praise. In simple terms, rave reviews will mean a long run, a trashing will mean imminent doom, and faint praise will probably mean a slow death even after a lot of hard work. Of course, it's not that simple.

Most shows must find their own way into the hearts and minds of the ticket-buying public. Even if the critics rave, it may take weeks before the message reaches the general public and translates into sales. Broadway budgets have contingency funds to cover unpredictable expenses, but these funds are also intended to provide a buffer for the immediate weeks following opening night.

A show that is selling half of the theatre and only at discounted prices is most likely taking in less money than it is spending. If the *New York Times* calls the show "miraculous," the producer will want to spread the word immediately hoping to change half a house to a full house, and discounted tickets to full price tickets. Without a sufficient contingency line in the budget, there is no money to survive the week's loss, and not enough money to advertise extensively.

Clive Barnes, writing for the *NYT*, reviewed the play *Moose Murders* as "the worst play he had ever seen." Nothing in any review said the show was boring, just awful. His review was the talk of the town, and the producers quickly closed the show. But just like a train wreck, there was interest generated. Some questioned whether the show could have survived a few weeks on its terrible reputation alone.

The point is that there is a difference between a boring show and a bad one. Finding the exciting words and phrases in a review can motivate audiences to give the show a try. The public wants to be entertained and/or challenged emotionally and intellectually. But critics are reporters and analysts, not paid promoters. Critics and the public don't always agree.

Producer David Merrick was noted for his clever, sometimes questionable, publicity stunts that often helped to extend the run of a badly reviewed show. In 1961, Merrick invited seven people with names exactly like those of seven prominent reviewers of the time. He then used quotes raving about the show and attributed them to the men who had the same names as the reviewers. His musical *Subways Are for Sleeping* ran an extra six months.

Among David Merrick's promotional escapades is his 1954 musical *Fanny*. He plastered stickers on men's room mirrors across midtown saying, "Have you seen Fanny?" and then had a nude statue of the show's belly dancer erected in Central Park only to call the police and press. Merrick bought the first-ever full-page newspaper ad and radio and TV ads too. The show received mixed to bad reviews, but it became the most profitable show in history to that date.

Today's producers seem more conservative in their approach and follow a well-trod path with their advisors. When the reviews are void of raves, the ad meeting on the morning after opening night (ON) can mean life or death. Everyone is motivated to keep the show open, but the struggle can test the most creative minds in the room. Nothing can happen until the lead producer and general manager (GM) announce their intention to keep the show open. At that point, the press agent will call editors with immediate story ideas; the marketing director will suggest newsworthy events to get the public's attention, and the ad agency will suggest the most effective placement of ads with quotes and images. The GM will have to explain the budgetary constraints, and the lead producer will have to make the ultimate decision about each expense.

The negative comments in a mixed review are sufficient to depress everyone on the show, yet the positive statements may offer hope for a future. Step one in the marketing of the show is finding the quotes that brand the show in a positive light to sell a lot of tickets.

A review of 2013's *Motown: The Musical* includes the following excerpts from critic Charles Isherwood (*NYT*): "The musical, mechanically directed . . . flashes back to the beginnings, when a young Berry [Gordy]—Junior to his large, loyal, and loving family—is casting about for a career. A brief stab at boxing fizzles (cuing one of the show's few and unfortunate original songs) . . . The dialogue is often vinyl-stiff . . . I often had the frustrating impression that I was being forced to listen to an LP being played at the dizzying, distorting speed of a 45."

These are not exactly glowing comments, yet the musical was selling out. Later in the same review:

"The hit parade reels on seemingly forever in *Motown: The Musical*, a dramatically slapdash but musically vibrant trip back to the glory days of Detroit . . . [Motown's stars'] indelible styles are being effectively recreated by a blazing cast of gifted singers impersonating this crowded pantheon of pop-chart immortals . . . the audience lapped up virtually all of the musical numbers . . ."

Within these words, there is silver, if not gold. Those attending the ad meeting after opening night "pull quotes" to put a positive spin on the show. Can you find the phrases with the most impact, known as "money quotes" from the above? Did you find "A musically vibrant trip back to the glory days of Detroit!" and "A blazing cast of gifted singers!" and "The audience lapped up virtually all of the musical numbers!"?

It is essential not to mislead the public by using words that imply the entire show is great. Nothing can destroy a show's reputation more than unattained expectations. The chosen quotes need to heighten those parts of the show that the audience will agree are positive.

A money review is what made the 1964 musical *Fiddler on the Roof* a worldwide smash hit. Powerful critic Walter Kerr of the *Herald Tribune* did not particularly love the show, but there were lines outside the box office the next morning. The other newspaper reviews were better but focused on the extraordinary performance of star Zero Mostel. "It might be an altogether charming musical if only the people of Anatevka did not pause every now and then to give their regards to Broadway," joined other reviews fearing that once Mostel left the show, it would fall apart. Seven years later it became Broadway's longest running musical and retained that title for several more years. No show gets perfect critical reviews (well, maybe *A Chorus Line* and *The Book of Mormon*). Extraordinary praise in just the right categories can overcome all other negatives.

The 2012 *Wall Street Journal* review of the hit Disney musical *Newsies* stated: "Imagine, if you dare, a cross between *Waiting for Lefty* and *High School Musical*. Should you find such a combination appealing rather than appalling, you'll like *Newsies*, the droningly earnest new Disney musical about the newsboy strike of 1899. Harvey Fierstein, who wrote the book, has turned all the characters into flimsy cardboard cutouts, and the songs, by Alan Menken and Jack Feldman, are namby-pamby pop-rock sprinkled with phony-sounding period touches. Christopher Gattelli's somersault-laden choreography is repetitive but excitingly lively, and the boys in the chorus tear into it with thrilling zest, especially the knockout tap ensemble at the top of the second act. I also liked Tobin Ost's fire-escape set. Otherwise, this one's a loser."

No, it was not a loser. The audiences loved it, and even in this review, there are great quotes that sell the show.

Media editors will need motivation to write an article about a show receiving mixed or bad reviews. They must believe that their readers want to hear about the show. Press reps will look for connections to current news items and trends, hoping to get their play mentioned anywhere they can.

Direct marketing, email, or snail-mail to a specific interest group, unless they are regular theatregoers, rarely works. A show about mental illness may be of little interest to mental health professionals, just as a show about dogs may be of little interest to veterinarians, because they wish to leave their jobs at the office. Broadway-oriented websites (Broadway.com, BroadwayWorld.com, see Appendix Resources) deliver the show's message directly to known ticket-buyers and for that reason, are cost-effective.

For the most part, only regular theatregoers read the entire review. Tourists may only see the display ads with quotes. Reviews fade; quotes stick in the public consciousness. Anything that gets these positive notices into the public's eyes is important. Testimonial commercials (see Chapter 5: Advertising) can be produced quickly.

When the musical smash hit *The Book of Mormon* was overwhelmed with excellent reviews, its ad execs branded their own style of TV commercial by filling the screen with words of varying sizes and fonts and a voiceover quoting aloud a few choice comments from well-known comedians and critics. It is a simple, irreverent, and effective presentation.

Good reviews don't promise ticket sales by themselves. *After Midnight*, a 2014 musical revue of Harlem's golden age, with fantastic dancers, singers, and orchestra onstage, featured alternating celebrities like Fantasia, Vanessa Williams, and Patti LaBelle. With quotes like "It doesn't get any better than this!" and "The #1 Broadway musical of the season!" it was one of the big delights of 2014 and was nominated for the Best Musical Tony Award. This should have been a major hit according to the critical raves. But it closed without repaying its $7 million dollar capitalization.

What could the producers have done differently? In hindsight, the issues are many. Audiences prefer storyline shows and *After Midnight* was all music and dance. Also the show's songs were older standards from the 1920s, not as familiar to a younger audience. On the other hand, *Ain't Misbehavin'* was a 1978 musical revue, featured the classic songs of Fats Waller from the 1920s and 1930s, and was a big success.

Perhaps *After Midnight* cost too much or spent too much on a slew of television commercials. The television ads featured the performers, and might have been more effective if they featured the public raving about the show as they exited the theatre. Perhaps Broadway finances are now tied to the taste of tourists. Maybe the scripted portion of the musical needed revisions. Perhaps it was the theatre location. Perhaps it was just one of those things.

To the producers' credits, the musical was hailed as being artistically wonderful, and thoroughly entertaining. Even with weekly box office losses, the show was kept afloat, reaching a significant, if discounted, audience for over eight months.

At this point, the producer's job becomes finding new ways to return money to investors through subsidiary rights, such as a television special, a national tour, or selling the movie rights. The 2004 Tony Award Best Musical *Avenue Q* ran for six years on Broadway, but found a new audience in an Off Broadway theatre where it continues to run. *Peter and the Starcatcher* was a critical success but failed to engage the Broadway audience at the Brooks Atkinson Theatre. It too moved Off Broadway, but not successfully. There are no simple answers; each show has its own personality and challenges.

Hope springs eternal on every Broadway production. A wise producer learns to expect difficulty in competing in the marketplace alongside familiar brands such as *Wicked*, *Mamma Mia!*, and *The Phantom of the Opera*. Without a significant contingency line in the budget, the best ideas have no chance of seeing daylight.

The general rule of thumb is that empty seats have no value to anyone and any money in the box office has value. That's why so many shows send their empty seats to the TKTS ticket booth on West 47 Street and Broadway. On the day of the show only, the public can wait on line for tickets at 20 to 50 percent off. While most shows cannot pay their bills with only half-price tickets, the cash helps. Also that day's audience may not return for weeks or years so get them in the seats while you can. Shows hire people to walk the TKTS line to talk up their product. It's a hard sell technique but there may be as many as thirty Broadway and Off Broadway shows available on any particular day. TKTS also runs two remote ticket windows in lower Manhattan and Brooklyn where the public can buy discounted seats for the following day.

The most common way to sell tickets, regardless of the reviews, is to give the show a recognizable and marketable quantity such as a popular celebrity, title, or subject matter. That's why *Motown* attracted so many. That's why Denzel Washington made the latest revival of *A Raisin in the Sun* such a smash hit.

The selling of all of these shows requires money. A hit show has the money to play with, but can lose its way with bad ideas. A mixed-review show needs money to activate as many good ideas as possible. Bad reviews can be overcome with a lot of money, but only if the audience doesn't feel the same way as the critics. In retrospect, David Merrick's stunts may be worth studying.

PART 3
THE BIG
SURPRISES

Chapter 10
Producing and Investing

Success running a multimillion dollar company such as a dry cleaning chain or a stock market brokerage does not naturally segue into a life as a successful producer. Quick decisions should be educated ones and while a business degree or a theatre degree provides worthwhile tools, learning under a seasoned producer before graduating to a lead producer job may be your best avenue to success.

The Broadway League, the association for producers, theatre owners, and other professional presenters, offers many services and tools for statistical analysis, marketing, union negotiations, and education. Producers and theatre owners each must contribute more than $300 each week to fund and benefit from the activities of The Broadway League (see Appendix). The membership dues are deducted from each show's box office proceeds each week.

Veteran producers have favorite directors, designers, press reps, and managers, eliminating the need for new people to apply. On the other hand, new projects often come with creative staff attached. Broadway is a relatively small community aware of who is who. When producing your first few shows, hiring the right advisors helps. There are enough decisions to be made to keep a producer busy day and night for a very long time. An experienced general manager takes a lot of this pressure, but won't mitigate the stress and time needed to stay ahead of the deadlines.

Of course, all you really need to be a Broadway producer is the ability to raise enough money to fund a show.

If you have ever sat on the Board of Directors for a nonprofit organization, you immediately understand why people give money: a personal relationship with the person asking, and a captivating or important mission, coupled with the ability to give money freely.

Investors in a Broadway show are similarly motivated. Producers must have personal contacts that have their own personal contacts, all of whom have disposable income. The producer then sells these prospective investors on a business plan and marketing vision that will undoubtedly insure that this Broadway show becomes a blockbuster. It is a long process and it is not easy.

So why would anyone buy the pitch for a Broadway show? Corporate investors, such as Paramount Pictures and Disney, have corporate reasons that include continued branding and merchandise.

The rest of us have different reasons. Yes, there's a potentially rare windfall of profits. More importantly, we love theatre and welcome a bit of adventure and excitement by being associated with a new Broadway show. We may get to meet a star, or converse with an emerging playwright or director. We may have personal reasons to invest in the producer. We may have disposable income from financial investments and are looking for new unexplored high-risk avenues of wealth. Most investors are family members of the playwright, composer, producer, or director. We say to ourselves, "If I am going to take a chance with my money, it might as well be used to support my beloved family member."

The young composer and lyricist of a financially unsuccessful, albeit well-received, musical, were asked how they cleared the hurdles to become a new writing team on Broadway. They answered: "Our relatives funded the entire show." This young creative team has not been produced on Broadway a second time.

Each Broadway show is its own company, in the form of a limited liability corporation or LLC. For example, *Fiddler on the Roof* investors wrote their checks to the Fiddler Company Inc. Each show's budget is unique to the playwright's script, the vision of the director, the designer's drawings, and the producer's ability to raise funds. The general manager is the person responsible for analyzing these areas and using past experience to translate them into dollar signs.

A tool for the producer to raise investment money has always been the backers' audition, where "angels" bring their checkbooks and decide to finance a show, or not. Often held in the producer's living room or a large room at a social club, the backers' audition invites friends and associates to listen to a short presentation of music and dialog (or just dialog and plot description) featuring a cast of talented performers.

Very few investors, if any, know how to read a script with the analytical foresight to make an educated decision about the show's potential. Many producers lack this ability as well. Producer Joseph Papp once explained that he had a better chance of producing one Broadway hit by sinking small amounts of money into a hundred plays than he did by spending money on his three preferred scripts. His point was that his taste in scripts could be questionable, and that after a play has been worked on by a director, designers, performers, and marketers, the finished product may not look anything like it was originally envisioned from the initial read. Producing is a crapshoot.

Some producers have a creative soul and actively involve themselves in many of the artistic developments of their production. After all, a producer is responsible to the investors to present the best show possible and increase the chances of it being a long-running success. Producer Kermit Bloomgarden attended most rehearsals, and is known for pulling a director aside to say, "Scene two isn't working. I want it fixed by tomorrow." Not all producers are comfortable directing their directors.

The common question among Broadway audiences after seeing a flop is: "Why did the producer think that awful show would be a hit? There are so many more worthwhile plays out there and yet they wasted all that money on *this* one!" The only possible answer is that no one can predict a hit. Even superstar producers like Harold Prince, Joseph Papp, Kermit Bloomgarden, and David Merrick have produced bombs.

The original 1976 production of *Chicago* directed by Bob Fosse, starring two big Broadway stars, Gwen Verdon and Chita Rivera, closed quickly. A decade later, producers Fran and Barry Weissler saw an *Encores at City Center* presentation of the show with a small orchestra sharing the stage with the actors. The Weisslers decided to produce that version of *Chicago* on Broadway. So the once failed *Chicago* is now the longest running revival in Broadway history and won an Oscar as Best Picture. Same show, different version, different times. On the other hand, a new production of the critically appreciated musical *Side Show* was revived in 2014 and was a financial flop for the second time.

The good news is that a hit show can bring in huge profits for investors. A $10,000 investment in *Hair* in 1967 returned over $400,000 within two decades or so. *Wicked*, now a decade old, is estimated to be returning a 250 percent profit annually to its original investors with no end in sight. The Dramatist Guild's newer rules allow producers and investors to receive 20 percent of author's income from future revivals of the show up to forty years after the original Broadway production closes.

But, for every one hit, there are eight or nine financial flops. Statistically, that means an investor might be better off investing blindly in ten shows rather than placing the entire bet on one show. Possibly. Gambling is still gambling.

The losses in the vast ocean of Broadway shows are too large to list here with *Spider-Man: Turn Off the Dark*, *Shrek The Musical*, and *Dude* leading the pack with over one hundred million dollars in Broadway's graveyard.

The issues that determine profit versus loss are complex. Simply put, the weekly operating budget (all salaries and expenses to run the show for an entire week) must be as low as possible but high enough to support the quality desired. Ticket prices must be as high as the market will bear so that weekly income exceeds costs but low enough to attract a wide audience. Of course, it's never that simple.

Unlike movies seen worldwide during a few weekends of release, theatre has a precise number of seats in one and only one Broadway theatre. Impresario David Merrick once considered opening his hit musical *42nd Street* in two theatres at the same time, but the idea never took wing.

Weekly profits must first be used to repay the initial costs of getting a show to its opening night. A large Broadway musical will spend around $15 million up front. A small Broadway drama might cost $2 million. Doing the math, a struggling large musical earning a low $50,000 profit per week requires approximately six years to repay the musical's production costs. Not an encouraging scenario. The small play would require less than a year to recoup its original $2 million costs with $50,000 profit per week. However, very few dramas have a life span of a year.

Included in the 1976 investor's prospectus for a Broadway drama, the producer anticipated reaching "breakeven" in twenty-two weeks of full audiences as an indication of the best possible scenario. The *New York Daily News* reported during the run of Disney's *The Lion King* that, because of the exorbitant costs, it would be many years before they would realize a profit. Each show is different, but the way the producer expects to spend money, especially on scenery and promotion, directly affects the gamble.

General managers calculate the weekly survival of a show on 65 percent of the theatre's sales capacity to break even each week. The budget for a particularly risky drama might be based on 50 percent of the theatre's capacity. This budgeting concept acknowledges that shows offer hefty discounts on group sales, discounts at the TKTS booth (that sells half-price tickets on the day of the show), and discounts for schools. They also give away tickets to charities, to industry folk to fill seats when critics attend, at Tony Award time, and to radio stations ("trade comps") in exchange for promotions. These discounts add up quickly. New shows rarely sell out, so these discounts plus empty seats explain the purpose of 50–65 percent "breakeven" budgeting. It is better to surpass financial expectations based on realistic projections, rather than fall short of a rosy picture. As Broadway begins to embrace premium and dynamic pricing (see Chapter 13: Box Office), expectations are being surpassed beyond comprehension for shows in demand.

Struggling shows will hover around the breakeven point each week, and use every marketing technique available for promotion. This is why many managers say that lukewarm critical reviews create more work than handling a big hit or a big miss.

Sometimes the critics will pan a show that the public loves. To some extent, that was the case with *Cats* and *Evita*. There are absolutely no guarantees and each show may have a different fan base. The team (press agents, managers, advertising reps, etc.) is the producer's best resource for healthy advice.

The first three months of a show can often be sustained with sales to local audiences in the New York area but traditionally struggle if the show has not found visiting tourists to buy full price tickets after those initial months. Because dramas often appeal only to audiences that see more than one show in a year, the drama must use every trick including casting celebrities in the lead roles and quoting out-of-town rave reviews to create excitement, a buzz, and demand.

A healthy plan is driving early ticket sales by announcing a limited engagement, and then budgeting the show to repay its costs within an extremely short time. Operating costs must be kept at a bare minimum, often under $250,000 for a play, to allow the show to work through many weeks of low attendance. In principle, musicals should have low operating budgets, but New York visitors expect a level of spectacle with a musical, so a reasonable operating budget of between $500,000 and $800,000 is usually the case.

Sometimes there's no way to save a production. When a show is dying, and cash in the bank is extremely low, a potential savior arrives with the best of intentions, often recruited by an investor. The savior with deep pockets loves the show and says she or he is willing to invest additional money as a priority loan, meaning that they will be repaid before any other investor. The savior's money will be earmarked for a new marketing plan and will cover losses while the producer develops a post-Broadway touring schedule. The only thing the savior requires is to be courted, including dinner with the show's stars, an introduction to the cast, and a lot of attention from the producer. More than one manager can testify that no savior has ever come through with the money. Ever. Manager's advice: "Let the show die and move on."

Investing is a multistep process. The investor writes a check after carefully reading (please!) and signing a prospectus, also known as the legal offering, that is drawn up by the show's entertainment attorneys. This prospectus is governed by New York State law and if the show has out-of-state investors, it is governed by federal law as well. There are government fees and legal fees required to prepare this prospectus. No money can be legally accepted without it. The purpose of the prospectus is to protect the investor from Bernard Madoff schemes and other con jobs.

The prospectus states the history and previous success rate of the producer. It also clearly states the small chances of seeing a return of investment monies. The name of the escrow bank account and business offices are clearly stated and there's a lot of small print regarding the method and timing of payments. In most cases, there is also an overcall clause (see Chapter 11) explaining that the producer can ask for even more money from you under certain conditions.

The total capitalization for the show (what it costs to get the show to its opening night) is chiseled in stone and written guarantees about when and how the money can be used are described in the prospectus as dictated by law. The capitalization and the production budget totals should be the same, which is why a general manager, the person who creates this budget, is so important early in the game.

Imagine that the producer is able to raise $13 million by deadline but the show is capitalized at $15 million. Without legal dictates, producers would try to produce the same show for what is on hand, $13 million. However, the budget is carefully designed to make sure that this gamble is done right. No investor should agree to a watered-down version. New York State laws protect the investor from this last minute desperation. Certainly, if the producer decides to adapt the show's vision to cost $13 million, then they are allowed to start over with a new prospectus and a new budget, and each investor will then get a new chance to decide whether to invest.

Investors' monies are deposited in an escrow account that cannot be touched by the producer until the entire capitalization has been reached. If the total is never raised, the monies are returned to the investors in full. However, producers need to spend money early in the game. This is called "front money."

Front money investors grant the producer use of their invested cash to pay expenses prior to capitalization. The front monies spent will not be paid back if the capitalization is not achieved, so there is a bigger risk to the front money investor. In exchange for the higher risk, a producer gives the front money investor an additional share of the profit pie. This additional share does not reduce the profits of the other investors, but comes directly out of the producer's share.

Front money investors receive double the profit normally due them. To clarify, assume an investor's share is 1 percent of the total capitalization. In exchange for using this 1 percent as front money, the front money investor receives 2 percent of the profits without investing another dime and the producer receives 1 percent less profit.

By law, the total capitalization must be in the bank by opening night. This explains why some producers are still soliciting and panicking during rehearsals. There are rare cases where producers have moved forward without having all the money in the bank. The results were disastrous. Small vendors were the ones usually screwed and paid 25 cents on the dollar when they thought they were working with a reputable producer.

Does every Broadway producer need to have a substantial bank account of their own? It helps. Many will say that it's absolutely necessary. Rich people like to invest with other rich people and especially rich, experienced people. The up-front costs of hiring an attorney and general manager, office expenses, and optioning the rights to the play require a significant up-front commitment. Prior to reaching full capitalization, unions will require security bonds and other personnel will be hired.

So how do investors earn money? The show goes "into profit" after all production expenses (through opening night) have been paid and investors have received their original investment back in full. The show has "broken even" and is now "in the black." After the show breaks even, all weekly profits are split between the lead producer and the investors, 50 percent to the producer and 50 percent split among the investors in proportion to the amount they invested.

Broadway investments do not come with the same tax incentives as films, although the industry is trying to even the playing field. After year end, the general manager's office will send out K-9 tax reports explaining how much the show has earned and how much your investment has earned. The investor does not necessarily receive all of the cash. The producer is entitled, and encouraged, to keep a significant buffer in the bank to handle intermittent weekly losses and unforeseen crises (weather, strikes, theatre damage, celebrities missing performances). The investor gets taxed on this money as well as the money received. The point is that the investor will see this money eventually. This often comes as a big surprise to first-time investors.

When a celebrity is involved, general managers will suggest performance cancellation insurance. The audience may want a refund or exchange if the celebrity is ill, and the loss of income from one show can be very expensive. Audiences are always offered a refund or exchange if the announced star is absent.

Cancellation insurance usually comes with a two-show deductible and many conditions, so it's not a catchall for short-term problems. Investors must rely on the knowledge and experience of their lead producer and general manager to weigh the cost of insurance against the potential losses. Another gamble.

How does someone get invited to invest? If you have significant money to invest, and you can be vetted as a serious and trusted investor, you can let producers know that you are interested. New York State requires large investors to be "vetted," showing evidence that they can afford to make the investment and have the cash on hand. There are cases where producers get bamboozled by would-be investors who back out last minute or who never had available money in the first place. Having a mutual friend recommend a potential investor will help to open doors to the producer.

The most accurate source for listing future Broadway shows, including contact information for the lead producer and general manager, is *Theatrical Index*. It's available weekly at New York's Drama Book Shop (see Appendix: Resources). Investors are generally the producer's associates, friends, or friends of friends, but the skyrocketing costs of producing a show usually means extending the pool. So there is often room to join the ranks of a Broadway investor.

When the show closes, if it has not returned its full capitalization to investors, the investors have lost money. However, the investors may see additional monies returned in the future (see Chapter 4: Dramatist Guild, and Chapter 17: Playwrights). The profits flow from many directions. Remembering that the script and music are licensed, not owned, by the producer, many of the potential monies will filter through the authors and their agents.

However, the show's investors participate in all money earned by the show and its extended activities, known as "subsidiary rights." Merchandise sales, original cast album sales, movie and television productions, international and national touring productions, printed scripts and sheet music, regional theatre licenses, and amateur rights (schools, community theatres) will add to the show's profits continually until the show closes on Broadway, and then for another forty years! Most likely, a hit show will have additional touring companies and the investors will be permitted to invest in those productions as well, increasing their take of the show's income. Producers and investors in a revival participate as well, along with the original producing team, as long as it is within the forty-year period.

Recent musical flops have found success in Europe and Japan, with new and revised productions. *Shrek The Musical*, *The Little Mermaid*, and *Legally*

Blonde are three such shows that have been retooled and produced overseas with better success. The new versions require new investment but bring in new income and give the show a new chance for significant subsidiary rights in the future.

Theatre is not a voting democracy. There is a lead producer, who makes important decisions, supervises all aspects of the production, raises most of the money, and takes care of legal and financial matters with the general manager. But when an investor is willing to bring friends with money to the table, the investor may want credit as an associate producer or a coproducer for the introductions. Sometimes a front money investor wants more than an extra profit percentage. That's why there are sometimes twenty-five or more producers getting "above the title credit" on the poster and in the program. Egos play a large part in the listing of multiple producers. In most cases, it is not negotiable. The lead producer's wishes and personal style determines if investors can negotiate for a producer credit.

An associate producer can also be a staff member responsible for important aspects of the producer's work. General managers can be credited as associate producers when they procure investments.

One of the biggest decisions after choosing the play is choosing the best venue. Some Broadway theatres have reputations that sometimes reflect the theatre owner's faith or lack of faith in the success of the show. Theatres on West 44th and West 45th Street between Broadway and 8th Avenue are considered prime locations because of the walking traffic that passes by. However, every theatre has had its own successes.

Some theatres have an orchestra section (the main floor with prime seating) that looks slightly down onto the stage, otherwise known as raked seating. Some theatres have a flat orchestra section looking dead on to a raised stage. When a director or choreographer stage a show with "depth," meaning that the actors are moved in attractive or meaningful formations that are aided by looking down on the proceedings, then a show may be received best with a raked audience. Shows that never have more than a few actors moving left and right at the front of the stage may reach the critics and audience best with flat orchestra seating. The producer will want to bring the director and designers into the theatre decision for this and other reasons.

The number of musicians required in a theatre under Local 802 regulations can be a positive or negative. Unfortunately, the producer does not often have a choice of theatres. There are many long-running shows that are housed in wonderful theatres. Other shows may be struggling but may not be willing to commit to an evacuation date. Theatre owners have a waiting list of shows looking for theatres and they have experience knowing what kinds of shows work best in each.

The time of year that a show opens can greatly affect its success. The Tony Award deadline in April creates a traffic jam of new shows with opening nights backing up against each other. The critics get tired, the media has limited space to cover so many shows, and there may not be enough of an audience to fill all the seats. Opening after the Tony deadline has its own issues. Summer doldrums, fall school schedules, Jewish holidays, and gift shopping for Christmas, all take precedence over theatre attendance.

Each experienced producer has their own style, some strictly adhering to the budget, others flexible with expenses. Some offer free tickets to staff members and celebrities; others don't want to offer discounts to anyone ever. Some watch the budget like a hawk; some accept reports from management blindly. Some talk to investors regularly; some leave communications to office staff. Some like to finance a major advertising campaign ahead of previews; others let the reviews decide if the show is bankable. Some are mean control freaks; others are benevolent parents.

The creative wizard behind Broadway's 1985 *The Wiz*, Geoffrey Holder, and the show's producers gave the mothers in the cast with young children a day-care room backstage. There are no such union requirements. Each producer gets to determine their own attitude toward the behind-the-scenes environment. There are other successful producers who are known as terrors, refusing to spend a dime on their workplace unless required by union rules.

Ninety-eight percent of producers share the same financial structure, the limited partnership LLC or corporation. Each show is its own company under the law, and is incorporated as such. The rare few, like impresario David Merrick (*Hello, Dolly, 42nd Street*), are sole owners of their productions. One hundred percent of the money invested came from his personal checkbook and 100 percent of the profit went back into his personal checkbook. There was no public accounting required, no state audit necessary, no investor reports generated. The payroll account was covered by a transfer made from one account to another each week once the total was calculated.

Under the law, producers with less than three investors are also exempt from many state filings and regulations. However, producers with out-of-state investors have the additional burden of filing with the federal Security Exchange Commission (SEC).

The limited partnership structure begins with two equal halves of the pie: the general partner(s) and the limited partners. The show's lead active producer, which may be more than one person, owns 50 percent of the profit pie. The financial investors in the Broadway show own the other 50 percent of the profit pie. Simple in its conception; increasingly tricky as the business unfolds. Front money investments, previously mentioned, and overcalls (see Chapter 11: Overcalls) can muddy the lines in the pie.

Until a show recoups, paying back every penny of investment monies to its investors, the lead producers, also known as general partners, do not earn money from the pie. That's why they receive a weekly fee ($2,500–$3,500), a weekly office fee ($2,500–$3,500), and a royalty (usually 2 percent). Once the show reaches recoupment, the general partners receive 50 percent of the profit, in addition to the fee, office fee, and royalty. It is at this point that the lead producers are rewarded for their hard work and stressful lives.

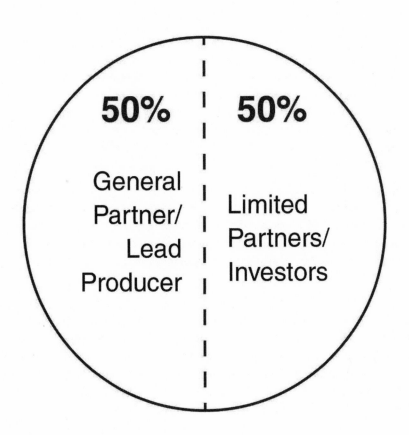

Let's call our example the Make Believe Company LLC for the new imaginary show *Make Believe*. If there are one hundred investors, and they each invested the same $100,000 in the show, equaling a capitalization of $10,000,000, they would each be entitled to 1 percent of half the pie, otherwise known as the limited partners share of the pie. Since people invest different amounts, the actual calculations are a bit more uneven, but are calculated based on the amount invested.

In addition to overseeing the entire company, the general partners are personally liable for the financial and legal aspects of the show. The limited partners are not liable, hence their being called "limited."

During rehearsals, money is spent, but no money is earned. By opening night, the entire capitalization is either spent or owed. Officially the bank accounts may be considered empty, except that the unions and the theatre have returnable bonds, and some contingency monies may remain intended for an early ad campaign, and to cover box office losses during losing weeks.

When previews begin, the bank accounts are replenished little by little with box office sales coming in and operating expenses going out. This process continues after the show has opened.

As the bank account builds with weekly operating profits over time, management provides weekly statements (yes, weekly) and then makes disbursements to the limited partners at irregular intervals. The initial investment monies are returned to the limited partners bit by bit.

If the show continues to run, these disbursements will eventually pay back the entire capitalization to the investors. This is when the show announces that it has recouped, having reached and returned full capitalization. Not a single penny of weekly operating profit has gone to the general partners at this point, only to the investors. The general partners have been living on weekly office fees (each between $1,500 and $3,000 per week) and a weekly royalty of 2 percent.

Once the show has returned its full capitalization, a few contractual changes kick in. Some stars and creative staff may see an automatic increase in salary or royalty percentage, and some vendors invoices rise, having given the production a discount to help them in the early days of the run. The weekly operating profits continue to build in the bank; however, they are now distributed 50 percent to the general partners and 50 percent to the limited partners. Reports are generated weekly, but payments are sent out as deemed appropriate by management.

In television, film, music, music videos, and other online programming, producing and executive producing have very different job descriptions and duties than the theatre. This may be why the Broadway world confounds

California film executives. Large entertainment companies hire multiple personnel to "produce" pieces of the total project, from individual scenes to special effects to financial accounting.

Producing on Broadway is itself a creative venture and no two investment campaigns are alike. Now and then, solo and concert performers negotiate a television broadcast deal from HBO, Comedy Central, and other networks to finance some or all of a live Broadway run. Shows based on hit movies carry financing support from the controlling film studios. The comic book industry has jumped into the game as well. As the cost of capitalization reaches dizzying heights, the need for new and richer funding sources grows.

There is technically no limit to the number of producers that may be listed above the show's title in a Playbill or on a poster. On one hand, seeing these producers' names won't sell any tickets and adds to printing costs. Names take up program space that might better go to promoting the performers and creative team. On the other hand, producers whose careers are tied to the theatre need to advertise themselves in order to continually raise money for the next project. At the present, the trend for more and more producers/investors continues.

In general, competition is not a motivating factor on Broadway. Broadway shows don't really compete with each other, except on the Tony Awards. One hit show helps bring new audiences to Broadway in general, and that in turn helps bring new audiences to other shows. Historically, attendance improves industry-wide when a new smash hit arrives, and all shows struggle a bit more in a year without a new blockbuster. So everyone cheers when their neighbor has a success.

Producers rarely compete with each other, except for the rights to transfer an acclaimed production from London or from an American regional theatre to Broadway. Investors are often personal contacts and do not come from a general pool. Those with enough money to invest in one show can be enticed into investing in a second and third show.

Chapter 11
Unique Broadway Financials—Overcalls, Royalties, and Royalty Pools

The fine print related to Broadway investing, producing, and employment is never ending. The prospectus given to investors before they write a check is filled with legalese and warnings, as well as legal protections that often surprise the most experienced producer. Each union has over a hundred pages of rules with penalties if the important ones are ignored. Box office financial statements can be pages long with dozens of ticket prices that can change from performance to performance. Before the producer gets his or her weekly settlement check from the theatre, the house manager collates pages of invoices, theatre payrolls, pension payments, and box office statements that are checked and double-checked by the show's managers and theatre owner's central staff.

There are four serious financial surprises whose details are rarely discussed except among Broadway managers. They are overcalls, royalty calculations, royalty waivers, and royalty pools. Each one requires a major education to fully understand.

OVERCALLS

Under the law, each and every investor must send in an additional 10 percent above their original investment money when requested. This is called an "overcall." It's very rarely invoked and usually occurs when a producer believes that the audience is building and the show will soon begin to earn a profit. In order to cover the losses for a few weeks, or to mount an advertising campaign for the same purpose, the producer needs additional cash. In practice, not every investor delivers on their legal obligation, nor does the producer report on how many investors actually sent in overcall money. The authors are unaware of any instances where an overcall has saved a show.

ROYALTIES

Royalties are calculated on a weekly basis from either the gross or net box office receipts. Royalties are paid to the producer, director, choreographer, librettist, composer, and lyricist. When applicable, royalties are due to the copyright owner of the original story, also known as underlying rights owners, such as a book publisher (*Bridges of Madison County*), a film company (*Rocky*, *The Lion King*, *Kinky Boots*, *Matilda*), record labels and music publishers (*Tommy*, *Beatlemania*, *Rock of Ages*), historical artists (*Jersey Boys* for Frankie Valli and the Four Seasons, *Beautiful: The Carole King Story*), comic book publishers (*Spider-Man: Turn Off the Dark*, *Superman*), and so forth.

Designers receive flat royalties, not based on a percentage of box office income, known as Additional Weekly Compensation (AWC). There are no calculations to consider (see Chapter 4: Unions).

In order to save time and money in negotiations, the industry has agreed on standard royalty rates. In contrast, underlying rights owners negotiate each deal with the producer. They hold the upper hand since the producer will not be able to move forward without these rights.

Dramatic shows have used songs during scene changes, and snippets of a song have been sung onstage. In these cases, song publishers usually settle on a small flat fee, as little as $10 per week. This low payment acknowledges that copyrighted songs like Orem and Forman's "Happy Birthday," or Paul Anka's "My Way," or Nelly's "Hot in Herre" can be exchanged for another tune if the price isn't reasonable. And the song benefits from being heard during the show.

To calculate royalties, we first need to find out how much income the eight shows (Monday through Sunday) earned at the box office. The box office statement will show a few deductions for the ".045" (see Chapter 4: Unions and Pensions), group sales commissions, credit card fees (between 2.5 percent and 5 percent depending on the credit card), and other items that can not be considered pure income for the show. For some people, this is regarded as "net income" because of the deductions. On Broadway, it's called "gross income" because although it's collected by the box office, it's not collected for the show's coffers.

Even when the ticket sales remain constant, royalties will change every week because group sales commissions, multiple discounts, and credit card use will vary. There is literally no way to be sure what a royalty check will be until after each week is over.

Using a director's royalty payment as an example, either the company manager, or someone assigned from the general manager's office to handle royalties, calculates 2 percent of this gross income and a check is written and mailed to the director the following week. If a show's gross income is $800,000, then the director earns $16,000 that week. Hit shows like *Jersey Boys*, *The Lion King*, *Wicked*, and *The Book of Mormon* earn well over $1 million every week. While not even close to the money earned by movie grosses, the regular weekly royalties based on Broadway income can add up nicely.

The total royalty payments, when added to the show's other weekly operating costs (salaries, repairs, props, rent, utilities, etc.), may be larger than the box office income in any particular week. For a struggling show, the royalty participants will continue to earn money even though the investors see no profit distribution. The producer is a royalty participant for exactly this reason. Otherwise, his daily office work as a producer may go unpaid. Of course, when profits abound, the producer earns his royalty as well as his general partner's share of the profits, two sizeable checks.

ROYALTY WAIVERS

Investors have asked the obvious question: Why should royalties be paid at all if the show is losing money? Broadway's response is the royalty waiver. While no one is willing to return a paycheck, the royalty participants have been willing to suspend their royalties on the condition that all royalty participants, including the producer, agree to waive payments. A producer will explain the show's need to save money in order to keep a show running. Sometimes this includes promises to reinstate royalties when the show starts improving at the box office, but in most cases, the request for a royalty waiver means the show is nearing its end. The waiver allows the show to maintain performances for a few additional weeks to keep its beloved cast and staff on payroll or to lock in a pending tour.

When the reason for a show's collapse is due to winter storms or other unpredictable events, royalty waivers have remarkable power to keep the show afloat while audiences find their way back to the seats. This was true during 9/11 and Hurricane Sandy. When producers began to abuse this policy, the unions set limits on how many weeks can be waived and how often the producer can use this technique.

ROYALTY POOLS

Royalty pools were invented in the 1980s as an alternative to the "simple" method of calculating royalties and to further confuse everyone. For a while, the managers and box office anticipated, when possible, the months that box office income would slump. They then contacted the appropriate unions and royalty participants to explain that the next four weeks would operate under a royalty pool. Four weeks was the minimum time period to lock in this option.

Today, Broadway shows must decide from the start which method of royalty calculations will be used for the entire run of the show. There is no longer the ability to switch back and forth between these two systems.

The standard royalty system is the simplest. The box office gross each week is multiplied by the royalty percentage to arrive at the amount of money to be paid. Example #1: A composer with a 2 percent royalty would get $16,000 on a show that earns $800,000 in the previous week (2 percent x $800,000 = $16,000).

The concept of a royalty pool is to calculate royalties from a pool of 40 percent of the operating profits, not the box office gross. For example, using the above $800,000 weekly gross, we first determine the operating profit by deducting total weekly expenses from the box office gross income. Let's say costs are $700,000. $800,000 minus $700,000 leaves a profit of $100,000. We multiply this by 40 percent to arrive at our pool. $40,000 is now used to calculate royalties.

For this example, let's say that the combined royalties of director, authors, producer, etc. equal 16 percentage points. Sixteen is divided into the profit pool of $40,000, and that means that each royalty point equals $2,500. A composer with a royalty of 2 percent now receives a payment of $5,000 for the week ($2,500 x 2). In this case, the composer makes $11,000 less under the royalty pool, providing a better survival chance for a struggling show.

However, the concept rests on the notion that any reduction of royalties must be balanced with a potential to make more royalties. Under the royalty pool, the risk to a producer is that the show may have to pay the maximum 110 percent of the standard royalty if the show does well.

Example #2: We have the same sixteen percentage points for our royalty participants. If a show earns $1,000,000, a standard royalty of 2 percent will yield $20,000 for the composer.

Under the royalty pool, with operating costs of $550,000, its operating profit is $450,000. 40 percent of $450,000 creates a royalty pool of $180,000. Each percentage point will be worth $11,250. This earns the composer a royalty of $22,500 ($11,250 x 2 points).

But the royalty pool's $22,500 will be cut down to $22,000 because the maximum payment is 110 percent of the standard calculation of $20,000.

The royalty pool in this example will still pay this composer an extra $2,000 over the standard royalty for the week.

The Dramatist Guild, a members-only association, not a union, was the only one to codify the royalty pool in its rulebook, and all royalty participants and producers have agreed to follow it.

Chapter 12
Good and Bad Surprises

Broadway has its share of surprises. While every industry has a million stories, Broadway tales are as hilarious and horrific as the masks of Thalia and Melpomene (comedy and tragedy).

AGE AND TYPE ARE RELEVANT

A high school graduate was planning to apply to Juilliard's prestigious acting program. He was lucky enough to know someone who arranged to have his audition material tested in front of a professional casting director, two working directors, and a manager. The unanimous opinion was that he was already a perfect type who would likely find work immediately, but Juilliard did not permit students to audition for nonschool projects. He chose to follow their advice and postponed school. He booked three Broadway shows, two television series, and a film within the first four years of auditioning. By the time he was twenty-eight, he was no longer the right age for his type. School would have gotten in the way of his brief career. Surprise.

UNDERSTUDY ABUSE

Actors' Equity Association (AEA) states if an understudy is instructed to get into costume, hair, and makeup, but the actor they are replacing suddenly decides they can continue, the understudy should be paid as if they had gone onstage. One celebrity in a Tony Award–winning Broadway musical would claim daily during intermission that she could not perform Act Two. When the celebrity saw that her understudy was dressed and ready, she would smirk and say, "I'll be able to finish the show after all." After three or four of these bluffs, the understudy appealed to her agent. Her agent asked AEA if there was any way to protect her from this ridiculous behavior. AEA ruled that the next time the understudy got into costume, she would be paid from the star's salary, whether she performed or not. This has become common practice.

SOME STARS SHINE

Actors are just as surprised by the friendliness and generosity of celebrities as the general public. David Hyde Pierce, Tony-winning star of *Curtains*, took the entire cast, crew, and theatre staff out to the Hamptons on a Monday, their day off, for a wonderful party by the beach. Yul Brynner, Tony-winning star of *The King and I*, was invited to the home of one of the show's dancers to meet with his large family, and he showed up. Carol Burnett met with a family backstage after her premiere in *Once Upon a Mattress*, then when the family stopped by the theatre six months later, she remembered all of their first names!

CASTING COUCH

In one case, a director was given carte blanche over all casting. When a superstar was hired to replace the older lead actor during his eight-week vacation, the director knew how advantageous playing opposite the superstar would be for the young costar's career. The young actor had refused the director's sexual advances so the director switched him with his counterpart in the same play in another city for the eight week run. Everyone in the producer's office knew that this was retribution, but because of the director's sole authority over casting, the producer was unable to overrule this decision. The casting couch can still be found in rare instances on Broadway.

BROADWAY REALLY DOES CARE FOR ITS OWN

Every year, the Broadway community produces over one hundred special events in order to raise millions of dollars for arguably the best charity in the entire world: Broadway Cares/Equity Fights AIDS. Broadway Cares distributes its proceeds to over four hundred fifty AIDS and family service agencies including The Actors Fund, Phyllis Newman Women's Health Initiative, the Al Hirschfeld Free Health Clinic, the HIV/AIDS Initiative, the Dancers' Resource, and the Stage Managers' Project. In addition, some funds provide personal financial assistance for rent, health insurance payments, medication and supplies, utilities, living expenses, and more to thousands of people in the entertainment industry. Twice a year, the casts interrupt their curtain calls to explain the work of Broadway Cares, auction off signed posters and programs, and greet the audiences in the lobby with baskets to collect donations. The shows compete to raise the most funds and then raise even more with four afternoon performances of original spoofs and skits, not advertised to the general public: *Gypsy of the Year* and *Easter Bonnet Competition*. This effort has raised over $5 million dollars each year, improving lives and funding research. The Broadway community stands together and donates their time and talents in support and admiration of their work.

The Actors Fund is another shining star supported by the Broadway, film, music, and television communities, and is one of the charities supported by Broadway Cares. They provide affordable housing, free and affordable health care, and education for industry people transitioning into other professions. They run three assisted-living retirement homes in New York, New Jersey, and California. The doctors in their free clinics volunteer their time, as do accountants, IT instructors, and all enlisted professionals. This is a full-service organization in every sense of the word for every member of the entertainment industry and their families. Every Broadway show adds one extra performance to their workweek, within the first three months following the opening night, and donates the box office proceeds to the Actors Fund. This is repeated every twelve months throughout the run of each show. The majority of the Broadway unions work for free at this performance.

CAN YOU FIRE A DRUNK?

The short answer is yes, assuming there is a risk to the production. The unions expect stage, general, and company managers to give warnings and keep proper records, and will then make a determination at a union grievance committee meeting. If the problem is real and just, the union will support the managers. However, the union is there to protect its members, and so the consequences may still include paying the employee his salary for a couple of weeks, even though they are in the wrong.

THE UNIONS MAKE EXCEPTIONS

If union rulebooks didn't exist, then each producer would need to negotiate minute details of pay, benefits, and working conditions for each job. Yet some theatre owners and producers negotiate special deals. What makes these exceptions surprising is that the union workers are not included in the terms that are ultimately agreed upon.

Nonprofit organizations that own their own Broadway venues, like Manhattan Theatre Club and Roundabout Theatre, have negotiated lower salaries for actors by using Actors' Equity's League of Regional Theatres (LORT) rules and pay scales. Certainly the rates are higher than Off Broadway salaries, but the standard weekly minimum of $1,861 on Broadway is reduced to about $1,345. And these shows have Tony Award eligibility. Their shows are usually short-runs of sixteen weeks or less with large subscription audiences. In most cases, salaries rise to the standard AEA production contract minimum level if the show extends beyond its original limited run.

The Lion King employs so many people in a variety of on and off stage capacities that Disney Theatrical Productions was able to negotiate lower than standard Equity wages for the launch of its extravagant hit musical. Due to the physical requirements of the show, Disney provides a chiropractor and massage therapist backstage. Disney has its own rulebooks for the employees of other unions as well.

Broadway's smallest theatre, the Helen Hayes Theatre, has paid reduced salaries (usually 20 percent less) for stagehands, managers, and others, and will most likely have its own negotiated rates having just been purchased by the non-profit Second Stage Theatre in 2015.

EXTREME MAGIC

Every show brings its own surprises. Each show and each producer has the ability to invent magic that inspires audiences and enhances the Broadway image. *ACL #3389*, the brainchild of director/creator Michael Bennett, is one such piece of magic.

ACL #3389 celebrated the day in 1983 that *A Chorus Line* became Broadway's longest running show with its three thousand three hundred eighty-ninth performance. Invitations were given to every performer who had ever been in the show throughout the world. Four hundred fifty participated. The cost of this one performance, including hotel rooms, airfare, hundreds of additional union salaries, costumes, rehearsal rooms, scenery changes, videography, a second theatre used for additional dressing rooms, security guards, a tented street party for celebrities, and lots and lots of press coverage, was estimated at over $500,000 (in 1983 dollars). When New York's city engineers arrived to inspect the theatre for safety, it was announced that the Shubert Theatre stage could not support the weight of all four hundred fifty performers. Overnight, the crew built supports under the stage and the show went on without incident. Considering that the musical had already earned over $300 million by 1983, perhaps it was not such a big deal for producer Joseph Papp to spend this kind of money. The publicity for this one performance is credited with giving the musical another seven years of life on Broadway. That one September day was a glorious surprise for all in attendance.

CLOSING NOTICE

A closing notice can shock the cast, crew, and public. Unions only require one week's notice to close a show. When a show has opened with mixed reviews, an excellent marketing campaign may be a life raft. A producer and general manager once bought a three-week radio campaign to bolster sales without apprising the accountant and company manager. The cost of that radio campaign wiped out the entire remaining bank account and the show suddenly needed to close in a moment's notice. No one will ever know if that radio ad would have boosted sales and put the show back on solid ground. Over a hundred people were instantly out of work. This has happened more than once. Surprise!

CLOSING "THE POLISH"

You would never know that the unimpressive Edison Cafe, a diner on West 47th Street just west of Broadway that did not accept credit cards, and known to the Broadway community as "The Polish Tea Room," was the locale of many major Broadway deals between theatre owners and producers over soup and coffee. Neil Simon's comedy *45 Seconds from Broadway* is based on the activity in this diner. The roped-off alcove near the street entrance was held for just such meetings. The "Polish" lost its lease at the end of 2014 to make way for a new high-end restaurant as part of the Edison Hotel.

SOME FUNNY UNION RULES

The house manager pays the stagehands and the musicians before the evening show on Wednesday. The company manager pays the cast and other crew on Thursday evening before the show. That's just the way it is.

The theatre workweek begins on Monday and ends on Sunday . . . except for stagehands and musicians who work from Sunday to Saturday. That's just the way it is.

SCENIC MISHAPS AND TRAGEDIES

Scenery is not always perfect. *Poor Murderer*, written by Pavel Kohout (who later became the President of Czechoslovakia), had one large semicircular wall pieced together across the entire stage. Measurements were wrong and it curved so much it blocked the audience's view from one side of the stage. Rather than rebuild it, stagehands overlapped sections of the wall and braced them from behind. The show ran for months, but closed before the set was fixed.

The musical *Titanic* had to tilt and sink their ship onstage at every performance. For weeks, the elevator under the stage that allowed the ship to sink failed to work properly. Opening night was postponed until they got it right.

For composer Andrew Lloyd Weber's musical *Starlight Express*, the Broadway Theatre was reconfigured with a circular roller-skating racetrack. Known for its many skating injuries, one performer tragically lost a limb.

During previews of Julie Taymor's *Spider-Man: Turn Off the Dark*, Spider-Man leapt off a platform but did not fly as planned and wound up in the hospital for weeks. He recovered and the jump sequence was redesigned with extra safety features.

A featured performer in Disney's *The Little Mermaid* plunged twenty feet through an open trap door in a boat overhead. While the actor thankfully survived, a wonderful career was ended.

Twenty-plus skates were custom-made for each dancer in a roller skating number in *Sugar Babies*, starring Mickey Rooney and Ann Miller. The skate's special ball-bearings didn't prevent one dancer from rolling off the stage into the orchestra pit. The dancer recovered. The number was cut and the skates were sold off. (This book's author bought a pair.)

THE LONGEST AND SHORTEST RUNS

The walls of Joe Allen's Restaurant, located on West 46th Street between Eighth and Ninth Avenues on Restaurant Row, only displays window cards of major Broadway flops. It's a lesson in humility. These shows have lost hundreds of millions of dollars for investors. The dozens of hanging posters include *Marilyn: An American Fable*, *Dude*, *Moose Murders*, *Carrie*, *Nick and Nora*, and the new king, *Spider-Man:Turn Off the Dark*.

Broadway's top twenty longest running shows are all musicals except *Life with Father* and *Tobacco Road*, both produced in the 1940s. After decades of new dramas and comedies, it is surprising that these plays remain on the current list. Six of the top twenty (*Phantom*, *Chicago*, *The Lion King*, *Mamma Mia!*, *Wicked*, and *Jersey Boys*) are still running. Here's the list as of 2015 according to Playbill.com and the Broadway League, although current shows will be moving up on the list. (1) *The Phantom of the Opera* (over 11,400 performances and counting); (2) the revival of *Chicago* (over 7,700 and counting); (3) *Cats* (7,485 performances); (4) *The Lion King* (over 7,300 and counting); (5) *Les Miserables* (6,680); (6) *A Chorus Line* (6,137); (7) the revival of *Oh, Calcutta* (5,959); (8) *Mamma Mia!* (over 5,600 and counting—scheduled to close in September 2015); (9) *Beauty and the Beast* (5,461); (10) *Rent* (5,123); (11) *Wicked* (over 4,800 and counting); (12) *Miss Saigon* (4,092); (13) *Jersey*

Boys (over 4,000 and counting); (14) *42nd Street* (3,486); (15) *Grease* (3,388); (16) *Fiddler on the Roof* (3,242); (17) *Life with Father* (3,224); (18) *Tobacco Road* (3,182); (19) *Hello, Dolly* (2,844); (20) *My Fair Lady* (2,717); Honorable mentions go to *Hairspray, Mary Poppins, The Producers, Avenue Q,* and the Roundabout Theatre revival of *Cabaret.*

PART 4
WHAT THE PROS WANT YOU TO KNOW

Chapter 13

What the Box Office Wants You to Know

The box office wants you to know that they are stuck in a small room with one or two other treasurers for a full day so when someone approaches the ticket window with impatience, or becomes irate because they didn't bother to decide ahead of time the date, show time, the number of tickets to buy, or read the lobby signs, that the box office has the right to not smile at you.

> Abbreviations used in this chapter and in the theatre world at large:
> B.O. = box office
> GM = general manager
> CM = company manager
> HM = house manager
> TDF = Theatre Development Fund

A question like "What date can I get the best tickets?" doesn't come with an easy answer. For some, a seat in the fifth row off to the side is better than a seat in the twelfth row in the center. Others prefer the first row mezzanine for the unblocked view of the stage.

The B.O. wants you to know that you should not hide your disabilities from them. If you are in a wheelchair, each theatre has excellent locations on the main floor at a special discount. Some people in wheelchairs show up with balcony tickets and expect the theatre to miraculously find them a seat in the orchestra section on a sold-out show. Many of the older Broadway theatres do not have elevators, so unless the ticket seller is notified in advance, seating options may be disappointing to say the least. The B.O. wants to help, so if you are hard of hearing, or extremely obese, or use a cane, please let them know before buying a ticket. If the show's special locations are already used, the B.O. may be able to suggest a compromise or suggest that you come to a different performance. Sometimes they can't help you and getting angry with them will not help.

If you leave your tickets at home or lose them, you can still get in with the following information: the name of the company where the tickets were purchased, the name of the person who purchased the tickets, the credit card that was used, and/or the location of the seats (always put the seat numbers in your phone or wallet). Thanks to computers, the B.O. may be able to verify your seats and let you into the theatre.

If you bought your seats from a broker online or in person, the box office cannot give you a refund or exchange your locations. A ticket broker at the Marriott Hotel is a separate vendor, like Macy's and Walmart. You can argue with Marriott but not with the theatre box office. For the record, every box office and every ticket stub clearly states that there are no refunds or exchanges. Luckily, house managers are human beings, and when not abused and only if possible, will try to accommodate audience members with last minute problems.

If you discover the half-price tickets you bought at the TKTS booth in Times Square are balcony seats and on opposite sides of the theatre, it will not help to lie to the treasurers and tell them that you were told they were a pair of orchestra seats. That's because the box office assigns seats, including singles and partial view tickets to the TKTS booth treasurers who, as professionals, carefully explain to a fault what you are getting for your discount. On the other hand, when a show is not sold-out, the house manager may approve the box office moving your seats together within a similar price range, but that is done at the HM's discretion and often depends on how nicely you ask. Treasurers become a bit numb after a while, and bring their own brand of attitude to the job, but most of the time they are willing to bend over backwards to help when the theatre's rules allow them to do so.

If you miss the show because (a) a snowstorm; (b) you thought the tickets were for next week; (c) you just plain forgot, call ahead. Don't just show up when you want. Call the vendor from which you bought the tickets (a hotel, the box office, an online broker, etc.) and explain your situation. They will contact the box office directly and when possible will allow you to attend on another date. There is a common policy called "past-dated ticketing." The B.O. will give you a phone number to call on the day of a show, and if the show is not sold out, they will allow you to use the tickets you have. Just don't lose your ticket stubs or barcoded printouts.

Just one of today's hit musicals can earn over $2 million in a single week. Trusted union treasurers have managed this money without incident for decades, although the record unfortunately is not perfect. Union box office staff are uniformly respected and as a safeguard, they are all bonded, a form of insurance should money ever go missing under their watch.

As of 2014, a treasurer's minimum weekly salary is $1,751.21 plus benefits. An assistant earns $1,538.05. While membership in the national union of ticket sellers for sporting, concert, and theatre events is about seven hundred, only about three hundred of these sell theatre tickets. Many of these members began their careers working in Off Broadway and regional theatres, gaining a good reputation and box office computer skills.

Tickets are sold online through remote outlets like Ticketmaster, Broadway. com, StubHub, and Telecharge, through private group sales agencies like Group Sales Box Office and Matchtix, ticket brokers at major hotels, and elsewhere. There was a time not long ago when the box office had a monopoly. Broadway tickets could only be purchased at each theatre's box office or by mail. There was no Internet, and there were no remote outlets. Remote ticket accessibility has made it easier to attract a global audience now that they can buy their seats in advance from anywhere. This convenience attracts a larger audience pool and potentially results in a longer run.

It's important to note that none of the remote outlets reduce the income that arrives at the show's box office; they add a cost to the ticket buyer, up to $8 per ticket, to cover the convenience of buying without going to the theatre's box office. Telecharge workers are governed by their own union, Local B751, with a detailed seniority system and hourly wages based on the date of hire, plus benefits, sick days, and vacation pay.

The show's potential income is reduced by group discounts, group sales agent commissions, Broadway League membership dues, discounts at the TKTS half-price ticket booth, online discounting services, and other special advertised promotions.

While buying a ticket at the box office avoids adding the surcharge from remote ticketing agencies, the box office is not surcharge free. In the 1980s, someone realized that renovating theatres costs a lot of money and that rather than raising the rent to productions, the audience could pay an extra $2 per ticket above the price of admission. This is now a fixture at Broadway theatres and is called a "facility fee." The show's producers do not receive any of this fee; it all goes to the theatre owner.

The only personnel other than a treasurer admitted freely into the box office near show time is the show's company manager and the theatre's house manager, who together with the head box office treasurer must sign off on the financial statement right after each show begins. The three of them meet in a separate office within the theatre to "finalize" the box office statement.

While many producers balk that they are not always welcome in the box office, showing that you have respect for their space and time, especially right before a show begins, will go a long way to gaining entrance at non-rush-hour times. No one likes twenty bosses, so ticket requests and changes go through the company and house managers, not directly to the box office.

The box office closes fifteen to thirty minutes after the evening show begins, leaving enough time to give out tickets to latecomers and to process the financial statement for that performance. Patrons arriving after the box office has closed can get their tickets from the ticket takers.

HOW TO TALK WITH A BOX OFFICE TREASURER

The financial discussion among the managers and treasurers includes these terms:

THE WRAP

The wrap is the total amount of money collected from all sources within the past 24-hour day, from 12:01 AM through midnight. The wrap tallies all tickets sold on that particular day including future performances. The term comes from the paper band that banks wrap around money.

A preliminary wrap is usually reported to the producer and GM directly after the evening performance, but it's only a partial reference. The total daily wrap (at midnight) informs the producer of the trends in ticket sales.

THE GROSS

After deducting credit card fees, group sales commission, and the ".045" (see Chapter 4: Unions and Pensions), the remaining money earned is called the gross. Each performance has its own gross amount and includes only the ticket sales for seats purchased for that one individual performance. At the end of the week, the accumulated grosses for all eight performances should hopefully be higher than the anticipated costs of running the show, thereby providing profit for the investors.

The theatre and the show are two separate entities. The theatre box office collects all ticket sales, but does not release any money to the show's management until after a full week of shows has been performed. This is a safeguard to be sure the producer cannot use income from future performances to pay past or current expenses.

Each week, the HM calculates the theatre's expenses (rent, theatre payroll, departmental invoices, utilities, real estate taxes, and additional union pension amounts due). Then the HM deducts the totals from the total weekly gross income. The HM pays the balance to the company manager on the Tuesday following the previous week's final show. Hopefully, the CM receives enough money to pay all of the show's bills and salaries. Some weeks are better than others so the profit from one week may cover the loss from the previous one. The CM, HM, and GM watch these numbers like a hawk.

THE ADVANCE

Ticket income sits in the theatre's B.O. account waiting for each performance to occur. Every night, the income from that day's completed performance(s) is subtracted from the account total so that the producer and managers can know how bright or bleak the future looks. If there is a million dollars in the bank as of Thursday, but only $500,000 in the bank as of Monday, then the show's advance is going down, a bad sign.

The managers analyze the advance and wrap data to determine whether to boost television coverage, offer discounts, subsidize the loss for a short time, or close the show.

Just thirty-five years ago, computers were not yet used in the B.O. The tickets and the cash were counted and triple-counted by hand, making for very long evenings for the treasurers, CM, and HM. After their count was complete, the ticket stubs were messengered to a separate location called the count-up room. The stubs were recounted overnight, and the results were compared to the finalized B.O. statement. Mistakes were easily possible.

HOUSE SEATS

A small number of prime location seats strictly reserved for industry associates, VIPs, the producer's family and best friends, investors, cast, and crew, are set aside as house seats. The director and other creative staff often negotiate to control their own house seats. A phone call or email placed to the general manager's office can buy these great seats at full price. Nowadays the general manager's office has become a private remote box office handling between thirty and two hundred seats for each performance, sometimes requiring a separate staff member and special work hours to accommodate all of the requests for a hit show.

There are "regular" house seats that, if unused, are made available for sale at the box office at 6:00 PM two nights before the actual performance, even to shows that are otherwise sold-out. A handful of "24 hour" house seats, if unused, are released for general sale at 6:00 PM one night before the actual performance. Then there are usually four seats whose sole purpose is to accommodate a last-minute call from the President of the United States, or the producer's nephew who suddenly shows up without any notice. These seats are called "emergencies" and are carefully guarded by the CM. Even these seats can be released for public sale two hours prior to show time if unused. The box office will not and cannot sell these seats without the express permission of the GM or CM.

House seats are either paid for in advance using an emailed credit card or must be "guaranteed" by someone connected to the production. If the tickets wind up being no-shows, the guarantor must pay for the tickets.

STATUS

The computers are constantly reprogrammed for new prices, discounts, and categories like house seats or broker assignments. Each ticket grouping is given a status number. For example, regular house seats may be found in "Status 9" while emergency house seats will be placed in "Status 10." Each price category (discounts, premiums, TKTS, upstairs, downstairs, side, partial view, comps, handicapped, etc.) is given a different status designation on the computer.

The individual box office treasurers can move seats from one status to another. Leftover seats, for shows that are not as big a hit as *The Book of Mormon* or *Wicked*, can be moved into different price categories last minute. This easy movement of seats opens the door for mistakes, so treasurers will usually call the manager to let them know when they are making status changes.

The programming of new prices is done in the central office of the theatre owners, not in the box office. This means that the managers must plan ahead when asking to add new pricing.

GROUP SALES

These agencies are usually private companies with direct access to the box office. Most big shows will offer a special presentation to group sales agents and ticket brokers to encourage them to start selling tickets well before the show has begun performances. A bad or uninspired presentation can kill a show. A great presentation can convince the agents to become ambassadors long before previews begin.

Group sales agents may hold the show's early success in their hands. Discount pricing for groups must be carefully determined to help the agents sell tickets even before the show has made a reputation for itself.

Not only can they match a particular group's interests with an appropriate show's style and subject matter, but they will also help groups put together a major trip including meals, hotels, and other activities.

The general manager will prepare a separate budget for these presentations. Since the show is weeks or months away from rehearsals, this presentation is only a representation of what the show may be. As an incentive for agents to attend, free food, CDs, and t-shirts are often given. These presentations can be expensive but extremely valuable for a musical.

ICE

One method of box office theft is called ICE. It involves hiding some prime seats from the general public, then selling them last minute to a broker or a hotel concierge for more than the ticket price and pocketing the difference. Of course, the broker charges even more to the rich people who want to see a big hit without advance planning and are willing to pay through the nose to get those seats. Since the show itself earns the full price on the original tickets, the theft didn't really happen, or did it? CMs are trained to watch for this practice and to stop it dead in its tracks.

PREMIUM AND DYNAMIC PRICING

Another scam involves scalpers on the street or through a ticket broker's office who buy up great seats at full price and then offer them at highly inflated prices. New York State law cracked down on scalpers but the practice couldn't be completely contained. With a sold-out hit like Mel Brooks's *The Producers*, the scalpers were making more money than the box office.

So in 2001, *The Producers* began selling premium seats and inflated the prices for the best seats at the box office to outsmart the scalpers and brokers. A $175 orchestra seat was now $450. To everyone's surprise, these expensive seats were gobbled up. Box office income soared. It worked so well that today most shows offer a limited number of great seats for hundreds of dollars more than the usual price. In addition, a show starring a popular film celebrity can double the number of premium-priced seats being sold.

Ironically, it was the common practice with shows in the 1950s through 1970s to offer lower pricing on extreme sides and first and last rows of the orchestra. Prices were also cheaper on Wednesday matinees and weeknights. In the 1970s it evolved into one-price-fits-all orchestra and front mezzanine seats, and eventually weekday and weekend prices became one. Then again, the top price at *A Chorus Line* in 1976 on a Saturday evening was $15.50, so comparison is not exactly fair. Ticket prices have risen drastically, but so has audience expectations for amazing and costly sets and costumes.

Now in 2014, the next step to increase box office income is called variable or dynamic pricing. It follows the successful, albeit obnoxious, airline ticketing system. Airlines change their prices daily based on how many seats are unsold on a particular flight. Following supply and demand, why not charge more for the theatre ticket locations and dates that are most in demand, and less at times when ticket sales are slow?

Spring vacation draws more people to Broadway than there are seats, so by raising the prices for that week, shows can double their grosses and still sell out. The week after spring break, prices return to some semblance of normal. The box office lets management know if there is price resistance and complaints, or when there might be a demand for more premium-priced seats.

The only people left out of the mix are poor and middle-class theatregoers. Some producers have instituted lotteries two hours prior to each show where inexpensive tickets are sold. The seating locations are sometimes questionable and the quantity is not large, but the seats are only $25 to $45 each. Would-be audiences fill out a card outside the theatre and wait until 6:00 PM when names are drawn out of a basket. This is similar to rush tickets that sell the cheaper seats first-come, first-served, on the day of performance only. Rush tickets and lotteries are very popular among all ages and also cater to the show's fan base, some of whom return to see the show hundreds of times.

HARD TICKETS

This is an ancient term for physical cardboard tickets that were in use during the precomputer era. Box office personnel may still use the term for vouchers given out when suddenly someone runs up begging to buy a full-price seat to that evening's performance after the box office statement has been finalized. The box office never says no to a sale. A hard ticket sale will be posted on the next day's statement.

THEATRE DEVELOPMENT FUND

There is one organization that helps Broadway shows sell seats that would otherwise go unsold. Theatre Development Fund (TDF) offers large discounts to preview performances and slow periods. TDF has a large membership of regular theatregoers who are willing to take a chance on an unknown play. Seats may not be great.

TDF also offers subsidies to new worthy plays that are opening with a perceived handicap, such as no celebrity actor in the lead role, a difficult topic, or a very limited budget. The show's producer must submit the script months ahead of previews to qualify for this subsidy.

TKTS, the half-price ticket booth in Times Square, is also a product of TDF. TKTS sells tickets on the day of the performance only and seats are limited by each theatre's box office.

DISCOUNTS

Making a decision about discounts or special promotions without box office input is ridiculous but many producers and marketing consultants move quickly without talking with the CM first. The CM is on a direct communication line with the B.O. in order to process the discounted prices in the computer and keep track of the discount's success. Before a discount can be advertised, the following should be determined: 1) beginning and end dates; 2) ticket codes (status); 3) black-out performances (dates when the discounts are not valid); 4) number of available seats at that discount; 5) and it can't interfere with other prices being offered group sales agents and other promotions. Shows have created ill will with the public and lost tens of thousands of dollars because of these kinds of omissions. Many producers also offer a friendly conciliation of discounted tickets to cast and crew for their friends, family and industry reps, traditionally called Staff Tix, that is administrated by the CM backstage.

REPORTS

When the B.O. statement detailing that day's activities has been finalized (around thirty minutes after the evening show begins), the CM and HM will email, text, phone, or fax basic financial information to a small list of people who wish to see this information (and who hopefully understand how to use the data) so that marketing and other decisions can be made first thing the next morning. Each general manager or producer requests different details, but everyone wants to know the wrap, the gross, and the advance.

The B.O. treasurers are the experts who provide data, analysis, and advice based on years of minute-by-minute experience on how to get the most out of your ticket sales. They will let you know good and bad audience feedback regarding discounts, premiums, and dynamic pricing, and if there is a demand for the show at all. They are the producer's allies and often they are the only face the audience sees before attending the show.

Sometimes the public makes it a lonely life and unnecessarily difficult.

Chapter 14

What Press Agents Want You to Know

Press agents, critics, and editors have a special relationship. They learn to trust each other's professionalism, to call or email each other for ideas, facts, and requests. They also share gossip and theatre stories. It takes a lot of back and forth to lock in a story and to get a story right.

There is an official contact list of critics and editors who receive press releases and are invited to opening nights. This list is maintained and approved by the Broadway League that represents producers and theatre owners, and is carefully guarded by press agents. Without their union and control over these lists, a producer might try to by-pass press agents to save a buck.

The media receives hundreds of announcements daily and have developed methods and filters to weed out notices from questionable sources. Just as celebrities appreciate protection from paparazzi, the media appreciates protection from people who don't always understand nor appreciate their methods.

Press agents rely on their past value to the reporter or editor; perhaps having provided access to a celebrity or having given an exclusive to one newspaper. In return, a press agent will ask favors to help a future production. Sometimes it works; sometimes it doesn't; but a producer has no clout whatsoever. An experienced press agent will know which editors will be interested in the news being pitched, and can reach out personally via phone or email.

The headline of a press release must capture the importance and relevance of the topic in an exciting way. The first paragraph must include all pertinent information because no one will read any further when making a decision to cover a story. In local news outlets, where the number of writers may be small or freelance, the entire press release may be printed word for word, so it is important to write a release worthy of reading.

Press agents operate in a separate division of ATPAM, electing separate members to the union's Board of Governors. Their needs and procedures are very different from company and house managers. Press agents will accompany stars to morning shows like *Good Morning America*, or after show events like opening night parties, and charity dinners arranged for the purpose of publicizing the show. Getting a mention in a local blog or gossip column can keep a show in the minds of potential ticket buyers. Actors will often forget to mention pertinent information, even the name of the show, and the press agent is there to fill in omissions and act as a fact-checker for the interviewer. This work is very time consuming.

Press agents also manage television crews, critics, important bloggers, and paparazzi photographers on theatre property. The cost of filming inside the theatre with plugged-in cameras is significantly more than filming with battery-operated cameras in a dressing room or outside in front of the marquee. This is because any use of electrical outlets requires the head electrician, head carpenter, and head property master in attendance. The press agent knows the rules.

The day is spent making deals with the media, designing newsworthy ideas, and negotiating time and locations with editors to get their clients coverage. The success rate is not usually high due to the extreme competition for free media space. It takes great effort to get even a tiny mention in a New York–based publication. Getting articles into small-town papers, where a particular actor was born, may not be difficult, but it rarely impresses a producer.

Producers want results and no excuses. This may be the reason that producers have been arguing for reduced salaries for press agents after the first few years of a show's run. Press agents argue that the amount of effort increases over time even if the return rate is lower.

The past twenty years has seen the invention of large publicity offices on Broadway, the largest being Boneau Bryan-Brown, started by Chris Boneau and Adrian Bryan-Brown, with a stable of working press agents and dozens of interns handling the work of multiple shows and companies. The union's contract with Broadway was built on paying individuals as employees bringing benefits like health insurance and pensions. Hiring a publicity office changes the playing field completely. Press agents operate under a system called multiplicity. Each show has its own union contract, and after the first three contracts representing multiple shows, they must hire additional union agents and/or union associates, no matter how many interns are on board. Who exactly is entitled to the union benefit package? Can the press office CEO decide to divide the union salary and benefits among his employees as he sees fit? What are the legal ramifications of hiring a complete office when the union agreement calls for individual payments?

Perhaps due to this change, press agents were now at risk of losing their union status altogether. Contract negotiations resulted in the use of IATSE contracts (the stronger parent union) rather than ATPAM contracts (the local NYC union). Producers won the right to reduce press agent salaries by 25 percent after three years of work on a show, and 50 percent after seven years. The press agent or press office won the right to withdraw from the show rather than accept the reduced rate, then necessitating a replacement union press agent who would be willing to accept reduced compensation. This provision of the latest contract for press agents has yet to be tested. As with most union negotiations, the new rule will be revised, updated, improved, or ignored—only time will tell.

Furthermore, the debate about whether to work with one exclusive press agent or be shared by an office of press agents continues to this day. Each producer ultimately makes that decision. Often the show's star power has more to do with a successful press campaign than the chosen press agent. Each press agent, whether as an individual or a team, needs something to bargain with, to entice the media, and build a campaign.

In addition, each press agent has office expenses that need to be reimbursed, such as copying charges and telephone. Similar to attorneys, these reimbursements are mandatory and yet they are negotiable. Not every press agent will negotiate but if a press agent is slack in his billing, there are producers ready to ignore the charges. In very rare cases, the producer has given the press agent a tiny percentage of profits in exchange for discounting fees and expenses, or the opportunity to invest in the show. In almost all cases, the press agents take their union salaries, and avoid the risk.

Press agents and performers have a unique relationship. They need each other. Together they promote the show. A press agent needs to be present backstage or at rehearsals to chat with actors and find hidden gems of personal information. That's where ideas for media stories are born. Often an actor who has received a local award in her home state will not think to share this information with a press agent. The son of a famous sports figure may not include his father's name in his bio. An article about technology may be written without mentioning an actor's contribution to an important invention.

With the advent of Internet blogging, a single press release can be copied and resent to thousands of otherwise unreachable readers around the world. With free services like Google Alerts, clippings arrive daily to everyone's computer desktop. Gone are the days when companies were hired to collect press clippings or anything that mentioned the name of the show, and to send the clippings as evidence that the press agent's work was reaching people around the world.

While Facebook, Twitter, Instagram, and many more social media sites are front and center in the collective minds of the world's marketplace, they have created new challenges for creating a message that the general public will want to resend to their friends until it goes viral. This is a new challenge for press agents and marketers, especially considering the 140-character limit in a Twitter campaign.

Because social media is so time-consuming, it has become the domain of interns and entry-level employees who are used to spending hours each day doing nothing more than enticing theatre audiences and responding to their comments. Press agents, for the most part, are still on the phones and computers with editors, critics, and journalists looking for a mutually agreeable topic for an article that will actually get printed.

While this activity is similar to public relations in most businesses, as well as Off Broadway and regional theatres, Broadway still gets special attention. When the Tony Award nominations are announced, there is little room in the major press for any theatre outside of the Broadway district. And yet, there may be twenty-five shows vying for the same two articles in the *New York Times* arts section. The press agent's job requires a constant onslaught of good ideas and the awareness of how to help an editor sell papers.

Employment for Broadway's one hundred eighty or so press agents doesn't fall out of trees. Often a general manager who appreciated the PA's work on a previous show will make the call. Sometimes the PA must call a general manager to express interest in an upcoming production. Other times, there is just no work to be had.

In 2015, ATPAM press agents earn approximately $160 more per week than company or house managers recognizing that they rent their own offices, and pay for utilities and office equipment year-round. CMs and HMs do not. A press agent's minimum weekly salary is $2,162.08 plus 8.5 percent vacation pay added on to each paycheck for a total of $2,345.85 weekly.

Since press agents often work on more than one project at a time, and since every producer expects 100 percent of the PA's attention day and night, the pressure can be extreme. PAs need a sense of humor and a solid home life to withstand the pressing demands.

While performers begin as the PA's best friend, anticipating lots of media attention, the relationship sours when the media blitz doesn't happen. When a show has a star, the rest of the cast has little chance of publicity because the media decides who gets covered. PAs will work doubly hard to get coverage for the other elements of the show, but there's little chance of winning that struggle. Producers, writers, designers, and directors, unless celebrities, are not of interest to the media. But egos continually make demands on PAs. Each major article in a major media outlet may require weeks of work to convince the editor that the space on their pages is well spent on the PA's pitched idea and the show in general.

In an office of multiple press representatives, there is a company owner. Only the owner of the office can agree to take on a client and set the minimum fee and salary. ATPAM regulates the minimum cost of hiring a press agent for a Broadway (and Off Broadway) show but it has no influence over the cost of representing other projects, such as individual clients, special events, and concerts. When a PA is assigned to a Broadway show, a nightclub, and a charity event, all at once, time and money are precious commodities.

Now and then, a producer asks a PA to work exclusively for a single show, and may even invite the PA into the producer's office in order to keep an eye on promotional activities. Rarely is this viable since the producer's one show can close quickly leaving the PA without a job or office. The only incentive would be a higher fee, and producers are loathe to increase union wages.

The union has a strict training program, including seminars and an apprenticeship program. It also requires a written and oral test before someone is given the right to work under an ATPAM contract.

There seems to be a very special personality that allows a successful press representative to overcome the non-stop pressures of the job. And most PAs remain in the profession for a lifetime.

Chapter 15
What Actors and Stage Managers
Want You to Know

At any one moment, more than 88 percent of all union actors in New York City are unemployed in the acting field. Even before their show closes, actors are already auditioning for their next job.

Diversity in casting is still a concern, especially as nonwhite audiences are increasing. Actors' Equity reports that its national membership is 85 percent white, 7 percent African American, 2–3 percent Asian American, 2–3 percent Hispanic American, and 3 percent multiracial. In 2013, minorities played 25 percent of all Broadway roles. This breaks down to the following: African Americans played 19 percent of the roles, up from 7 percent in 2006; Latinos on Broadway dropped from 5 percent in 2010 to 2 percent in 2013; Asian Americans remained about the same 2–3 percent of roles; Native American and others were a blip on the radar. Equity's membership is almost 50 percent male and 50 percent female in both Caucasian or other ethnic categories.

When nonwhite performers are cast without considering ethnicity, it is called nontraditional casting. There is no reference to ethnicity in *The Normal Heart*, *Company*, *Richard II*, *Rocky Horror Show*, *Much Ado About Nothing*, or

> Abbreviations used in this chapter:
>
> US = understudy
> PSM = production stage manager
> SM = stage manager
> ASM = assistant stage manager
> AEA = Actors' Equity Association
> SAG/AFTRA = the merged unions Screen Actors Guild and American Federation of Television and Radio Artists
> AGVA = American Guild of Variety Artists
> AGMA = American Guild of Musical Artists

Who's Afraid of Virginia Woolf? to name a few, but they have been traditionally cast white. Currently, Actors' Equity reports that approximately 10 percent of Broadway roles are cast nontraditionally. The 2014 revival of *You Can't Take It With You* stars James Earl Jones as the patriarch of an otherwise Caucasian family, and Norm Lewis made Broadway history as the first African American Phantom in *The Phantom of the Opera*.

Actors ought to go into this field knowing these statistics before they start. However, so many are still surprised, anticipating a broader opportunity.

Talent sometimes takes a back seat to other casting concerns. Height, weight, age, perceived beauty, and other factors go into hiring performers. You may have given the best audition, but were too tall/short, thin/fat, old/young for your corresponding partner. If you've done your best, that's all you can do.

This reality is not specific to the Broadway stage, but Broadway represents the top of the acting chain and therefore failure may hit harder and success may bring a greater sense of accomplishment.

The stars of Broadway earn far above the Equity minimum. Weekly salaries range from $2,500 a week for a featured role to over $100,000 per week plus a percentage of the box office gross (very rare) for the celebrity whose name alone can sell out a show.

Until a show starts earning income, it is understood that a production cannot afford to pay large rehearsal salaries. That's why Equity contracts provide the same minimum salary of approximately $1,861 per week to all performers in all roles, including leads, until the first performance.

Of course, there are ways to earn more. For talent that lives outside New York City, per diem (nontaxable money to cover hotels and food expenses) and housing assistance are given. For stars, minimum rehearsal pay is sometimes supplemented with special treatment like car services, personal assistants, and more.

Each show must decide its "point of organization" before it hands out contracts to actors. This can be a costly or cost-saving decision. It doesn't matter where the actor resides; it does matter what city the show calls home. The show must pay per diem to all talent when working outside the point of organization. Approved originating cities are Chicago, Los Angeles, San Francisco, Boston, Toronto, Washington DC, Philadelphia, Honolulu, or New York City. New York City is the obvious organizational point for Broadway shows.

Actors' Equity follows the federal government limits on how much per diem is nontaxable. The cost of living in a "high-end" city like New York or a "low-end" city like Omaha is different. For high-end cities, producers pay $134 daily above contractual salary and for low-end cities $128 per day. Actors are expected to pay for their hotel rooms and all meals from this money. Managers are required to provide affordable hotel options while on the road.

So if the show is being developed or tested outside New York City, the producer will be required to pay per diem somewhere. A show can save a lot of money paying per diems in Chicago for a month, for example, before moving it to New York. The per diem for a twenty member cast in New York City could total $18,760 per week or $975,520 for the year versus $75,040 for a month in Chicago.

There will also be per diem for every crew and staff member working out of town, subject to their union agreements. The cast and crew are responsible for their own living expenses whenever the producer is not required to provide per diem.

All Broadway Equity production contracts include pension and health benefits, but health benefits are not automatically earned. A minimum of twelve weeks of work receives six months of health coverage. Twenty weeks of work receives a year's coverage. Most theatre people don't work continuously like other jobs, so performers, designers, and crew may lose coverage within any given year.

The 2013 Affordable Care Act (Obamacare) helps to fill that gap, but by the time the actor applies and purchases healthcare, they may have landed a job that provides coverage. It's tricky, and may cause actors to have months without health coverage waiting for the next show's coverage to begin. There is a three-month grace period in Obamacare to accommodate people without continual work, but there is a tax penalty after three months with no coverage. These rules may change as Congress makes adjustments and corrections to the healthcare law.

Broadway's extravaganzas must compensate an additional $20 per week called "extraordinary risk" for precarious moves such as climbing ladders, flying across the stage, jumping from balconies, gymnastic flips, and more. Without health insurance, this pay increment is a token acknowledgement of the fact that an actor's career may end with one wrong move (see Chapter 12: Surprises).

Other weekly increments that help boost an actor's salary include the role of dance captain ($361.40/week), solo chorus parts ($20/week), and understudy assignments ($50/week).

Actors in small roles understudy the larger roles. It usually doesn't make sense to have a large role understudy another large role since the domino effect can disrupt the entire cast. A few actors are hired solely as understudies for large roles but do not perform in the show, an expensive but often necessary choice. Celebrities or lead roles may have a "standby" who does not need to show up at the theatre, but is required to be within easy distance from the theatre in case of an emergency.

"Swings" are understudies for chorus performers, generally one male and one female. They learn all the songs and choreography for all chorus members, a difficult task considering that one chorus member may move left, while the other moves right. Swings are generally not on stage during the show, although they can be asked to sing backstage to supplement the voices on stage or perform some other specific tasks.

Every role on Broadway must have an understudy. This is an expensive rule. Equity mandates an understudy must be hired or assigned no later than two weeks after the first public performance. Some understudies are not assigned until previews because directors wait to get to know their actors and managers want to save money. So much is going on before opening night that understudy rehearsals take a back seat to everything else, and may only last a short time, with the stage managers supervising them rather than the director.

Still understudies must be prepared to go onstage in a moment's notice and some actors understudy more than one role. From opening until the show closes, the understudies perform a weekly brush-up rehearsal to keep them fresh in case they have to perform. Each time they go onstage, they get an additional one-eighth of the their own weekly salary (based on eight performances per week). This is above their usual weekly pay. Under certain conditions, an understudy to a star will instead earn an additional $300 per performance when they go onstage.

There was a time when no understudies were required. At that time, when an actor took ill, the stage manager and producer would call upon friends, colleagues, and Actors' Equity to find a last-minute replacement actor. That actor would go onstage with script in hand and do the best they could. The producer of course had the option of cancelling that evening's show rather than use the understudy provided. The gamble for the producer was saving money on understudy salaries versus devastating losses from cancelled shows. Eventually the current system was developed, requiring an understudy for each and every role.

When an actor gets sick, sometimes they get paid and sometimes they don't, depending on how long they have been employed on the show. Broadway actors accrue one sick day for every four weeks on the job, allowing them to receive full salary during missed performances. The show may have to pay double salary for those shows, to the absent performer as well as the understudy. Very highly salaried actors, often celebrities, do not receive sick pay at all. If they miss a show, they lose that portion of their weekly pay.

Vacation days, like sick days, are accrued over time.

When all is said and done, receiving an Equity contract for a Broadway show is very exciting. The first day of rehearsal begins with a full company meeting with the producer, managers, press agents, designers, and director (along with Danishes and coffee). After introductions, everyone who is not an Equity member is kicked out of the room for about an hour's time to allow a union business representative to discuss healthcare, pension, dispute procedures, actor responsibilities, and possible extra duty payments. A vote is taken to elect the Equity deputy, a cast member who must know the rulebook and intercede between cast and management, if and when complaints occur. The deputy keeps the complaints anonymous to prevent possible retribution from management. There is no additional pay for the deputy. After the meeting, the usual first step is a read-through of the script with the entire cast sitting around a table.

Because the nature of the creative process often results in script changes affecting an actor's participation, Actors' Equity rules become extremely important. Actors, at times, rely heavily on the Equity deputy and union rep to save their jobs and money.

For example, actors in a musical developmental workshop are entitled to a small percentage from all first-class productions (Broadway and national tours) thereafter. What happens to the actor's percentage when the actor's featured role is cut or reduced during the workshop? The actor may be offered a chorus role at a lesser salary or one month's Broadway salary as severance pay per Equity rules.

What does the show owe the actor if the actors have already signed production contracts for the Broadway run with their roles clearly noted? In this case, the producer has made a very expensive mistake by presenting the cast with contracts before the workshop's changes are complete. The actor is probably entitled to his full salary and first-class percentage payments. If the actor insists on full payment, the actor's reputation may be ruined among producers as a troublemaker, affecting future hiring. The contractual battle is emotional and financially risky for both actor and producer. Without union rules, the actor would surely be out on the street without a chance.

In addition to rules for the producers, Equity has rules defining actor responsibilities. Late actors are not to be tolerated although an important actor may get some slack. Call time for all actors is thirty minutes before the announced curtain time although many show up hours ahead to review lines and choreography, get into makeup and wigs, and prepare for an emotionally stressful role. Actors must sign in on the backstage callboard by 7:30 PM for an 8:00 PM show. Under union rules, because of the time needed to prepare, an actor who is even one minute late does not go on stage at that performance.

After this time, understudies are told to get ready and the wardrobe department is busy adjusting costumes. The rest of the cast makes the mental adjustment for the new actor's interpretation of the role, and stage managers prepare to support the understudy should there be a lapse in memory.

The stage managers (SM) keep detailed files for each performer and for each performance. If the director or SM has issues with an actor, the SM registers these comments with the union in preparation of future action or even removal. Consistent lateness, disputes with other performers, and actions that affect the quality of the performance can all be reasons for discipline, but must be evidenced by a stage manager's notes.

Arguably, the most respected position on every show is the production stage manager (PSM). Many stage managers enter Actors' Equity as performers and soon discover that they are more interested in running a show than being in it. All shows have a PSM and at least one SM if for no other reason than there are two active wings on each side of every stage and someone's got to supervise and observe the potential chaos. On shows with large casts there can be five or six stage managers on payroll. Rarely, but sometimes to save money, a stage manager is asked to double as an understudy. PSMs are never allowed to understudy.

The PSM "calls" the show from behind a podium. Every change in scenery and lighting (known as a "cue") is numbered and documented in a master script written and controlled by the PSM. Broadway shows can have as many as six hundred cues. No curtain is dropped or raised, no light is turned on or off, no chair is moved into place unless the PSM announces the cue over a headset. For example, the PSM announces: "Warning. Lighting Cue #65." Then "Lighting Cue #65—Go." Even if the electrician knows that the lights go off as soon as a particular word is spoken on stage, the electrician knows to wait for the PSM's call. This keeps mistakes to a minimum and allows for stagehand substitutions without technical disruption.

There can be as many as five or six assistant stage managers (ASM) on larger shows. They work under the PSM as a first ASM and second ASM, etc. The first ASM is eventually trained to "call the show" and take over at the podium when the PSM performs other important duties or takes a break. Rarely does this happen until many weeks of performances have passed, allowing everyone to settle into a confident routine.

After opening, the director is rarely at the theatre and trusts the PSM to act on their behalf in the same way that the general manager trusts the company manager to handle all daily management duties at the theatre. The PSM monitors the performances by regularly watching from the audience and/or backstage and taking notes, then holding ongoing brush-up rehearsals for the cast. Reports are emailed to all senior creative and management staff by the PSM after every performance detailing the show's running time, latenesses, illnesses, attitude issues, technical and staging mistakes, special visitors, and the like. These reports also serve as a record of problems that may lead to disciplinary action in the future.

Stage managers designate a dressing room as an office with copier, laptops, printers, and Wi-Fi. Stage managers are Equity members like the cast, and this allows them to both represent and discipline their colleagues. Their responsibility is to ensure that the audience at any given performance is seeing the best performance possible. Quite simply, SMs manage everything that touches or affects the stage. Company managers and stage managers, although in different unions, maintain the health of their show from two different perspectives, and rely on each other to keep order and stay on top of potential problems and solutions.

Equity contracts come in many shapes and sizes, even within a single Broadway production. Broadway contracts come in two parts. The first part is a preprinted "face page" provided by AEA that refers to the *Production Rulebook*. The second part is called a "rider" and is written by management. It includes any special conditions negotiated with the actor or actor's agent (e.g. hair color or cut, extraordinary risks, specialty roles, program billing, and so on).

AEA "Production" contracts are only used for Broadway and national tours that originate out of the Broadway producer's office. There are contract variations for principal and chorus actors, and stage managers, under "Standard," "Term," or "Run-of-the-Play" conditions.

Principal actors and chorus members sign different contracts stemming from the time that they belonged to two separate unions. The 1955 agreement to merge the two unions included a stipulation that some conflicting regulations and benefits would remain intact forever, and therefore required each show to strictly designate chorus roles. Until recently, one regulation prohibited the payment of agents' commissions for chorus roles because most chorus people are paid minimum and have little need for an agent to negotiate. There are different rules for chorus members who understudy principal roles, and special rates for chorus members who perform small parts. Swings are considered chorus people.

The "Term" contract locks in a termination date for the actor, used when the actor is hired to replace someone who has left but plans to return, or has limited availability. A "Run-of-the-Play" contract locks in an actor to a minimum run of three months, six months, or longer, with extreme penalties if the actor leaves the show early. Celebrities see this kind of contract most often. "Standard" contracts allow two or four week advance notification to quit the show. There are additional differences explained in the detailed *Production Rulebook*. All contracts should be written and signed before rehearsals begin.

Two contract clauses that save many negotiations promise fairness among cast members in terms of compensation. Management can offer a "Favored Nations" or "More Favored Nations" clause. The first says that all actors in a category (chorus, featured roles, leading roles, etc.) will get exactly the same compensation and if any of them earn more, so will the other actors in that category. The second assures a performer that she or he is making more than the other actors in their category and if anyone earns equal compensation, this actor will get an automatic raise to assure that she or he is still making more than the others.

The traditional musical has a cast of approximately twenty, yet there are two character and forty character musicals. Cast size affects the weekly operating budget, of course. Dramas and comedies usually remain under eight characters to be profitable. Now and then Broadway invites large casts, such as 1990's Tony Award–winning *The Grapes of Wrath* with over forty actors, knowing that there is no chance that the show will ever return its investment. Broadway can be a strange mixture of art and commerce.

When children are involved, the *Annie* rule requires height and weight to be documented and maintained within certain parameters because children grow unpredictably, and the children in a show must remain looking and sounding like children. This was placed into the rulebooks because the musical hit *Annie* employed so many prepubescent children whose bodies developed beyond the young character roles they portrayed. Case in point, young Simba in the long-running *The Lion King* may have been eight when he started but would be over eighteen now, so he obviously needed a replacement.

Child labor rules also require backstage tutors and wranglers (guardians that baby-sit and ensure young actors remember their cues). These rules are sometimes needed to keep stage parents at bay. Producers need to be aware that there are strict laws about parents collecting salaries on behalf of their child actors.

With special Broadway projects come special Broadway exceptions. A known rock band, an opera, or a solo performance might come under the jurisdiction of two other performer unions, AGVA and AGMA. This gives producers an option to operate under a different set of rules and salaries. The 2001 *Blast!* was an Indiana-based marching band that performed a variety of instruments in choreographed routines that won a Tony Award for Special Theatrical Event. It was not an Equity production. Baz Luhrmann's *La Boheme* was a 2002 critically acclaimed musical based on Puccini's opera that performed under the auspices of AGMA. John Leguizamo's solo shows *Freak* and *Sexaholic* were both performed in Broadway houses under AGVA, as were Tony Award–winning shows *Lena Horne: The Lady and Her Music*, *Jackie Mason*, *Dame Edna*, *Def Poetry Jam*, *Black and Blue*, and many more.

Employment for actors is a union's prime directive and with forty-nine thousand Equity members, and only forty Broadway theatres, the union is open to reasonable discussion if conditions warrant. There is rarely a good reason to ask the union to temporarily reduce actors' salaries to keep a show afloat. With a realistic plan to return the money plus more if and when the show regains its box office strength, a special request will be considered, but only after consultation with the cast itself.

An actor's work does not begin and end on the stage. Eight shows a week, sometimes performing physical and emotional feats, demanding preparation and repair, have been compared to running a marathon daily. The bare essentials include arriving a half-hour early to get into makeup and costume with a few moments of warming up the body and mind. If a show begins at 8:00 PM and ends at 10:00 PM, with preparation and getting out of costume, the work will total a minimum of three hours, eight times a week. That's only twenty-four hours at the theatre per week.

Some weeks there are group rehearsals and publicity that might add three or four additional hours. The balance of the actor's week might include classes in dance, acting, and singing, the gym, the chiropractor, meetings with agents, performing readings of new plays, networking, reviewing the show's script, dances, and songs to keep it fresh and prevent lapses, and therapy sessions. The energy exerted during a performance means that, after the show ends, many actors go out for dinner, drinks, and talk in order to relax sufficiently to fall asleep. It's a lifestyle, not just a job.

For a star, the workload can often double. The press and the public love "celebrity." Stars make more money because they sell tickets and may be the only reason that a fan will even know that the show exists. For this reason, a contract rider will include a provision that the star's name is billed above the title on a marquee, in programs, and on posters. Fans have been known to return to a show literally hundreds of times at full price to see their favorite star. After the show, the star walks past a small mob of fans that expect an autograph and a smile, or else Twitter will light up with negative reports.

The star must arrive early and in prime condition for a television morning show, then meet face-to-face with a reporter, who knows that no one cares about the show being discussed, but only the celebrity who is in it. The rest of the cast gets to sleep in. There's a lot of pressure on these stars who, in extreme cases, take time off from a mulitmillion-dollar film deal to be in front of a live audience on a weekly salary for several months.

Before any actor (except a star) is hired, Equity requires actors be allowed to audition. The competition among hopefuls is daunting. There are plenty of casting agents willing to give a new actor a chance. There are just too many performers auditioning for a handful of roles. For actors, the audition process is stressful, grueling, aggravating, and hopeless, yet hopeful.

There are many kinds of auditions and they each have a name (or a nickname) and conditions. There are interviews, general auditions, replacement calls, and callbacks for principal roles and chorus. There are cold readings, singing and dancing auditions, and agent submissions by appointment. Auditions by appointment cannot be scheduled until after a general audition on a first-come, first-serve basis to be sure that every union actor has a chance to be seen. Actors call these "cattle calls" because of the large number of attendees.

A union "monitor" attends every audition to check everyone in and make sure that rules are followed. There are rules about how many times an actor can be asked to audition without compensation. Nudity is not allowed at preliminary auditions even if the role requires it. No union actor can be asked to pay to audition. What sets Broadway apart is the long list of regulations that protect Equity actors.

Actors learn about auditions through detailed listings in online publications (see Appendix: Resources) and through the union. Actors with agents hear about them from submissions known as "breakdowns" that describe the roles, the show, the creative staff, and the producers. Getting an audition for a role on Broadway is not usually easy. Winning the role is cause for celebration.

Actors' Equity and British Equity have developed a relationship and understanding regarding the employment of each other's members. The most important obstacle to gaining a working visa is trying to explain why no American actor is capable of a particular role. The usual explanation is the

British actor is a celebrity and is already synonymous with the role and the show. Then comes the hard work of proving the actor's celebrity status using headlines, articles, and other promos.

When claims for a foreign actor are not easily proven, the cost and time applying for the visa can add up, but a producer or manager with political connections in Washington, DC, can greatly reduce the waiting time.

Productions that arrive intact from Britain using the entire original cast are rare, but have happened. One example is The National Theater's production of *The History Boys* that arrived with the original fourteen-member cast in 2005 and won the Tony Award for Best Play. In all such cases, the producers must agree that all replacement actors must be American.

Additionally, the unions have agreed on an exchange policy. For each British actor in the United States, there must be an American actor allowed to work in Britain.

Many working actors never join a union. Most theme parks, cruise ships, community theatres, and international touring companies do not hire union actors. The primary difference between non-Equity and Equity contracts revolves around pension and healthcare payments. Non-Equity shows, even when they pay good salaries, do not pay pension and health insurance. Broadway actors are union performers. Once an actor joins AEA, they are not allowed to work in non-Equity productions.

Those actors who make their living working in non-Equity theatres and tours sometimes decide to stay nonunion and there is a loophole on Broadway that allows it. Actors are allowed to perform their first Equity production without joining the union, but if they land a second union job within twelve months, they are required to join AEA. Most actors desire Equity membership. It is a badge of pride and provides access to auditions in professional productions across the country as well as Broadway.

Actors also get to celebrate with each other through the Gypsy Robe ceremony (Chapter 6: Opening Nights) and charity events open to the general public to raise funds for Broadway Cares/Equity Fights AIDS. Just a few of the fundraisers are: the Easter Bonnet competition (creative chapeaux), Gypsy of the Year competition (celebrating chorus performers), Broadway Bares (a live burlesque), Broadway Flea Market (all day street fair of donated memorabilia), Broadway Backwards (gender-reversed song performances), Broadway Barks (dog rescue awareness), and many star-studded cabaret shows held throughout the year on Broadway stages, streets, and nearby venues. Theatres also host memorials and dim their marquee lights for losses in the community.

Live theatre is like no other entertainment. The audience is a part of the show. Every show, for that reason, is one-of-a-kind. There may be over a hundred people working backstage, but actors are the ones who dialogue directly with the audience. Everyone is important, but actors are the face and voice of the show.

Chapter 16

What Stagehands Want You to Know

In 1912, a "Yellow Card" paper trail became the backbone of a stagehand's employment on productions headed to Broadway or born on Broadway and then on national tour. In 2015, the Yellow Card is an online resource at http://www.iatse.net/memberresources/yellow-card-shows/forms. This informational system guarantees that the approved number of local union crew is available and present to work the touring show when it arrives.

There are two union loyalties on each show, a Pink Contract traveling crew and a local crew. In simple terms, all crew are members of the International Alliance of Theatrical Stage Employees (IATSE, a.k.a. "the IA") as well as a member of their local neighborhood union, the "local." On Broadway, the local union is called Local One.

> Abbreviations used in this chapter:
> TD - Technical director or production supervisor
> IATSE or IA = International Alliance of Theatrical Stage Employees
> Heads = Three members of Stagehands Local One hired by the theatre: head carpenter, head electrician, and head property master.
> Pinks = Members of IATSE hired by the production: production carpenter, production electrician, and production property master

When a Broadway show prepares to travel to other cities, the producer wants to take trusted crew that is already familiar and experienced with the details and nuisances of the Broadway show. The out-of-town Local wants to provide work for its members. The compromise is a limited number of supervisory traveling crew working on an IATSE pink contract collaborating with a local crew performing physical labor and following instructions of the supervisors and stage managers. The Yellow Card is the official count of how many local crew will be hired in each department (electrics, carpentry, props, sound) and the official count of the union-permitted traveling crew that will oversee the production.

Back on Broadway, the Yellow Card determination begins at the first production meeting where the hiring of Pink Contract crew will be discussed with the technical director (TD a.k.a. production supervisor). By definition, the TD knows every possible stagehand worthy of supervising a large crew and keeping a show in top shape. The small pool of union stagehands makes this process sometimes difficult. At minimum, each show will hire a production carpenter, production electrician, production prop master, and a few assistants depending on the complexity of the production.

Historically, there has never been a rulebook for Pink Contract crewmembers, only a simple one-page pink-colored contract. These are trusted people and their roles have not been easily defined. The IA's minimum weekly salary for Pink crew is still around $1,000, much less than Local One stagehands. It would be considered embarrassing except that Pink heads are never paid the minimum. Their loyalty to the show and a real appreciation of their help translates into equal pay on par with Local One head stagehands, and often a bit more.

Not until the early 2000s did a printed rulebook for IATSE Pink crew exist. Up until that point, their rules and conditions were passed around by word-of-mouth. Unlike local stagehands, they are not paid by the performance nor with additional hourly and daily rates for repair work and special rehearsals. Pink Contract crews are paid a flat weekly rate. In principle, the Pink crewmembers are supervisors and their salary, like company managers, covers all supervisory stage work. Disney has negotiated its own "Pink" agreement that includes these IATSE stagehands, wardrobe, hair, and makeup artists all within one agreement. Rates are slightly different than those used by Broadway League producers.

There are two categories of work for Local One stagehands: those that help load the equipment into the Broadway theatre before performances begin, and those that remain with the show once performances have begun. The first division of load-in crew can number over two hundred stagehands for four to six weeks depending on the show's design. A load-in of six weeks can cost over $1 million in crew payroll.

After the load-in period, some of these stagehands will stay to run the show at performances. They receive a weekly salary, depending on their position, and extra increments for special duties and daytime repairs. The TD will have analyzed the show's needs based on the director's rehearsals and the designers' instructions.

If a castle having its own built-in lights needs to move onstage in scene three, the move, known as a "cue," may require a combination of computer operator, two or three carpenters guiding it, and an electrician watching the cables and flipping a switch. Or it may only need one carpenter and one electrician. Safety and accuracy are important considerations. The TD will experiment during rehearsals and even during preview performances, and then he and his Pink Contract crew may evaluate the operations and change their minds about the necessary number of crew for that particular move. This decision can cost the show a lot of money since one extra crewmember at $2,000 per week (with benefits) equals an annual cost of $104,000.

In addition, the number of stagehands working as of the official opening night determines the Yellow Card affecting the entire future of the show on Broadway and on tour thereafter. Once the Yellow Card information is set, it cannot be changed, except upon a complete redesign of the scenery and lights. Sometimes rehearsing the stagehands carefully during previews can save the need to hire extra crew when only one cue is the problem. The TD and Pink crew are the best resource for controlling the number of crew needed to run the finished show.

Unlike the IATSE Pink crew rules that allow for a wide range of work for one weekly salary, the Local One rulebook is very detailed during load-in weeks. Workdays operate in four-hour periods, 8:00 AM to 12 noon, and 1:00 PM to 5:00 PM. This schedule allows stagehands working in the evening on other shows to help with preparation of a new show at a different theatre.

Common practices that are not in writing include a short 10:00 AM coffee break with doughnuts and/or bagels paid in cash by the company manager to the head carpenter. Since the crew starts work at 8:00 AM, this is a courtesy, but also an expectation. At 8:00 AM on the first few days, the company manager will be on deck as a reminder that men are expected to be on time and as a liaison with the TD and Pink production heads.

Some of this load-in crew have regular work running a current show, and will not be present on matinee days, and may not be able to work overtime when needed. The TD must find other available stagehands for these times, often an opportunity for an apprentice to get experience.

The TD will have provided the company manager with the sizes and license plates of the expected trucks, the trucking companies' names, and their planned arrival and departure times. The company manager calls the police department with the details. This grants the trucks permission to park for a limited time on the busy New York City streets in front of the theatre so that the equipment can be unloaded onto the sidewalks by the Teamster truck drivers. The Teamsters do not enter the theatre. All equipment is left on the sidewalks and Local One stagehands take over from there. Rented equipment from lights and sound can fill up multiple trucks.

Load-in work begins by hanging pipes above the stage, and then lights are secured onto these pipes. This happens first because the new stage floor, the scenery, and moving props could easily interfere with ladders and genie equipment. Safety is rule one. The pieces of the set, with fireproofing certification and union shop stamps, will not get pieced together until the stage floor is laid down. In the case of an out-of-town show being transferred to a Broadway stage, the set will need to be rebuilt. Scenery is rarely, if ever, certified to New York City fire code standards.

There is always a false floor built on top of the theatre's actual stage to both protect the floor from custom design elements like painting and tracks cut into the floor to move scenery. Some floors are raked, meaning that they slope slightly downward toward the audience, allowing for better sightlines. There are strict Equity rules about raking a stage for dancers.

The traditional load-in period was as short as three days, but nowadays it usually lasts up to six weeks. Scenery now requires computer banks and a mile of cables under and around the stage. Stagehands, once considered blue-collar labor, have degrees in computer technology, fireguard certification, electrical licenses, design talent, and even architectural experience. They are also extremely handy with a hammer, a saw, and a paintbrush.

The theatre owners hire three Local One department heads (carpentry, electrics, props) to protect the theatre. Their duties are different from the load-in crew and the running crew. The head carpenter supervises all repairs including broken chairs in the audience; the head electrician supervises the power supply; and the head property master handles the glass cases and other promotional installations in the lobby and outside the theatre. No one may work on the stage unless all three House Heads are present in the building. Any interview in the theatre that needs to have a camera plugged into a wall socket will require all three House Heads. To save money, press agents arrange interviews in a star's dressing room or outside in front of a marquee, always with battery-operated cameras.

All three Local One House Heads are permitted to work cues for up to ten minutes at each performance, but no more. This is to make sure that the House Heads are not taking jobs away from the other local stagehands. The House Heads work for the theatre owners, not the production. The Heads keep the local crew payroll that they submit weekly to the house manager. House Heads accumulate severance pay with each year that they work for the theatre.

The smaller size of a theatre does not mean lower stagehand costs. Only the Helen Hayes Theatre, with just five hundred ninety-seven seats, and the non-profit organizations that own Broadway theatres, have negotiated slightly lower minimum salaries for almost all employees.

The theatre's Heads keep careful attendance that is double-checked by the Pinks, the TD, and the house manager before sending it on to the company manager.

Producers and theatre owners have long blamed the stagehands for the high cost of ticket prices. The high payroll for stagehands, with double supervisory jobs, Pinks and House Heads, is a source of budget aggravation. In the words of one electrician on a long-running hit, "Bring us a show without complex sets and cues, and a producer can save a lot of money on stagehands. But if the show can't run without a lot of stagehands, don't blame that on us."

When a show begins previews, the TD selects a running crew. If the director has asked for two spotlights to follow the stars on stage, then two electricians will be hired. If the action requires multiple cues occurring at the same moment, then multiple running crews will be needed, even if the remainder of the show doesn't otherwise require that many stagehands. The TD and director will col-laborate on ways to save costs if the artistic choices aren't negatively affected. Just as actors improve with time, so do stagehands. A two-stagehand cue may eventually be handled by one. The final decision about the running crew is made by opening night when the Yellow Card is created.

Changes and repairs on the physical production are accomplished at work calls. A simple fifteen-minute task will cost the production a minimum of four hours labor costs; therefore tasks are scheduled to make the best use of the stage-hands' time and the show's money. During previews this can mean work calls from 8:00 AM to 12:00 PM, rehearsing with the cast from 1:00 PM to 5:00 PM, then returning at 6:30 PM for that evening's performance and finishing at midnight.

These minimum four-hour work calls protect stagehands from being called to work at 8:00 AM for a short time and then expecting them to amuse themselves without pay until the evening show.

While the actors are asked to arrive thirty minutes before the show begins, stagehands are already busy refocusing lights, replacing bulbs, mopping the stage, checking wireless microphones, preparing props, and making sure that everything is ready for a flawless performance. Some preparations, like mopping, come with additional pay.

Most shows will have two or three sound people. The sound engineer will run the board from a location in the audience. The one or two additional sound people work backstage, replacing the batteries in all wireless microphones, fitting them in costumes and wigs, and handling any malfunctions, at every performance.

By opening night, the production has its official complement of carpenters, electricians, prop people, and sound engineers. Carpentry assistants have been hired to operate the ropes (mechanical or computerized) that lower scenery from the fly space. The union job is called a "fly man." The electrics department has follow-spot operators who work from positions above the audience. Other possible job titles, hired if needed, and each with their own pay scales, include winchmen, turntable operators, portable board operators, riggers, traps operators, pyrotechnic operators, flying rig operators, laser operators, and automated light operators.

Props have as many assistants as are needed to purchase and prepare consumed food (known as perishables) and to place all handheld items, including weapons, near the actor's stage entrance. If a prop is not in its right place, the entire show may grind to a halt.

If a chair is to be moved mechanically onstage, the prop department is in charge. If the chair also lights up, then both the electrics and props department supervise it. If a large staircase is moved on and off stage, the carpentry department supervises it. Every department knows its jurisdiction and learns how to maintain, operate, and store every item used in the show.

When the production finally closes, Pinks will supervise the load-out, taking as few as three days, if possible. A big musical may require up to two weeks to load-out the set, lights, sound, props, and costumes. After the theatre is emptied to its original four walls, the Heads will continue to restore the theatre to its original glory, under the direction of the theatre owners, before a new production begins its load-in.

The technical director's job is to know everything and everyone. The TD follows the intricate blueprints of the designers, prepares bids sent to a handful of union shops vying for the work, watches the progress of the chosen shops, and negotiates necessary changes. If the computer running the lighting cues freezes, the TD knows where to borrow a temporary laptop before Act Two begins. Considering that the older theatres were not built to hold today's computerized lights and scenery, the TD must consult with the House Heads, representing the theatre owners, to prepare for each show's intricate designs.

TDs must hire the best stage crew and builders, and troubleshoot a myriad of crises. The days when family credentials and nepotism were the only way to find work as a stagehand are gone. TDs need to know that the crew is prepared and able to handle all challenges. Stagehands, Local One, and IATSE Pinks, take the jigsaw pieces and put them together on, above, and under the stage, and in the wings left and right. In many cases, they need as much rehearsal as the actors. The best stagehands take their jobs as seriously as the stars.

Many stagehands learn their craft at the union shops that build, prepare, and repair lights, scenery, and sound equipment. Experience with computer design programs like AutoCad, as well as credentials in engineering and electrics, are increasingly essential. Safety procedures as regulated by the Occupational Safety and Health Administration (OSHA) are required knowledge.

New York City fire codes, the toughest in the world, require fire-certified stagehands, equally knowledgeable about building fires in the middle of the stage floor, and placing the right kind of extinguishers off-stage. Certified stagehands stand in both wings with fire extinguishers every time a cigarette is lit onstage. There has never been a fire in an occupied Broadway theatre.

It is not unusual for a Broadway production to lift an elegant mansion high into the air to allow for actors to perform temporarily underneath (*Sunset Boulevard*, 1994) or to attach a two-ton water tank to the architectural structure of the theatre over the heads of the audience so that the director can choreograph a twenty-two-minute rain storm on stage at every performance (*The Grapes of Wrath*, 1990). Theatres do not come with trapdoors, nor do the stages arrive on mechanical legs that effortlessly slide a regulation boxing ring over the first twenty rows of seats to create the illusion of being in the center of Madison Square Garden (*Rocky*, 2014).

Because Broadway productions are unpredictable, the rulebook for stagehands is very detailed, attempting to cover unexpected 6:00 AM publicity events, or new last-minute scenery, or the sale of a theatre to new owners. Union business reps show up backstage day and night to support their members when a rule is not as clear as hoped, and to be sure they are paid as required.

Of course, some shows are repetitious and not very challenging. Many stagehands do extra work on other shows, or have a second job during non-show times. They hang out with the rest of the theatre community only on special occasions. They are an insulated family of hard-working men and women, who appreciate their work and the Broadway theatre.

Chapter 17

What Playwrights, Directors, and Designers Want You to Know

Abbreviations used in this chapter and in the theatre world at large:
Guild = Dramatists Guild of America
SDC = Society of Directors and Choreographers
USA = United Scenic Artists
APC = Approved Production Contract
PSM = Production stage manager

PLAYWRIGHTS

When a producer asks to produce your show on Broadway, it is beyond exciting. It is the pat on the back from your parents that you always want, the feeling of winning the lottery, and falling in love all rolled into one.

Playwrights work for years on script ideas, character development, and dialog but rarely get the opportunity to have their plays considered seriously for production. As with actors, there are too many playwrights, far too few theatre companies, and too little production money. Unlike other nations like the United Kingdom and Canada, the United States government does not seriously support American theatres. Perhaps the large box office profits for a handful of hits on Broadway leads government officials to believe that the marketplace can handle its own financing. To date, the lack of tax incentives for Broadway and Off Broadway makes the production of new stage work less enticing than new film and television work that do receive tax breaks.

Many of Broadway's playwrights received their first production in a nonprofit regional theatre. Shows are workshopped and developed in front of sophisticated audiences and local critics drawing attention to the playwright and the play. Producer Joseph Papp, of the nonprofit Public Theater, once said that he was willing to (paraphrased) ". . . lose money producing a mediocre play by a good writer in order to help the writer move on and write the next play that will win the Pulitzer Prize."

Tony, Grammy, and Emmy Award–winning Lin-Manuel Miranda composed his hit Broadway hip-hop/rap musical *In the Heights* first as a college weekend production in 1999. It was then expanded and presented at the Eugene O'Neill Center in Connecticut where it was seen and transferred to Off Broadway by *Rent* producers Jeffrey Sellers and Kevin McCollum, who eventually moved the show to Broadway in 2008. *In The Heights* garnered several awards and made Lin-Manuel a new creative force to be watched. This process took over nine years. His hit Broadway musical *Hamilton* was developed at the Public Theater and has solidified Mr. Miranda as one of Broadway's favorite sons.

Stephen Sondheim's *Sunday in the Park with George* was first developed at Off Broadway's nonprofit Playwright's Horizons. Prolific playwrights Terrence McNally, August Wilson, and Neil Simon have had plays developed at institutions all over the country, like Chicago's Steppenwolf Theatre Company and Goodman Theatre, New York's Public Theater, Vineyard Theatre, and Second Stage Theatre, New Jersey's McCarter Theatre, Massachusetts' Barrington Stage Company and American Repertory Theater, Connecticut's Yale Rep, Washington DC's Arena Stage and Kennedy Center, and other nonprofits with the audience and budget for new works. Many hit productions also originate from London's West End like *War Horse*, *The History Boys*, *Les Miserables* and everything Andrew Lloyd Weber.

Playwrights, composers, and lyricists receive little if any income from the developmental process; rather, they are grateful for any opportunity. In so many ways, the lives of playwrights mirror those of actors, struggling to use their craft and their artistic expression, and willing to work for free. By the time they reach Broadway, the rewards can be spectacular or heartbreaking. Critics, poor marketing, disappointing direction, and last minute misguided rewrites kill shows. Or perhaps it's all about bad writing in the first place. However, it is important to remember that the 1968 Broadway musical *Hallelujah, Baby* closed in less than three months with mediocre reviews and audience apathy, yet won the Best Musical Tony Award due to a lack of serious competition that year. What a mixed message!

Broadway producers very, very rarely read scripts, unless it comes recommended from a trusted friend, theatre associate, or literary agent who vouches for its quality and sings its praises. Seasoned producers know that an acclaimed production in another city does not guarantee success in New York.

Broadway audiences do not necessarily have the same taste as subscription audiences in Minneapolis, Louisville, or Los Angeles. Since the producer must raise millions of dollars, the decision to produce on Broadway should not be an easy one. It isn't easy.

Working without a literary agent or an attorney is out of the question. Literary agents are difficult to attract; they earn a percentage of the money that a play earns, so they must believe strongly in the authors' work. They too only read recommended works. The authors' agreement, based on the Dramatists Guild's Approved Production Contract (APC), should not be casually negotiated. It covers distribution of subsidiary rights income for decades, including lucrative movie and television rights. The Guild is not a union, but a member services organization, and so technically everything is up for negotiations. A single word change in the authors' agreement can mean hundreds of thousands of dollars to the authors or the producer and investors.

On Broadway, playwrights, composers, and lyricists, collectively known as the authors, make money in three ways. The first is an "option." For a flat nonrecoupable fee, a producer acquires the exclusive right to raise money for the purpose of producing the play on Broadway. The production can recover this option fee from future royalties but only after the show has recouped its initial investment. The initial option period is six months or a year with additional six-month extensions. Each extension requires additional option fees. The option payments for members are standardized in Guild guidelines that set $5,000 as the minimum for a six-month option on a play and $18,000 for twelve months on a musical. Guild writers with a track record and a literary agent can command tens of thousands of dollars over the minimum. For unknown playwrights who are not using Dramatists Guild guidelines, an option amount has been as little as one dollar. The writer is restricted from trying to sell the play to other theatres or producers during this option period. The length of time and the track record of the producer should be carefully considered.

During the option periods, the authors will write any unfinished sections of their work, make adjustments during workshop productions, and participate in casting. When rehearsals begin, the authors are present as needed to make rewrites, including new material, right up to opening night. This is a full-time job in almost every situation.

The second moneymaker for playwrights is a royalty advance. When the play is finally scheduled to enter a rehearsal period with director and cast, the authors are paid an advance on their upcoming royalties, 3 percent of capitalization up to a limit of $35,000 for a nonmusical play, 2 percent of capitalization up to a limit of

$60,000 for a musical. Even if the show only plays one night, the authors are guaranteed this amount of royalty payments. After all, the author or authors have spent years writing their work with no compensation except their dreams.

Once the play or musical has ticket sales, the Dramatists Guild has set the standard for royalty percentages, minimum payments, and special conditions. A nonmusical author earns 5 percent of box office sales until investors' recoupment, then 10 percent thereafter. There is a myriad of adjustments and weekly conditions in the APC that help the production invest more in marketing and expedite returns to its investors.

For a musical, the standard division of royalties is now 4.5 percent until recoupment and 6 percent thereafter. This is traditionally divided one-third to the scriptwriter/librettist, one-third to the composer, and one-third to the lyricist. At 6 percent, the authors of a hit musical earning $1 million weekly at the box office will share $60,000 per week in royalties. But no matter what the condition of the show's gross box office income, the authors will never be paid less than $1,000 per week for a play and $3,000 per week for a musical. Authors' payments for out-of-town and preview performances are complex and require a lot of math on the part of management.

There is another popular and approved way to process royalties, called the "royalty pool." Shows and authors must agree to use the standard royalty system or the royalty pool from the start, and cannot change from the initial agreement. The pool may help reduce royalty payments if the show is not a blockbuster, but may mean more author royalties if the show becomes a major smash. This is another example of Broadway's toss of the dice (Chapter 11: Royalty Pools).

One of the reasons producers like to produce plays by William Shakespeare or Anton Chekhov is that there are no royalties to pay, no literary agents to contact, and no resistance to script changes, except sometimes by the critics and the audience. The Guild exists to foster plays and musicals that will hopefully join the ranks of the theatre classics.

Overall, the Guild protects both the authors' ownership rights of the material and the producer's investment in the work should it turn into a big hit on Broadway. The devil is in the details.

Producers must be "vested" in a production in order for investors to participate in the show's subsidiary rights. To be vested, the show must have an official opening night on Broadway, after which the sharing of subsidiary rights are secured. These rights include films, television, cast recordings, merchandise, regional, stock and amateur productions, international productions, touring companies, and a long list of potential opportunities. The general manager and literary agent will discuss different percentage packages based on written Guild categories. Producers of Broadway revivals also share in subsidiary rights often with smaller percentages.

Subsidiary rights are paid to the authors first who then distribute a percentage per Guild rules to the producers. In this way, even with a financial loss, a Broadway producer and investors can recover their investments and possibly earn a profit over time.

DIRECTORS AND CHOREOGRAPHERS

Early in the process, the producer and general manager hire the director, who is responsible for the overall artistic vision of the production, the conceptual interpretation of the script, and the staging of the actors. The director will cast the show and select the designers for the set, lights, and costumes, subject to the producer's approval and the general manager's budget. The seasoned producer may have casting and designer selections in mind, but rarely inflicts these requirements on the director. A great deal of trust between producer and director is necessary if there is to be a peaceful and successful project.

Directors and choreographers are paid in three ways, similar to playwrights: up-front fee, royalty advance, and performance royalties.

The job description of a choreographer varies more than one would think. In most instances, the choreographer moves the actors, using many styles of dance, to tell the story in concert with the music. A union choreographer will also be used to stage a big fight scene like in the drama *On the Waterfront* or in the musical *Rocky*. A small fight scene in a play like *Hamlet* uses a fight director or fight choreographer, a nonunion specialist in martial arts, weapons, etc.

Staging for the actors may have looked wonderful in the rehearsal studio, but may need adjustments once on the actual stage. Directors and choreographers should sit in all areas of the theatre to see if the entire audience can see and hear the show. Seats with limited sightlines are sold as partial-view seats, and in some cases, may not be sold at all. A director's eye for this kind of detail can save hundreds of thousands of dollars over the lifetime of a hit show.

A director may have less than a week in the actual theatre to concentrate on technical elements and designing cues for the show. This is known as "tech week." The seats in the theatre were covered with tarp from the day the stagehands began loading in the lights, the stage floor, and then the sets, in that order. The lighting, set, sound designers, and their assistants have set up makeshift tables on top of the seats to hold their computers, scripts, and coffee. The director, choreographer, and production stage manager (PSM) have chosen seats together within communication distance of the designers and walk the cast through the entire show, stopping constantly to create cues for the movement of set pieces, lighting effects, and other technical elements. The PSM keeps careful notes of cues and changes, as well as cast movement on stage. A piano and possibly drums play from the aisles until the orchestra is brought in toward the very end of tech week.

Between rehearsing cues and last minute stage work, the cast continues to add more depth and detail to the show under the ever-watchful eyes of the director and choreographer. Costumes are checked under the lights and backstage areas are designated to hold the many set pieces when not in use.

The director puts all of these jigsaw pieces together step by step, until the chaos of a dress rehearsal evolves into a messy but promising first preview performance. Audience reactions are seriously considered, but the director's vision determines what changes still need to be made to the script, musical score, staging, design, and performances. Even if the show is in great shape, it is not finished until the director says it is. Unfortunately, there is often not enough time during previews to make the necessary changes before the critics show up.

The ultimate goal is a successful artistic and financial hit. So sometimes an opening night is pushed back for days or even weeks. In 2010, *Spider-Man: Turn Off the Dark* postponed opening night multiple times before replacing the original director, rewriting the script, and going back into full-time rehearsal. While the extreme changes in this musical did not work out financially, a preview period on Broadway is an important chance to save a show.

More often, shows go through a birthing period out-of-town, when the critics and audiences in cities like Washington, DC, Boston, Philadelphia, New Haven, Dallas, Chicago, Atlanta, and Toronto let the producer and director know that something isn't working. Disney Theatricals has produced Broadway shows in multiple cities before showing up in New York and, in at least one case (*Aida*), has changed the director and concept between cities. In 1962, Stephen Sondheim wrote a new opening number to *A Funny Thing Happened on the Way to the Forum* after a less-than-spectacular run in Washington DC. The audience wasn't laughing. When the show opened on Broadway with the new song, "A Comedy Tonight," it became an instant musical comedy hit. Audiences still debate if the 2014 Tupac Shakur musical *Holler If Ya Hear Me* would have survived if the creators had given the show a trial period in other cities to develop the script and make changes before bringing it to Broadway.

It is more expensive to open a show out-of-town since the cast, designers, and staff must receive per diems and travel costs. It also involves building and trucking scenery, a separate load-in into another leased theatre, a separate marketing campaign, etc. However, in the long run, it may be an important investment. The director and producer must agree if a pre-Broadway run will be valuable. But since the producer holds the purse strings, they have the ultimate word on whether it will be done or not.

The role of the director has changed over time. According to producer Kermit Bloomgarden (*The Miracle Worker*, *The Diary of Anne Frank*, *Equus*), the title "director" came into wide use for Broadway plays sometime in the 1950s. Until that time, instead of "directed by" credits, the programs of many plays read "staged by." In an era where one-set living rooms were common, the primary purpose of a director was to keep the actors from bumping into each other on stage. Famous leading actors like John and Ethel Barrymore were considered to have directed themselves. Musicals, on the other hand, had a rich tradition of revues like Florenz Ziegfeld productions and Busby Berkeley extravaganzas, yet with the story-based *Show Boat*, *Oklahoma*, and others, the roles of choreographer and director did much more than stage the production.

In time, directors discussed motivation with the actors, and as stage elements became more complex and mechanized, directors began staging scenery movement and lighting effects as well as actors. Tony Award–winning director Harold Prince (*Company*, *Follies*, *Pacific Overtures*) anchored his theatrical concepts around the brilliance of set designer Boris Aronson as if the set were part of the cast. As technology developed, design elements have added to the complexity of directing and choreographing shows, from *Equus*, *The Lion King*, and *War Horse* utilizing life-size puppetry, to the revival of *Sunday in the Park with George* enveloping a painter's mind in the video projections surrounding the actors, to 2014's *The Curious Incident of the Dog in the Night-Time* where the stage becomes a technological interpretation of the mind of a brilliant, autistic child.

The ultimate achievement of a director is probably Julie Taymor's production of Disney's *The Lion King*. Hundreds of her stunning personally designed puppets are inhabited by a large cast of actors playing animals and moving scenery, to bring a beloved movie to life on a stage. On today's Broadway stage, directors oversee it all and sometimes conceive and design it too.

Some directors began as stage managers and actors. Mike Nichols was one-half of the famous Nichols and May comedy team prior to earning awards as a Broadway director (*The Odd Couple*, *The Real Thing*). Austin Pendleton began and continues as a film, television, and stage actor while directing Off Broadway and on (*The Runner Stumbles*, the revival of *The Little Foxes*). Former dancer/

choreographers like Jeff Calhoun (*Newsies*), and Rob Marshall (the revival of *Cabaret*) have become well-respected Broadway directors.

Some directors are also successful playwrights and producers. George Abbott (*Pajama Game, Pal Joey, Fiorello, Damn Yankees*), who worked on Broadway until the age of 107, was an award-winning playwright. Director Hal Prince (*Phantom of the Opera, Sweeney Todd, A Little Night Music*) began his career as a producer (*West Side Story*). George C. Wolfe wrote and directed plays Off Broadway before moving to Broadway as the writer/director of *Jelly's Last Jam* and director of many other Broadway hits (*Angels in America, Bring in the Noise/Bring in da Funk, Lucky Guy*). James Lapine both wrote the script and directed *Into the Woods, Act One*, and *Sunday in the Park with George*. David Hare is both the director and writer of award-winning plays like *Plenty* and *Amy's View*.

The choreographer can be a second director, helping actors to develop their characterization through dance. Since contemporary theatrical dance often moves the story along, choreographers make a significant difference in the flow and tempo of a musical. Jerry Mitchell, choreographer for *Hairspray*, is given codirector praise by the show's Tony Award–winning director Jack O'Brien, after which he became director and choreographer for the Tony-winning musical *Kinky Boots*. Michael Bennett held director, creator, and choreographer titles for *Dreamgirls, Ballroom, A Chorus Line*, and more, before his untimely death. His career began as a dancer on TV's *Hullabaloo*, and then choreographer for *Promises Promises, Company*, and *Follies* (that he also codirector with Harold Prince).

Directors and choreographers own their own work, and only lease it to the Broadway producer. This was not true a few decades ago but has been advanced by agents and the Stage Directors and Choreographers Society (SDC) together. The work of Jerome Robbins on *West Side Story*, Michael Bennett on *Dreamgirls*, and Agnes de Mille on *Oklahoma* helped make these shows a hit. Script rental organizations like Samuel French, Inc. and Musical Theatre International now carry program credit requirements and include payment to original directors and choreographers for both professional and amateur productions.

Most directors and choreographers see each show as their baby. While they move on to the next project, they want to be sure that their baby stays healthy. Contractually, they are required to revisit the show on a regular basis, when their schedule permits. Production stage managers are their eyes and ears between visits, holding brush-up rehearsals weekly to keep the show fresh.

Directors have been known to show up every six months and fire a few actors on the spot. Choreographers have been known to scream at their dancers until they are happy with the results. The creative spirit of directors and choreographers can make them extreme and volatile. The pressure of a $15 million production resting on your shoulders, as well as the frustration of matching the reality on stage to the artistic vision in your head, can make for intense sensitivity.

DESIGNERS

At the beginning of a run, it doesn't make sense to buy expensive and powerful lighting fixtures not knowing if the show will hit or miss. And so lights are always rented. The bulbs are purchased.

The invention of moving lights has greatly reduced the number of lamps hanging over a stage, although the cost, and the work-intensive computer programming required to create the effects, has added expense and time to the process of putting the show together. Moving lights provide serious flexibility and quality to a production, especially for big splashy musicals, therefore costs be damned.

Today's designers have had to adapt their skills and talents to the computer age. The basic principles have not changed. Lighting designers must tailor their choices with the style and color of costumes and scenery. A minimalist set can mean that the lights must create time and place. A strong lighting effect will create special effects in costumes. This is why production meetings are essential and why a fashion designer does not necessarily make a great stage costume designer, and why an architect does not always make a great scenic designer.

Producer Harold Prince tells the story about his first invoice from *West Side Story*'s costume designer Irene Sharaff. When he saw that the denim jeans worn by the Jets and Sharks cost over $25 each, he inquired about the cost, knowing that jeans in the late 1950s regularly cost about $5. The designer had individually dyed the jeans to make each one unique under the stage lights. Mr. Prince requested that she build jeans for future cast members at the street price. When he returned a few months later, the subtle difference on stage was so disappointing, he apologized and allowed the costumer to dye the jeans as originally planned.

The mechanized dress worn by Bernadette Peters in the opening scene of *Sunday in the Park with George* reportedly cost $150,000. Ann Hould-Ward's Tony Award–winning costumes for Disney's *Beauty and the Beast* (the tea pot, the dresser, forks, knives, and spoons, etc.) added up to about $3 million. The Woody Shelp hand-beaded hats in the finale of *A Chorus Line* cost $2,000 apiece in 1976!

The design and creation of specialized or period costumes requires an extra layer of research and execution. Costume designers are therefore paid by the number of costumes and receive an extra pay boost if the costumes are not contemporary.

Multiple sets moving on and off stage require more blueprints, construction, and time. Therefore scenic designers are paid at different rates based on the number and kind of scenery they are asked to design, build, and install. These extra sets also require more work from the lighting designer.

The technical director (TD), also known as the production supervisor, will oversee the discussion among the designers and shops that build the designs, under the artistic eye of the director. Communication is essential. Stress is often high. Things can go wrong, and often things go very right.

The finale costumes for *A Chorus Line* looked pink to the naked eye backstage, yet under the lights and against a wall of mirrors, they reflected a brilliant silver to the audience. This was not a mistake.

Boris Aronson's dragon with big disturbing eyes in 1976's *Pacific Overtures* was an accordion that slithered toward the audience to become a large shipping vessel complete with live sailors on board. The lights did not reveal the trick before it appeared. The sailors' costumes did not pull focus away from the dragon until the right moment. Sets, costumes, and lights worked together in artistic harmony. And the musical score created a reason for the audience to applaud the scenery. It was a very magical moment.

With the exception of the design offices inside the Disney Theatrical offices in New York, individual designers must find and pay for their own workspace. The United Scenic Artists (USA), their collective union, makes sure that designers and assistants receive health insurance and pension contributions. Many scenic and light designers supplement theatre income by designing for films, concerts, retail stores, and corporate offices. However, if theatre is their first love, then their other businesses must provide some flexibility. In reality, they just work multiple jobs at the same time, hiring additional assistants at their own expense, and hoping for a little recognition.

Chapter 18
What Management Wants You to Know

Abbreviations used in this chapter:
GM = general manager
CM = company manager
HM = house manager
PA = press agent/representative
ATPAM = Association of Theatrical Press Agents and Managers
League = Broadway League
IATSE = International Alliance of Theatrical Stage Employees
FOH = front of house
TDF = Theatre Development Fund

Each house manager has stories of rude, despicable, selfish, stupid, or sickly audience members. Here are a handful of true stories:

At the end of one show, the house manager listened to the complaints of the last couple still in the theatre who thought they should not have been asked to vacate the theatre. "We weren't finished with our conversation," said the irate customer. At the beginning of another show, the manager took complaints from people who were refused admission because their tickets were for a different day. At intermission, one manager helped a nun in full garb into the ambulance after an apparent heart attack. Fifteen minutes before the end of the same show, one man wanted his money back and refused to understand that he had already seen the entire show, that the box office was closed, and that the tickets clearly said "no refunds or exchanges." A family of five wanted the manager of a sold-out hit to move all of their seats together and to a more expensive section (which was not available). The range of complaints and situations handled by a house manager on Broadway cannot be fully explained or understood. Yet the house manager's job is often called "easy."

172

The company managers' stories include star divas demanding pink dressing rooms, a drunken producer demanding a reason why a group of students are being loud in the balcony, investors asking for free seats because of "who they are," and stagehands demanding money up front before they will do work. Keeping track daily of available cash and budget expenditures while juggling emergency wardrobe expenses when the dry cleaner fails to return an important costume are a few of the talents that CMs have learned. Unions are often months behind in processing benefit checks, and payroll companies make errors. Cast, crew, and staff are rarely willing to wait a few days for an adjustment check. Everything must be fixed immediately and the CM is in charge of "fixing."

General managers are stuck with the larger problems of celebrity negotiations, budget overruns, union disputes, lawsuits, a troublesome producer, and disciplining staff. Negotiating how to list the names of performers on the billing page of a program, on the marquee, and in advertisements can take weeks of heated discussions with the actors' representation. When a producer authorizes an expensive ad campaign without consulting the GM, or signs off on a special event without a finalized budget, the GM resolves the crises.

The CM is hired by the GM. The HM is the employee of the theatre owner. Together, these three managers are the backbone of the financial and legal success of every show. Woe to the producers who think they don't need these three managers.

All three deal with the Broadway unions. Overlooking or ignoring a union rule can result in very expensive penalties and costs. That's one reason why general managers, company managers, and house managers play such an important role. It is impractical if not impossible for a show's producer to read, learn, and understand the detailed union agreements that were forged over many decades of negotiations between the Broadway League and each individual union.

General managers usually maintain an office space at their own cost. In the case of a long-running hit, producers may bring both GM and CM into their production office. There is no one office situation exactly the same.

New York City offices are very expensive so the general manager's approximate $3,500 per week paycheck is not as lucrative as it may imply. This salary begins just before rehearsals. Prior to receiving a salary, the GM is paid a flat fee, $35,000 or more, for a limited amount of time and preproduction work that can be extended upon further payment. General managers can supervise more than one show at a time.

About a week or two before rehearsals, a company manager gets a desk in the general manager's office. Proximity is important so that both managers can communicate easily and often. The company manager will only handle one show at a time, and with rare exception, will not be offered more than the union minimum pay of $2,002.23 (as of September 2015) plus 8.5 percent vacation pay for a total of $2,172.42 per week. This is because GMs must compete for each show, so they try to impress producers with how low they keep management costs.

General managers and company managers work six and a half days a week on average. They are at the beck and call of the producer and the entire production staff. Crisis management is the name of the game. If everything is good at rehearsals, there will no doubt be a problem in the wardrobe department. If everything is good in wardrobe, there will be a problem in the box office or a deadline at the advertising agency. Communication between departments is the responsibility of these two managers, with the company manager handling more of the day-to-day issues like payroll and benefit payments, while the general manager works on the longer range issues like promotion and negotiations.

There are approximately four hundred ninety company and house managers, and one hundred eighty press agents, who belong to the Association of Theatrical Press Agents and Managers (ATPAM), a very small *national* union that in 1994 joined the International Alliance of Theatrical Stage Employees (IATSE), the same parent union of Broadway stagehands. IATSE provides negotiating clout as well as additional benefits such as healthcare options, a pension and annuity plan, and retail discounts.

ATPAM members can work as a house manager one year and a company manager the next because they are trained and experienced in each other's dealings. The public relations people, called press agents or press representatives, can work solo or as part of a larger office (Chapter 14: Press Agents). The general manager is not a union position, but may nonetheless be a member of ATPAM. Very often GMs have previously worked as a CM or HM where they collected their wealth of experience and large pool of professional contacts that qualify them to be a general manager.

ATPAM members come in two categories: certified and noncertified. Certified managers have apprenticed for a minimum of two years under a working company manager, attended many seminars covering topics such as box office and union rules, and have passed a six-hour written and short oral test. To prepare for this test, ATPAM members meet in study groups, similar to law school, and sweat it out. Noncertified members do not go through this process.

Right-to-work laws in New York State permit people to be hired without union membership. When this happens, it's often because the manager had a previous working relationship with a producer at a non-Broadway theatre. By law, nonunion workers must join the union after thirty days, even though they get all union benefits without membership. In practice, there is some freedom in the length of time, especially if a show looks to have a short run. If they are lucky enough to be hired for a second job, there is no grace period.

Each Broadway production is required to have three ATPAM workers as part of their management and public relations team. The GM will hire an ATPAM company manager and press agent, and the theatre owner will hire an ATPAM house manager.

It should be emphasized that the title of company manager means something radically different in regional and stock theatres where company managers handle housing, travel, and social events for staff and acting members of the theatre company. On Broadway, CMs also handle housing and travel, but their primary job is the day-to-day business of production in all its aspects including finances.

During the load-in weeks prior to the first performance of the show, company managers carry up to a thousand dollars in cash to cover unforeseen expenses for tools, sets, lights, props, sound and costume materials, coffee breaks for the crew, and signage problems outside the theatre. When the Teamsters arrive in their trucks, they expect immediate payment for their services and while there are no union rulebooks explaining this, it is considered "past precedent." Only Teamsters are allowed to unload a truck. No one wants deliveries to be held up, so they are paid as requested. Otherwise, the show is paying lots of idle stagehands waiting to move the equipment from the sidewalk into the theatre.

Company managers meet once a week with the show's certified public accountant to submit all collected invoices and receipts and explain them. This weekly financial report is used to determine profit and loss from which all royalties and investment returns are calculated. The CM writes the checks, but may or may not have signatory power over payments. In the case of larger offices, there may be someone else assigned to write checks, but the CM is responsible to the GM for timely payments and accurate accounting.

CMs are also responsible for calculating vacation pay, annuity and pension payments, vacation approvals, processing discounts, and overseeing box office procedures and FOH signage, and more. Since lawyers are expensive, managers learn to write their own basic contracts and contract riders. Hiring and firing at all levels of production is under the jurisdiction of a general manager, but the process is often transferred to the company manager.

CMs go backstage prior to each performance to confer with stage managers, actors, stagehands, and musicians before going to the box office with backstage and office house seats (Chapter 13: Box Office). After the start of each performance, CMs finalize the box office statement with the house manager and head treasurer.

Company managers hand out paychecks every Thursday night. House managers distribute paychecks every Wednesday evening. This makes them very popular, for a short time at least.

Company managers have no dedicated assistants on most productions. None are required although the union has wanted to make it mandatory on large shows. In case of illness or days off, the pressure to go to work is enormous. Those larger offices that hire ATPAM associates are few. Administrative assistants are sometimes used temporarily as "covers" to be available at the theatre and box office before a show, but they are not thoroughly trained, and cannot be held responsible for financial mistakes and union issues the same way that ATPAM members are.

Each show is different and managers are constantly presented with unique situations. Since no union rulebook can possibly cover every situation, the managers become the catchall for all business and production issues. There are no union instructions on who budgets a show's participation in the Macy's Fourth of July fireworks televised concert, or for an all-night cast album recording, or a producer's birthday party, or a cast member's memorial. The CM has his or her hands in every pot.

House managers are hired by theatre owners on an annual basis. When a producer leases a theatre, the HM comes with the lease. HMs work inside the theatre, with almost all theatres providing a dedicated office space, computer, phone, and Internet. Some house managers also have workspace in the theatre owner's corporate offices to consult with the owner's centralized executives and financial people. The HM's payroll is very different from the CM's payroll, yet the CM ultimately reimburses the HM for theatre payroll and theatre expenses.

The payroll for stagehands, musicians, and other theatre staff, property taxes, union pensions and benefits, box office expenses, and other costs at each theatre can total over $100,000 per week. It is the house manager's job to collect, process, and total this invoice, subtract it from the box office weekly income, and submit this invoice to the company manager ("house settlement") along with a check for the balance of the income from the box office ("settlement check").

Even though the financial staff in the theatre owner's central office and the CM will double-check the HM's work, accuracy is not ensured. Time sheets and unexpected invoices may arrive later in the week, and misinformation from department heads may require adjustments from a previous week.

The theatre lobby, marquee, box office signage, and photo display cases are collectively called "front of house" (FOH), another domain of the house manager. While the GM, CM, press agent, and other marketing people will determine the content to be displayed in the FOH, the HM will get approval for and arrange for house staff and crew to install the signs. House managers also supervise the custodial staff that keeps the theatre clean and presentable for the public. Everything that touches or maintains the physical theatre goes through the HM first, and the costs for such work go onto the HM's payroll. Above all, when a house manager is able to add a welcoming smile or an easy solution to a patron's needs, the job has fulfilled another important responsibility not found in rulebooks.

Primarily, the house manager is there to supervise the opening of the house for audiences, deal with audience issues, and get everyone settled in during the thirty minutes prior to show time. Theatre owners each have different personalities in structure and attitude that define responsibilities and limit or expand the house manager's work in subtle ways.

All house managers (and a few theatre engineers and crew) have fire guard certificates issued by New York. They sign a logbook before every performance guaranteeing that all daily fire safety procedures have been performed. The New York City Fire Department shows up for surprise inspections just before curtain time to be sure the book has been signed and that instructions continue to be taken seriously. To date, there has never been a serious fire in a Broadway theatre.

The house manager's weekly hours may look something like this: Monday off, Tuesday 5 PM to 11 PM, Wednesday matinee day 12:30 PM to 11 PM, Thursday 4 PM to 11 PM, Friday 7 PM to 11 PM, Saturday matinee day 12:30 PM to 11 PM, Sunday matinee only 1:30 PM to 6 PM. Every show keeps a slightly different schedule. The theatre's payroll is submitted on Sunday after the matinee. If there are payroll questions, the HM receives a phone call on the day off.

A company manager's work hours change with each show as well. One example of a workweek may be: Monday partially off (subject to finishing the show's payroll), Tuesday 11 AM to 8:45 PM, Wednesday 10 AM to 8:45 PM, Thursday 10 AM to 8:45 PM, Friday 11 AM to 8:45 PM, Saturday 12 PM to 8:45 PM, Sunday matinee 2 PM to 3:45 PM. They also answer emails from producers after hours, while sometimes taking breaks for errands or an occasional lunch.

Since the company and house managers are peers, there is usually great cooperation between the show and the theatre. Their employer allegiances are different, but the goal is the same: a profitable, audience-pleasing show.

Some general managers with multiple shows work harder than both the CM and HM combined. Other general managers purposefully restrict their workload to producer meetings and staff supervision. After a show closes, the GM is the watchdog over future subsidiary income and royalty payments for the show, unless the producer elects to take on those tasks. In the case of a hit musical like *Les Miserables*, this work could go on for decades.

Broadway management is a lifestyle. House managers are rarely free in the evening. Company managers have late night free time only. General managers are on call 24/7. Dating and family life often take a backseat to the demands of the job.

At the beginning of a run, so much information is exclusively in the GM's and CM's heads, that taking a day off for a cold or a family event is nearly impossible. The supervisory position of a general manager, like a producer, is unique and has no substitute. Company managers don't have regular subs but, when the show is a bona fide hit, there is the possibility of adding a dedicated ATPAM associate, apprentice, or office associate to cover a night or weekend at the theatre and take over some basic management tasks. House managers have less trouble finding union subs from an available pool that is kept by the theatre owners. While HMs are permitted three paid sick days each year, personal days are docked.

Early on, it is difficult for a director and producer to gauge if the show is working if audiences are small. It is important that critics see the show with a lively audience reaction. To this effect, managers fill early houses with "comps" and low-priced tickets.

"Comps" are free tickets discreetly given to theatre industry staff and their guests, as well as select theatre groups like TDF, Manhattan Plaza residents, Hospital Audiences, and select schools. The number of comps range from a few tickets to thousands. There are literally dozens of organizations hoping for these offers and ready to supply theatregoers. Managers remember who failed to respect the rules, and those organizations are denied future comps. Discretion is essential so that the general public doesn't get a negative impression and stops buying tickets. Since there is no union job assigned to dealing with comps, this task falls to the company manager in almost all cases.

So much of a manager's job description is covered by the term "crisis management." The phone rings with worried calls from investors, or urgent emails are waiting requesting favors from the theatre owner, or equipment being held for payment due, or cast illnesses, or arguments in rehearsal, or problems at home. These all divert attention from the manager's original plans of budget analysis or contract writing. Since theatres operate on a six-day schedule, new information arrives for analysis and action every day.

Company managers are the only Broadway staff that literally know what's going on with all the other departments and employees, from family births to deaths, from illness to schedule conflicts. The CMs know what everyone earns, and what everything costs. And the managers supervise the spending of millions of dollars leading to opening night. It's an exciting job requiring six but needing almost seven days a week for the first few months of a run. Just when it seems it will slow down, the Tony Awards happen, or a cast recording, or some other special event.

Company managers are disturbed that Equity stage managers earn higher salaries, sometimes over $1,000 more per week. In many aspects, stage and company managers are peers and collaborators, even though company managers are technically the stage manager's boss. This salary gap is the result of years of contract negotiations. Perhaps management's worth in the eyes of producers and theatre owners, or the power of a large union (Equity) versus the smaller union (ATPAM), created this large discrepancy.

And then the show closes. They all do eventually . . . even *Cats*, which famously advertised "Now and Forever." If the first show of the week is a Tuesday, then the notice must be on the backstage callboard by the half-hour call on that day. Not wanting to blindside your creative staff, technical director and crew heads, theatre owner, promotion staff, investors, and stars, they are often notified earlier in the day, and the ad agency may know even sooner to prepare final ads. Actors on Run-of-the-Play contracts are required to receive individual notification.

This closing notice releases all union members from their contracts permitting them to accept new work the following week. Of course, the show may suddenly see an upswing in ticket sales based on a rush to see the show before it closes. In that case, the company manager will take down the callboard notice by half-hour of the final performance of the week. The cast and crew now know that they have at least one more week of work. In some cases, this up and down pattern goes on for weeks driving everyone crazy.

After the final performance, the house manager makes sure that signs go up on the lobby doors telling the public how to get refunds for future performances. The technical director will have organized a load-out of all scenery, lighting, costumes, and props in the shortest time period possible, usually two to three days for a simple production and ten days for a monster production. In the short time between posting the notice and the final performance, a large supplemental crew must be hired and trucking secured. Whether a show will soon start touring, or just die a quiet death, will determine what will happen to scenery, props, and costumes: storage versus trashing versus donation versus selling. Restoring the theatre to its original four-wall status will be discussed with the theatre owner.

The house manager and company manager will be paid through the end of load-out. The managers may get a few extra days if there is additional closeout work and payroll to complete. Thereafter, the general manager handles all leftover paperwork for the show, and the theatre owner looks for the next tenant.

Hit shows never truly die and the general manager stays on to collect subsidiary rights, pay out investor profits, and oversee plans for future tours and productions. The company manager looks for employment with another show, often after a much needed rest. Since house managers are signed to annual contracts with the theatre owner, from September to August, they wait sometimes for months without pay to hear about the next show entering their assigned theatre. There is always the possibility of extra days of work subbing for fellow vacationing house managers.

And then it starts all over again with the next show.

Retired general manager Robert Kamlot documented a previously unwritten professional code for all managers, known as *Kamlot's Six Rules of Management*:

1. Never assume anything.
2. Never give out gratuitous information.
3. When in doubt, do nothing. Sometimes, no action is an action.
4. Never play around in your own backyard.
5. Never speak to the press.
6. Diplomacy is at least as important as being right.

With time and experience comes wisdom.

Chapter 19

What the Ushers, Ticket Takers, and Porters Want You to Know

While the vast majority of audiences are respectful and polite, ushers receive the brunt of rude, drunken, sick, and troubled audience members. Their experience and people skills are called into action almost daily policing illegal use of cameras and cell phones before, during, and after performances, ejecting unruly customers without major disruption of the show, working with EMT workers and theatre managers to carefully and quickly move a heart attack patient out of the theatre, and so much more.

The actual job description of an usher has them arrive one hour before show time to stuff inserts into Playbill programs, hand out the Playbills, direct the public to their assigned seats, answer questions about bathrooms and hearing devices, and maintain crowd control, while eyeing the clock to be sure the show begins as scheduled. All of this is done by unionized workers who give up their free nights and weekends for approximately $400 a week before taxes. They are given a small weekly stipend of $4 per laundered item in their uniforms. These items have changed over the years from white embroidered collars to company-branded scarves and ties.

The head usher, sometimes at the same theatre for over thirty-five years, takes attendance and schedules the ushers. The head usher, the ushers' "director" (second in command), house manager, and entire staff are trained to evacuate the theatre quickly and calmly during fire, bomb scares, and other emergencies. Ushers are the largest number of theatre staff on duty at the start of every show. Some are scheduled "short" (two hours until just after the curtain rises) and some are scheduled "long" (four hours or until just after the audience departs).

The audience rarely notices an usher's work once the show has begun. Ushers are the ones who confiscate a camera from a patron who ignores the "no photograph" law, or who gently removes a patron from the wrong seat when the actual seat holder arrives late. They will signal the house manager while comforting a heart attack victim or moving a potential fight among patrons from the seats to a quieter location in the theatre so that the show can continue.

Most importantly, it is said that if you want to know if your show is going to be a hit, ask an usher. Arguably, no one in the theatre sees more performances, observes more audience reactions, and has a longer history of comparison than an usher. Smart producers and directors talk to the ushers rather than wait for the critics.

The Shubert, Jujamcyn, and Nederlander organizations hire their own ushers. The union protects their benefits and establishes working conditions. Applications are also taken at the nonprofit Roundabout and Manhattan Theatre Club offices, as well as the independent Circle in the Square theatre. Ushers begin their career as subs, then regulars. Over time, a few graduate to ticket takers.

Ticket takers are members of Local 306 as well. They have thirty minutes to admit from six hundred to eighteen hundred patrons into the theatre, answer questions, catch tickets for a different date and sometimes for a different theatre, watch for drunk audience members or other potential disturbances, and scan each ticket or barcoded print-out for every patron and send them to the correct aisle or level for seating. Problems are referred to the head usher and house manager who are usually positioned just inside the doors.

The ticket takers are the first to welcome people with physical challenges arriving in wheelchairs. The ushers guide these patrons to specially designed and priced locations. If a physically challenged patron has not given advance notice, the head usher will ask the house manager to try to exchange seats, when possible. The public often creates its own problems by not alerting the box office or online ticket services about special needs. An elderly couple that arrives at an older theatre with tickets requiring two flights of stairs may be surprised when there is no elevator and the show is sold out. The front-of-house staff (house manager, head usher, ushers, and ticket takers) is experienced in solving these preventable problems.

Double ticketing, when two people show up with tickets for the same seats, has all but disappeared due to computers, but tourists are sometimes the victims of crooks who sell counterfeit tickets on the street or online. Tickets clearly state that all sales are final. Ushers, ticket takers, and the box office treasurers can accommodate seating changes with the house manager's approval and assuming seats are available.

At every backstage door sits one person, 90 percent of the time a male, to collect messages, packages, notices, answer questions, and prevent access to the unauthorized public. Each member of the company is assigned a mailbox, and a bulletin board posts notices approved by the show's managers. Notices can include cast party announcements, ads for massage therapists, rehearsal schedules, and the dreaded closing notice.

No one enters the theatre—no cast, no manager, no crew—unless the doorperson is on duty. This means that there are usually two scheduled people per day beginning as early as 8:00 AM through 11:00 PM or midnight, depending on the day's activities. Local 306 builds in two hours of overtime into the doorperson's forty-hour workweek, but during load-in and special events, there can be many hours of overtime at time and a half pay.

After each performance, it is the doorperson who has a list of who is permitted backstage to visit with a cast member. In the case of a major celebrity, the doorperson is often supplemented with a person to keep the stage exit clear. The Shubert Organization maintains a large force of security personnel and is given much credit for pressuring New York City to clean up the Times Square district. In addition to the Shubert force, many shows hire their own security personnel to check packages as patrons enter the theatre, and help with disruptive audience members (see Chapter 22: Theatre Owners).

Most stage doors are situated to the left or right of the main entrance of the theatre. There are significant exceptions. The stage doors for the Majestic, Golden, and Jacobs Theatres are found in a common alley between the Row Hotel and the Golden Theatre on West 45th Street. The stage door for the Imperial, American Airlines, Lyric, and Belasco Theatres are on a separate street behind their theatres. The Minskoff, Gershwin, and Lincoln Center's Beaumont Theater stage doors are on side streets away from the public entrance. Circle in the Square's stage entrance is below ground and takes the cast through an office building on West 50th Street, or actors can exit with the audience through the main lobby.

Porters and cleaners belong to a separate union, Local 32BJ. They work quietly around the public and the performance schedule. When the audience exits after a show, they drop Playbills, candy boxes, drink containers, umbrellas, cell phones, gloves, scarves, and jewelry between and under seats. Lost and found is collected by the cleaning staff, and delivered to the house manager should someone call. All Broadway theatres take pride that the next audience will find a spotless theatre.

There was once a union position known as "matron," a woman assigned to maintain and clean the women's restroom while in use. This position no longer exists. All restrooms are now maintained by the custodians known as "porters." Before each performance, porters stand in front of the box office directing traffic, answering questions, and generally keeping the public outside until the doors open a half hour before show time. At intermission, they may be stationed near the restrooms or in the lobby. At the end of the show, they wait for the last patron to exit and then padlock as many as two dozen doors. A custodian is the last to leave the theatre and go home. Even the house manager must exit before the last door is locked. Strict fire codes require that padlocks be removed from every door before the public is allowed in the theatre, and that too is the responsibility of the porter.

There are forty-hour, thirty-two-hour, and twenty-six-hour porters, titles that represent the basis of their workweek and salary. In 2015, the head forty-hour custodian earns a base pay of $778 per week. A twenty-six-hour custodian makes $475.80 for his partial week. Each theatre uses a combination of these differently scheduled employees. Whenever printed inserts are added to the Playbill, they are paid an additional $2 for that week.

All front-of-house staff responds to the directives of the house manager; however, they are hired and fired by the theatre owners who schedule and oversee their training.

Ask the house staff about their other careers and you will discover teachers, actors, writers, social workers, parents, grandparents, and students. For some, this is a family business spanning two or three generations and a source of great pride.

Chapter 20
What Wardrobe Wants You to Know

If you wore the same clothes six days a week under physically challenging circumstances, you would need a wardrobe specialist too. There are many people who love theatre, have good people skills, and have grown up with a natural talent for sewing and mending.

Wardrobe people spend more time with actors than anyone else. They see actors naked, both physically and emotionally, in dressing rooms and quick-change booths that are common in the wings.

Of course, their real job is tending to the specialized materials from which long-lasting costumes are built. Some costumes have to be dry-cleaned overnight every night. Most costumes require heavy-duty washers and dryers. Some theatres have them from a previous production; others don't. Each show purchases and/or replaces what it needs.

The wardrobe supervisor is in charge of scheduling assistants whose numbers can range from a few to a multitude. Some stay late to prepare for the dry-cleaning pickup, and others arrive early for the in-house washing.

Wardrobe people are backstage to help actors get into their costumes and make costume changes during the show. They also make temporary modifications to costumes for use by understudies. With the exception of Disney who is jokingly known for casting people because they fit the preexisting costume, most understudies don't fit the original costume.

Modifications happen more often than most people think, especially during the preview performances when managers are loathe to spend money on making duplicate costumes until they know the show will last beyond opening night.

The original costume design and building budget may exceed $1 million, but eventually shows duplicate each costume for emergencies.

Purchasing undergarments for each and every actor is a must. This includes stockings, skullcaps, dance shoes, and more. Actors' Equity rules do not permit actors to wear any personal item that has touched the skin of another actor, for obvious health reasons.

Audiences expect spectacular costume designs. The materials used must last for years and look fresh at every performance. Some costumes cost over $100,000 each. Wardrobe staff does not build these costumes. Costume construction is bid out to expert shops with talented sewers who, under pressure of deadlines, sometimes work nonstop in order to deliver dozens, if not hundreds, of costumes to the theatre, ready for the final fittings on the actors.

Fittings are held as early in the rehearsal process as possible as soon as actors are officially on the clock. Knowing that a male actor wears his shirts large is not enough. Detailed waistlines, inseams, arm lengths, chest, neck, and hip sizes are needed to turn the designs into practical garments. Dance clothes including shoes are carefully measured to allow for flexibility and comfort. They need to last a long time, hopefully.

In some cases, actors are asked to use their own shoes or other clothing. The production rents these personal items as dictated by the Equity rulebook. The wardrobe staff will clean, store, and maintain these items as well.

During tech week, time is found to parade the actors in costumes under the lights on stage. Although built, the costumes are not yet fitted to the actors' bodies. Wardrobe is working with the designer right up to the very last second. The final one or two run-thru performances without an audience, known as dress rehearsals, is when the dressers learn who needs special help getting into costume, and where costumes need to be placed backstage. Quick-change booths are built last-minute when it is discovered that there isn't time for an actor to run back to the dressing room, change, and get back for the next cue on stage.

When Disney's *Beauty and the Beast* was suddenly moved from the Minskoff Theatre to the Palace Theatre, the new lack of backstage space created major problems. Some of Ann Hould-Ward's award-winning costumes, like a human-size tea pot and dresser drawers, couldn't fit through doorways or down the stairwells, so set and costume changes had to be choreographed in the wings within an inch of its life. Curtains were lifted and lowered on either side of the stage to create a private space for actors to quickly change and get into places, then the change curtains rose back up so large set and prop pieces could move on and off stage. Additional wardrobe people were added to work in the wing space while the original staff worked with the dancing knives and forks in the wardrobe room downstairs.

Great designers know how to match color and materials to work with lighting and set designs for maximum effect. Protecting these costumes can save the show a lot of money, and continue to wow audiences night after night. The wardrobe supervisor understands this and hires people who take the work seriously.

Newly hired wardrobe people usually begin with hourly part-time assignments. When they are provided with full-time employment, there are union (Local 764) initiation dues to pay, $1,000 up front, plus $55 quarterly, and 2 percent of salary thereafter. These dues are similar to most other Broadway unions. Some wardrobe people begin their Broadway careers as actors and designers. This work keeps them in the theatres they love.

For productions with a huge number of costumes and subsequent touring productions, costume studio space is rented. For example, *Wicked* has multiple costume shops that handle repairs and re-creations for their worldwide productions. These outside shops are another source of employment and a backup staff for the Broadway show.

A wardrobe supervisor, as of August 2014, earned at least $1,551.87 per week plus benefits (Disney's separate agreement with Local 764 pays a tad more). Wardrobe supervisors work so closely with designers and actors that they can rise to a celebrity-like status that carries them from show to show. Assistants and dressers earn at least $1,448.18 weekly. Overtime is common, especially during final rehearsals and special promotional events such as photo calls, the Tony Awards, and Macy's Thanksgiving Day parade.

Stars have personal dressers, except when budgets do not allow, or if there are no significant costume changes during a show. The ability to make a star feel supported and attended to can mean a lifelong friendship, and possibly a job with the star beyond the show.

Before each performance, costumes are delivered to the dressing rooms or the actor comes to the wardrobe room. Hair, wig, and makeup personnel share space in the wardrobe area. At the end of the show, wardrobe visits each dressing room to collect costumes. Long hours and repetitive work in rooms with no windows can be tiresome except for the company of actors who appreciate them. A successful wardrobe person cares about both the costumes and the people wearing them.

This union, along with many others, recognizes that people skills and leadership training help to make a successful career. To that end, the union provides classes for its twelve hundred members in the New York City area.

Hair and wig designers are specialists who work closely with costume designers, directors, wardrobe staff, and actors to bring the characters to life. Unlike wardrobe people who receive the costumes after a union shop has finished the primary construction, hair and wig designers earn a design fee and additional income in one of two ways: a flat rate for building a new wig or rental fees for the use of wigs they own. They will tell you that it takes just as much work to teach an actor how to style their own hair to express the character as it does to build an appropriate wig. The work includes keeping the production looking fresh as if every performance is the most important one.

Chapter 21

What Musicians Want You to Know

The musical skills required to get into a Broadway orchestra require much more than being a good player.

A small handful of musical contractors are the casting agents for orchestra members. They know who is reliable, who can hit an especially important high note on a horn, and who can read complicated musical scores at first sight with beautiful tones and musicality. The contractor can work on more than one show and can also hire himself as a musician.

Abbreviations used in this chapter and in the theatre world at large:
802 = Musician's Local 802
AFM = American Federation of Musicians
IATSE = International Alliance of Theatrical Stage Employees

A rehearsal pianist must be able to look at a new unseen song, as complex as anything Stephen Sondheim or Leonard Bernstein might compose, and on the spot, transpose the song into a different key for the selected star of the show. A rehearsal pianist will spend hours playing the same music over and over in a rehearsal studio, make edits and add new material whenever the composer makes changes. And this pianist may not end up in the orchestra of the show by choice or by design. They are paid by the hour and scheduled by the stage manager. The company manager translates the submitted hours into payroll including overtime if applicable.

Musicians Local 802 includes rehearsal pianists, orchestra members, the musical contractor, the librarian, orchestrators, arrangers, and music copyists, as well as the associate musical director/conductor. The musical director/conductor duties can be handled by one person or divided between two people. For that reason, the original musical director (MD) is governed by both Local 802, and its parent union the American Federation of Musicians (AFM), receiving a weekly salary from 802, and a supervisor's fee too. Just as IATSE Pink stagehands (see Chapter 16: Stagehands) may travel with the show outside of New York, the musical director will most likely travel with the initial tours of the show and must have membership in the national AFM.

Within the orchestra pit, there are some musicians with additional responsibilities. The librarian collects and distributes the music at the theatre. The printed music does not go home with the musicians in case a sub shows up at the next show, and to also make sure the score is not copied and sold. The librarian receives an extra weekly stipend.

Composers are not paid as members of 802 or AFM. Some composers, like Jerry Herman of *Mame* and *Hello, Dolly* fame, admit to not being able to read or write music. A great musical ear and talent does not necessarily come with the ability to write the language of music. It is the orchestrators that work from the composer's hand-written music and/or vocal recordings, choose which instruments should play in the orchestra, and then design the musical accompaniment to enhance the composer's songs into theatrical magic. This talent takes place in their mind's ear, hearing what combinations of sounds will work best with a variety of voices and the personality of each song and character. Then it is translated from the mind to paper, before moving on to the copyists, and then musicians.

The Tony Awards have acknowledged the work of orchestrators, but since it is not a glamorous profession, the category is omitted from the televised presentation. The minimum pay scale for this work is complex so general managers negotiate a high flat fee ranging in six figures.

The title "arranger" can be used for the orchestrator of a small band, or for someone who only works on vocal harmonies and/or dance interludes.

Each instrument must have its own "charts" from which to read. While most musicians can write musical notes, their handwriting may not be easy to read and this activity is terribly time-consuming. The specialists known as copyists have trained for years and often work through the night to get musical scores finished in time for rehearsals. Computers have taken over as a tool for writing out musical notes, but someone who can read the scratch sheets from composers and orchestrators must still do the work. They are literally paid by the type of musical note, the number of lines of music, and the hours worked, an extremely complex system of payroll probably designed to confuse management. The copyists submit detailed invoices that are paid as the invoices arrive. In general, a musical will budget from $75,000 to $150,000 for copying costs.

When a composer throws out a song during previews and replaces it overnight, the orchestrator, arranger, and copyists work nonstop to get the music to the conductor and musicians. The old movie musical storylines where a show is saved from disaster because of script and music changes do not capture the impossibly difficult creative work behind the scenes. Yet many shows have gone through this process. It is an important reason for out-of-town tryouts and for weeks of previews prior to opening the show to the press.

Networking is essential to a musician's survival. Without regular work in the larger music community, perhaps behind a concert singer, with a symphony orchestra, with a jazz band, on recordings, in a television special, etc., a musician may not be able to find new work after a show closes. This is recognized by union rules that permit musicians to bring in subs for up to 50 percent of every week, while being guaranteed their jobs in the show.

Subs are recruited by the musicians, and approved by the contractor and musical supervisor. Technically management must also approve, but realistically they have no idea which musicians are good enough to ensure the quality of the show.

The contractor keeps records of absences and subs and turns in a payroll chart each week to the theatre's house manager. That's because musicians are employees of the theatre, not the show. The contractor receives a 50 percent boost to the musician's base pay for these extra duties.

For previews leading up to press performances and opening night, the union denies the right to substitute musicians. When tempos are being set with the singers and dancers, and changes are being made to musical numbers and cues, substitutions might threaten the quality of the show.

Orchestras do not create the music; they play music that has already been written. Broadway musicians rehearse less than most people expect. Their musical skills are second to none and they are capable of delivering a polished performance under the direction of the musical supervisor with as little as three rehearsals prior to the first preview performance.

First, they will play together in a rehearsal room under the guidance of the musical director/conductor, with copyists in the room noting mistakes in the written music to be corrected overnight. Next, the cast is invited to the rehearsal room to sing along (known as a Sitz Probe); in most cases, this is the first time they will hear more than a rehearsal piano and drums. Finally, the orchestra is moved into the theatre by stagehands to work with the sound designer (who will assign microphones to each instrument). The next time the orchestra performs may be the first preview.

Time is set aside to perform a "SIM" sound test. That's when the sound engineer measures the theatre's audio frequencies in order to apply precise electronic corrections to the room's acoustics. This test requires no other rehearsing in the pit or on stage and can take a full hour or more.

Musicians who play on the stage, instead of the pit, receive a pay increment. The long-running *Chicago* has the orchestra on stage "front and center." 2014's *After Midnight* considered the orchestra to be one of the show's stars and featured them on stage during many musical numbers.

When in the orchestra pit, musicians are hidden from the audience and can wear casual clothes. They are paid extra if required to wear anything other than their own clothes or a tuxedo (formal attire has been declared part of a musician's equipment, along with the instrument they play).

When an Equity actor plays a musical instrument onstage or an 802 musician performs an acting role, the conflict between the two unions is resolved on a case-by-case basis. Almost always, the actor/musician must become a member of both Equity and Local 802 and will get paid the higher of the two salaries based on their role in the show. Producers pay health and pension benefits to only one of the unions. Musicals like *Once* and the revival of *Company*, where every actor plays multiple instruments, require management and union officials to talk before contracts are written and signed.

Musicians who play more than one instrument get additional weekly payments. This is called "doubling." For example, an acoustic guitar player who also plays the electric or bass guitar is considered to bring more than one talent to the orchestra. A clarinet player who also plays a flute or oboe, or a trumpet player who doubles on a trombone, are providing additional sounds to enrich the music, without requiring the full salary of another musician. They earn an extra $210.09 weekly for the first double, $105.05 for each double after that. They all receive a $50 weekly maintenance fee for providing their own instrument, except that the producer supplies keyboards and percussion instruments. A harpist gets transportation expenses as well.

Synthesizer players were not allowed for a long time, since they could provide the sounds of many instruments with only one salary. The negotiated compromise discourages the overuse of synthesizers by paying 25 percent more than the minimum. The associate musical director/conductor receives a 30 percent increment. The conductor's pay is 75 percent higher than the base musician salary.

A computerized orchestra was attempted during the last musician strike, antagonizing the Broadway unions that insisted on live music. The attempt failed because the digital sound was aesthetically inferior.

When a producer is looking for a theatre, orchestra size requirements are often a deciding factor. Some theatres are traditionally designed for nonmusicals yet have housed small musicals. The Booth Theatre, a dramatic house, was the original home for the Sondheim/Lapine Tony Award–winning musical *Sunday in the Park with George* using a small live band. Likewise, a small rock band played onstage every night at the Helen Hayes Theatre in *Rock of Ages*. Theatres with no minimum orchestra size requirement give shows the freedom to design their own sound and musical budget. When a theatre has orchestra size requirements, the union considers special requests for smaller bands through an "objective group of outsiders."

Here are the current musician minimums for thirty-three of the forty theatres on Broadway. Seven other theatres are minimum-free.

Three-musician minimum: Belasco, Booth, Circle in the Square, Cort, Golden, Walter Kerr, and Lyceum theatres.

Four-musician minimum: Longacre and Nederlander theatres.

Eight-musician minimum: Brooks Atkinson, Eugene O'Neill, and Bernard Jacobs theatres.

Nine-musician minimum: Barrymore, Music Box, and Gerald Schoenfeld theatres.

Twelve-musician minimum: August Wilson and Broadhurst theatres.

Fourteen-musician minimum: Neil Simon, Al Hirschfeld, and Richard Rodgers theatres.

Eighteen-musician minimum: Majestic, Palace, Lunt-Fontanne, Imperial, Gershwin, Shubert, and Winter Garden theatres.

Nineteen-musician minimum: Broadway, Lyric, Minskoff, St. James, Marquis, and New Amsterdam theatres.

Work on the original cast recordings must be offered to the performing orchestra, but is often supplemented to fill out the sound. In this digital world, the recording labels have other options as well.

Thirty years ago, one union practice was uniformly hated: walkers. Following an ugly strike and subsequent contract negotiations, the practice theoretically no longer exists. Walkers were musicians who were not needed to play in the orchestra, but fulfilled the required minimum number of musicians in that theatre. The union told producers, "Why not use all the musicians and make your sound better?" The producers told the union, "We don't need that many musicians for this particular show and we'd like to save the cost."

One well-known producer was so angry having to hire two "walker" musicians that he assigned them to entertain in the ladies lounge during intermission and in the lobby after the show. Another show that moved from Off Broadway with a small orchestra was forced to pay an additional ten musicians. When the show closed during the musicians' strike, it had a financial loss equivalent to the salaries of those ten walkers.

The former case involved the producer's sense of principle. The latter case had no room in its environmental scenic design to accommodate the extra bodies and chairs. From the union's perspective, both producers were cutting long-fought employment for its members.

The union went on strike a number of times to protect the musician jobs that Broadway had always maintained. These costly strikes caused some shows to close early and/or lose their investment. The union strike was not appreciated although the other unions mostly supported their cause. In 2003, a negotiated settlement reduced the minimum number of required musicians in the larger theatres from twenty-six to nineteen. This appears to have eliminated the existence of walkers.

Musicians are hired for the run of the show. If they want to take a hiatus from the show, the producer must approve it. A long-running show's steady income is a blessing, but its hefty schedule can be a curse too.

Chapter 22
What the Theatre Owners Want You to Know

Most of the shows that make it to Broadway are selected or approved by the major theatre owners, the Shuberts, the Nederlanders, and Jujamcyn organizations. They also have the right to kick them out if tickets sales dip below a certain dollar amount two weeks in a row. This "stop clause" is required in every rental agreement and protects theatre owners from carrying a struggling show.

The theatres are leased out to producers who pay both a flat weekly guaranteed rent and a percentage of the box office income, so it makes sense that theatre owners are looking for a show with great potential at the box office and a producing/management team with experience.

In recent decades a few nonprofit organizations have purchased theatres in the Broadway district. A handful of independent companies own and operate Broadway houses as well.

Locations for all Broadway theatres are noted at the end of the Appendix.

SHUBERT ORGANIZATION
The Shubert Organization owns and operates seventeen Broadway theatres as well as the city's largest Off Broadway theatre, the Little Shubert, and Philadelphia's Forrest Theatre. Their Broadway houses are:

- Ambassador Theatre
- Ethel Barrymore Theatre
- Belasco Theatre
- Bernard B. Jacobs Theatre

- Booth Theatre
- Broadhurst Theatre
- Broadway Theatre
- Cort Theatre
- Gerald Schoenfeld Theatre
- John Golden Theatre
- Imperial Theatre
- Longacre Theatre
- Lyceum Theatre
- Majestic Theatre
- Music Box Theatre
- Shubert Theatre
- Winter Garden Theatre

The Shubert Organization also operates the Shubert Foundation, a nonprofit that supports the arts and theatre in particular, providing unrestricted grants and other support to other nonprofits and artists.

NEDERLANDER ORGANIZATION

The Nederlander Organization owns and operates nine Broadway theatres and has significant ownership in other theatres across America and Europe, including theatres in London, Los Angeles, Chicago, Detroit, Durham, Charleston, San Diego, San Jose, and Tucson. The nine Nederlander Broadway houses are:

- Brooks Atkinson Theatre
- Gershwin Theatre
- Lunt-Fontanne Theatre
- Marquis Theatre
- Minskoff Theatre
- Nederlander Theatre
- Neil Simon Theatre
- Palace Theatre
- Richard Rodgers Theatre

JUJAMCYN THEATERS

The Jujamcyn Theaters derives its company name from the first letters of the original owner's three grandchildren: Judith, James, and Cynthia. Jujamcyn Theaters now owns and operates the following five Broadway theatres:

- Eugene O'Neill Theatre
- August Wilson Theatre
- Al Hirschfeld Theatre
- St. James Theatre
- Walter Kerr Theatre

INDEPENDENTLY OWNED THEATRES

The three Broadway theatres owned independently by individuals or by for-profit companies are:

CIRCLE IN THE SQUARE THEATRE

Paul Libin and the estate of the late Ted Mann are the owners of the only Broadway theatre with a thrust stage (audience on three sides of the stage) and located one floor below street level. They also operate an accredited theatre school below the theatre.

LYRIC THEATRE

The Lyric's previous names in its relatively short history were the Foxwoods Theatre, the Ford Theatre, and the Hilton Theatre. It is Broadway's second largest theatre.

NEW AMSTERDAM THEATRE

Disney Theatricals received tax monies from New York State as part of the 42nd Street Redevelopment project to redesign this former Ziegfeld theatre to new glory. To date, the New Amsterdam has been used exclusively as the home for Disney productions.

THEATRES OWNED BY NONPROFITS

There are six Broadway houses owned and operated by nonprofit theatres.

VIVIAN BEAUMONT THEATER

Lincoln Center Theater has this one Broadway house. The Beaumont is the only space situated outside the grid of the Broadway theatre district.

SAMUEL J. FRIEDMAN THEATRE

Manhattan Theatre Club has this one Broadway house. The Friedman was rebuilt and redesigned in 2009 on the site of the former Biltmore Theatre where the original 1968 production of *Hair* was presented.

AMERICAN AIRLINES THEATRE, STEPHEN SONDHEIM THEATRE, AND STUDIO 54

Roundabout Theatre Company has these three Broadway houses. Studio 54, now redesigned as a theatre space, was originally the infamous 1970s–1980s disco club known for its wild dance parties and concerts.

HELEN HAYES THEATRE

Until 2015, when this theatre was sold to the nonprofit Second Stage Theatre, Martin Markinson and the late Donald Tick were the sole owners of the Helen Hayes Theatre, housing Broadway's smallest audience capacity of five hundred ninety-seven seats. At the time of this book's printing, it is unknown if the theatre's name will be changed.

While many Broadway theatres have a rich history and glorious decor, it is important to realize that the current Broadway theatre buildings have only existed for approximately one hundred years or less. Before that time, Broadway theatres and opera houses first operated near Union Square at East 14th Street. The theatres later migrated to Madison Square at West 26th Street. (The world-famous sports arena Madison Square Garden was built and named for this site but later relocated.) Broadway theatres continued to migrate north to its current midtown district from West 40th to West 54 Streets between Sixth and Ninth Avenues.

Before producers Cameron Mackintosh and Disney Theatricals brought a corporate structure and way of thinking to Broadway in the 1990s, Broadway was very much a "mom and pop" operation. Producers and managers used their experience and acumen for analysis of pricing, marketing, and finances. As the costs of producing theatre and profit potentials rose, so did the need for more statistics and computerized data.

Perhaps theatre owners were corporate all along, with attorneys at the helm and dozens of centralized employees within each organization. Decision-making and financial controls sit with a handful of top-level executives. The politics and power struggles are sometimes no different from financial institutions like Citibank or Merrill Lynch.

Who are these powerful men, and a few women, who run Broadway, and oversee the selection of plays and musicals each season? Who is in charge of this billion-dollar-a-year industry? In the 1950s, three Shubert brothers were the powerbrokers. The following decades on Broadway were ruled by James Nederlander, Sr. and family, two of the Shubert's surviving attorneys Bernard

B. Jacobs and Gerald Schoenfeld, and after its original owner James H. Binger passed, Jujamcyn's president and owner Rocco Landesman.

The Nederlander family is still intact to this day. Jujamcyn is now run by the industry's youngest entrepreneur, Jordan Roth, who is a co-owner with Landesman. The Shubert dynasty is now run by Philip J. Smith and Robert E. Wankel. Each organization has specialists in theatre design and restoration, human resources, I.T., promotion, finance, real estate, and politics. A handful of vice presidents and executive assistants are some of the most powerful people on Broadway.

The Shubert offices live in two locations: above their Shubert Theatre in Shubert Alley between West 44th and West 45th Streets, and upstairs from the famous Sardi's Restaurant, both paneled in rich wood, soft in tone and quiet power. The Nederlander offices are on 1450 Broadway south of West 41st Street. Jujamcyn's home base is a series of offices off one long rectangular hallway above the St. James Theatre on West 44th Street. These offices each employ more than two dozen people.

In contrast to the theatre owners, show producers use smaller offices, sometimes with no more than two or three people sharing one room overseeing the entire $15 million production. Producers handling multiple shows and/or massive hits like *Wicked* and *The Phantom of the Opera* have larger staffs, but it's still nothing like corporate America.

Every theatre in New York City is regulated by codes and inspected by city and state government. The Occupational Safety and Health Administration (OSHA) makes sure that federal and state standards for working conditions and audience safety are followed. New York fire codes are the strictest in the world, requiring specially licensed stagehands. A fire can't be lit onstage in New York City unless the fire department has approved the safety features in place to protect audiences and workers. All asbestos fire curtains in older theatres have been replaced with water curtains or other contemporary protections. There has never been a fire in modern Broadway history.

There are also newer codes dictating the number of bathroom stalls for women (twice as many as for men), and handicap access (still lacking in a few older theatres where structural changes are restricted by New York State's landmark status laws).

City and state property taxes are very high and Broadway is prime real estate. In more troubling times, Gerald Schoenfeld, the former head of the Shubert Organization, was quoted in the *New York Times* as saying that the Shuberts would be better off financially by tearing down the theatres and putting up more office towers.

Theatre owners bear the cost of electricity, air conditioning, heat, plumbing, sewage, waste disposal, and building staff, not to mention the staff and supplies at the company's headquarters. These costs are reimbursed by the occupying production but when the theatre is dark for months at a time, the owners bear the expenses.

To cover the needs of today's high tech shows, the theatre owners provide and maintain superior electrical wiring. Otherwise there would be no way to accommodate the many computers and mechanical systems needed to move the scenery in magical ways, run the huge numbers of stage lights, and process the actors' and orchestra's sounds through both wireless and wired microphones from a super sound board and high-end speakers. Outside the theatres, theatre owners are adding marquees made of video screens to keep the theatre district modernized and appealing.

All theatre leases are "four-wall deals," meaning that all lights, sound, and scenery must be shipped in and installed by the individual show. Sound and lighting equipment are rented from union shops by the show leasing the theatre. All stage flooring with turntables, mechanical grooves, dance surfaces, and other tailored scenic requirements are layered on top of the theatre's basic stage.

When a show closes, the theatre must be stripped of all added equipment and restored to its original condition, even if the new equipment would improve the theatre. The money for this restoration is collected up front and deposited in an account with the theatre owners as part of the theatre lease.

The lease will also state the number of opening night tickets and house seats to be put aside for use by the theatre owner and executive staff. The lease lists the number of building and box office employees that the theatre owner will hire for the run of the show. All of this is negotiable, especially with a trusted general manager, but theatre owners usually win.

No matter how many producers are credited above the title of a show, theatre owners work with one key lead producer and general manager. Until the 1980s, it was uncommon to see more than a few producers named on a marquee or in a program. "David Merrick presents," "Harold Prince and Ruth Mitchell present," "Elizabeth McCann and Nelle Nugent present," recognized that investors put their money into the hands of the producers who made the big decisions. As the cost of productions increased from hundreds of thousands of dollars to more than ten million dollars, large investors wanted to be called associate producers and producers and not remain anonymous. But negotiations don't work by committee. Each theatre-owning organization will speak with one voice, usually the president himself, and each production is expected to speak with one experienced voice as well, usually the lead producer or general manager, depending on who has the most experience with the theatre's executive.

Because theatre owners receive a guaranteed flat rent plus a percentage of box office income, they have a vested interest in the price of tickets. The higher the price and the more tickets sold, the more rent they collect. The stop clause protects their interests and makes way for new shows that may be waiting for a theatre to become available. *The Phantom of the Opera*, Broadway's longest running musical, has monopolized the Majestic Theatre for decades. *Phantom* still sells out, brings in lots of rental income, and therefore is not in jeopardy of being forced to vacate.

However, theatre owners have another option should they decide that a new show should open in an already occupied venue. *Mamma Mia*, another long-running musical, inhabited the Winter Garden Theatre for ten years. Whether the reason had to do with softening ticket sales, or whether a decision was made that the new musical *Rocky* would benefit from the Winter Garden Theatre's design and location, a decision was made to move *Mamma Mia* to a smaller, well-located theatre between *Phantom* and the flagship Shubert Theatre. The move from one theatre to another is not cheap. Yet it can lead to additional years of life to a show as it gets older. *Chicago* moved to the smaller Ambassador Theatre and is now the longest running revival in history.

A theatre move can be a source for beneficial promotion. The 1983 Broadway production of *The Pirates of Penzance* starring Linda Ronstadt and Kevin Kline moved only three blocks but a pirate ship sailed the cast on the Hudson River along with photographers and reporters to announce the theatre change.

Disney Theatricals moved *Beauty and the Beast* from the Palace Theatre to the Lunt-Fontanne Theatre with a reduced cast, saving significant cast salaries. The cast reduction was very controversial and involved a little-used Equity rule that allowed the show to close for eight weeks, and reopen as a new production with new parameters and staffing needs.

Theatre owners sometimes dictate these moves and often advise producers about the potential benefits of making the move. The show's producer works with the creative team to maintain the creative quality of the show and minimize any changes that the audience will notice.

Considering the costs in maintaining, repairing, staffing, promoting, and supervising mostly low-rise single-use buildings that have no other income except ticket sales, the owners are responsible for a unique business model. New York City's regulations for safety, utilities, and taxation are tough. Even tougher is how much New York City depends on the Broadway theatres to bring in tourism and support businesses throughout the Times Square district. When Broadway fails, restaurants and retailers suffer deeply. During the World Trade Center bombing crisis in September 2001, it was the theatre owners through their association, The Broadway League, that joined with city officials to keep Broadway open and let tourists know that theatre was alive and well. In the 1960s when the theatre district was ridden with crime, the theatre owners fought hard for city policies that cleaned up midtown Manhattan. New York's transformation over the past decades owes so much to the theatre owners who recognized the problem and acted with political force.

Chapter 23
Life After Fifty on Broadway

Working on Broadway must be a good thing because no one seems to want to retire. There are some jobs that are held for decades, like those in the central offices of the theatre owners, and they do not open up until someone dies. Working on Broadway is generally considered a dream compared to the corporate world.

On the other hand, every time a Broadway show closes, almost all of its workers become unemployed. Salaries must outlast the workweeks and subsidize the unemployed time. At a certain age, the insecurity of work on Broadway requires reassessment of life's priorities and goals. It is a shame that many who have dedicated themselves to this business and art form struggle so much in their final years.

The bottom line is not completely dismal. Survival is a unique talent in itself. It requires careful planning and great effort to hold onto the career you love. If possible, finding a flexible job can provide financial security when Broadway isn't calling. But, it's even harder after a certain age to find security in a new life plan. The good news is that there is plenty of opportunity for advice and guidance.

The most precarious and inconsistent of Broadway jobs belong to actors. There are so few jobs and so many actors. Those that find work on the rare long-running show like *Cats* or *The Phantom of the Opera* are conflicted by the desire to move on to another show, grow as an artist, build their career, and challenge themselves rather than settle into steady employment. Of course all shows eventually close, so there really is no steady employment.

Some actors have a rich career in their twenties and then as they grow older find themselves "typed out" of acting roles. Unlike college productions where a twenty-year-old can play *Uncle Vanya*, or *Macbeth*, or the older sister in *West Side Story*, Broadway hires age appropriate, gender appropriate, and size appropriate.

The joke among New Yorkers is that without actors, the restaurant business would have to close. All over town, the bulk of waiters are hopeful performers. At some point, an actor may decide to give up and declare his profession as a waiter on his tax returns. For many actors, this doesn't happen until later in life with the decision to support a family. Ironically, for other actors, their careers begin at fifty, after the pool of older actors has dwindled and the casting agents need really good actors to fill older roles. Sometimes an actor doesn't have a unique look until they are more seasoned.

Actors seek secondary employment in part-time work or professions that provide some flexibility for auditioning. Besides restaurant work, some get certified in massage therapy, some tutor, some teach classes in singing, dancing, or acting, and some work for relatives. These work situations may not provide significant income. Marrying rich helps, but a recurring role on a TV drama or sitcom provides more than salary and benefits; it provides stability, confidence, a feeling of success (albeit temporary), and recognition.

As they get older, Equity stage managers find more competition, and like actors, explore new careers. Dancers' professional lives are even more limited by physical demands.

For those who think it's time to find steady employment and make a career change, the Actors Work Program (AWP) through the Actors Fund, and Career Transitions for Dancers offer career transition counseling and will cover the cost of retraining in another field and offer computer skills classes. Members of all unions are entitled to take advantage of these programs.

It is this later period of life when the cliché parental warning "Make sure you have a backup skill" comes into play. Some have heeded the warning; most have not. The local and national economies at various times make employment solutions easier or more difficult. Varying responsibilities will affect how much the new job must pay.

The reality is that it is a horribly difficult task to choose a new profession in midlife or later. The lure of Broadway and the fun times of being part of a theatre company make the move even harder. The lack of available entrance jobs for older citizens makes it sometimes impossible.

Company managers burn out with each closing show. Periods of rest between shows are often the norm. At fifty-plus years old, working from 8:00 AM to 11:00 PM during production weeks, and sixty to eighty hours a week thereafter, the burnout takes its toll. The logical move for company managers is to switch roles and work for a theatre owner as a full-time house manager and then retire.

House and company managers train together so they know each other's jobs. Both salaries are the same so the move from company to house management can be a desirable alternative. Some managers find jobs teaching or working in an office.

Many stagehands are experts in computer engineering and architecture. They may have mechanical skills and general contractor experience as well. Yet the physical limitations that come with age make it difficult to start a new occupation outside the theatre. Some sound engineers go into the music field. Managers, with knowledge of accounting and law but no license to practice, often find that other businesses don't know what to do with them.

Ushers may survive better because it's usually their second job anyway.

Broadway offers a great number of alternative careers within its community (see Chapter 2: Jobs). Some actors become wardrobe people. Some stagehands become engineers. Some ushers become merchandise salespeople. Some managers become box office treasurers, group sales agents, and find employment at Playbill or BroadwayWorld.com.

Teaching, whether privately for voice, acting, or dancing, or at a school or university is sometimes a good response to aging in the arts. In New York City, there are many respected teachers that were once performers or backstage personnel. Advanced degrees are necessary for college employment, which means going back to school.

Some unions provide educational opportunities including scholarships and training courses, helping members to adapt to ever-changing situations in employment and life.

Willingness to move to another city can increase work prospects and reduce living expenses. It's another difficult decision. Unfortunately, regional nonprofit theatres, according to management headhunters, like to hire from other nonprofits. Broadway likes to hire those with Broadway experience. There is very little crossover, and nonprofits. tend to pay less than Broadway minimums.

At first thought, moving out of town or changing professions means severing ties with the Broadway community. That's often the reason why the AARP generation of theatre professionals resists transition. However, there are ways to remain part of the community from anywhere in the country. Broadway-connected charities, especially Broadway Cares/Equity Fights AIDS (BC/EFA), utilize thousands of volunteers to raise funds for hundreds of causes, particularly those surrounding the scourge of HIV and AIDS. This disease killed tens of thousands in the entertainment industry in the early 1980s. Thanks to research supported with funds raised through BC/EFA, AIDS is no longer a death sentence, but a chronic disease supported by good medical care and personal management.

The Actors Fund is another charity supporting a myriad of causes and maintains multiple facilities for aging entertainment professionals in New York, New Jersey, and Los Angeles. No matter where you work, or where you live, you can join Broadway's support network and stay in touch with valued friends and coworkers.

There doesn't seem to be enough discussion about the second half of a theatre person's career. Actors, managers, designers, directors, composers, playwrights, crew, and waiters are on their own. Perhaps the best advice is to explore and develop talents in several areas of interest, acting, writing, cooking, skydiving, computer graphics, martial arts, drumming, homeopathic healing, gardening, etc., and keep them active.

If you someday decide to transition to another career, it is essential that you can show employment references. An internship or a paid job with a family member, or with anyone, will help establish your resume credentials should you need them.

Hopefully you will only have to work at what you love, but things are always in flux. So when you're making money, put a little aside for investing and retirement. You can plan for old age but get crushed by a car tomorrow. On the flipside, when that car doesn't take you out and you wake up over fifty, your priorities may change. You don't want it to catch you by complete surprise.

There is no singular path into or away from any profession and Broadway is no exception. After fifty years old, more people than you realize are questioning their ability to thrive on Broadway and in the entertainment fields. You're not alone.

Hopefully you can live your passions and your dreams to your very last days. In the event that you choose to make a change in your later years, the Actors Fund and Career Transitions for Dancers are leading the discussion.

PART 5
BUDGETS

Chapter 24

Production and Operating Budgets from a $15 Million Broadway Musical

Each Broadway show operates with two budgets created by the general manager. The *production budget* lets the producer and investors know how much money will be needed to get the show from inception to the official opening night. This may include preview performances lasting a few days or a few weeks.

The *operating budget* computes an average week of expenses and royalty payments. Many expenses are unknown at the time the budget is created, so budgets rely on the experience and expertise of the general manager.

To paraphrase Mark Twain, Nostradamus, and a handful of others: "Forecasting is difficult, especially in regard to the future." That's why a theatre budget is considered a living thing. It will, by necessity, change over time. However, while money can be moved from the costume line to the scenery line, the total must be carefully determined and considered gospel. New York State law requires a producer to lock in the capitalization (total money to be raised). This budget and capitalization amount is the jurisdiction of the general manager (GM). The GM's experience with budgeting can make or break a show's profitability and longevity.

Below are the categories in a production budget along with monetary allotments for an imaginary $15 million musical, compiled from three actual musicals. Below that is a weekly operating budget for the same musical. Each general manager may work with a different template and certainly every show has slightly different categories. Some shows will have special effects (the flying actors in *Spider-Man: Turn Off the Dark*), or walls of video (the 2008 revival of *Sunday in the Park with George*), or an entire cast playing musical instruments on stage (*Once*). The stage elevator that sunk the Titanic every night (in the musical

Titanic) cost more than $1 million alone. Foreign plays, Shakespeare, and other classic plays may require dialect coaches. The 2013 revival of *Pippin* hired circus consultants, and many shows from *Hamlet* to *Rocky* employ fight choreographers.

It is considered average to spend 20 percent of the precontingency budget totals on advertising and promotion but each show either raises or lowers that amount based on the producer's plan. For big musicals, physical production elements (set, lights, and costumes) can eat up 50 percent of the entire budget. Each budget has a contingency since no one can be absolutely sure about the expenses. Some producers anticipate a contingency of 20 percent and others feel secure at 10 percent. Contingency monies are also important as a buffer against anticipated losses in the early weeks of a run before the reviews kick in and audiences, hopefully, start buying tickets in droves.

There are no royalties included in a production budget because there is no income at the box office. Instead, royalty participants receive an advance on their future royalties in addition to their production fees. The projected profit or loss for preview weeks is included in the production budget to arrive at the total cost of reaching the opening night.

Significant cash reserves and union bonds must be placed aside to be sure that the producer doesn't disappear into the night before paying obligations. Many unions require two weeks of salary and benefits to be held in union escrow accounts, after past decades of stranded employees when producers left town without paying salaries. Unions may allow well-established and trusted producers to post a written bond instead of cash, freeing up a portion of the budget. Shows don't actually cost $15,000,000 to produce, but it takes that much cash to convince theatre owners and unions to allow producers to produce on Broadway.

The theatre rental agreement will dictate how much of a reserve the theatre requires to guarantee the first weeks of rent and restoration after the production closes. In some cases, the entire theatre is ripped out and redesigned, such as with *Cats*, the revival of *Candide*, and *Starlight Express*. In other cases, computer cables gobble up the entire backstage causing changes to the theatre space as they did with *Rocky* and Disney's *Beauty and the Beast*. Some shows spend upwards of $200,000 reconfiguring the seats in the orchestra section, like 2014's *Holler If Ya Hear Me* at the Palace Theatre, and must return the seating to its original layout when the show closes.

All first drafts of budgets attempt to pay creative people what they are worth: a lot. New producers want to be kind to the production assistants and other hard-working people by paying more than required, until they realize how much scenery and other production elements actually cost. Suddenly, $15 million is not enough to produce a show. The general manager knows this dilemma and will balance the need to be fair, while acknowledging real costs, union requirements, and the smallest realistic capitalization needed to produce the show.

Weekly operating budgets require amortizing many costs over time. For example, legal work may only be required once in six months, with a one-time invoice of $10,000, so the budget will assign a weekly cost of $500 that over twenty weeks will cover this expense. The same will apply to anticipated special events like the Tony Awards or the building of understudy costumes over a three-month period.

Decisions must be made before any budget can be compiled. For this imaginary musical, we have decided to have two weeks of preview performances, a large cast of thirty actors, a twelve-musician orchestra, and nothing flying or sinking on stage.

PRELIMINARY ESTIMATED PRODUCTION BUDGET FOR
Make-Believe: A New Imaginary Broadway Musical

CATEGORY	Royalty Advance	Fee	Salary	Total	Category Total
PHYSICAL PRODUCTION					
Scenery, prototypes and automation				$2,500,000	
Props				$ 300,000	
Costumes and shoes				$1,800,000	
Hair, makeup, masks, wigs				$ 150,000	
Electrics				$ 800,000	
Sound				$ 200,000	
Projections				$ 225,000	
Musical instruments				$ 30,000	
Departmental expenses				$ 25,000	
TOTAL PHYSICAL PRODUCTION					$6,030,000

Page 2: Production Budget for *Make-Believe*

CATEGORY	Royalty Advance	Fee	Salary	Total	Category Total
CREATIVE FEES					
Authors	$60,000	$20,000			
Director	$45,000	$40,000			
Director—assistant (8 wks)			$ 4,000		
Choreographer	$35,000	$25,000			
Choreographer— associate (8 wks)			$ 6,400		
Scenic designer @ 150%	$10,000	$47,000			
Scenic designer—3 assts (5 wks)			$22,500		
Costume designer @ 125%	$10,000	$42,000			
Costume designer—3 assts (8 wks)			$36,000		
Lighting designer @ 125%	$ 6,300	$30,000			
Vari-lite Design		$20,000			
Lighting designer—3 assts (4 wks)			$18,000		
Sound designer		$16,000			
Sound designer —associate			$ 6,000		

Page 3: Production Budget for *Make-Believe*

CATEGORY	Royalty Advance	Fee	Salary	Total	Category Total
Projections designer		$ 20,000			
Hair designer		$ 7,500			
Musical supervisor		$ 30,000			
Orchestrator & orchestrations		$150,000			
Dance music arranger		$ 20,000			
Music copying		$100,000			
Synthesizer programmer		$ 10,000			
TOTAL CREATIVE FEES					$ 836,700

Page 4: Production Budget for *Make-Believe*

CATEGORY	Royalty Advance	Fee	Salary	Total	Category Total
PRODUCTION FEES					
General manager		$80,000			
Casting director		$30,000			
Technical supervisor		$80,000			
Legal		$80,000			
Accounting		$10,000			
TOTAL PRODUCTION FEES					$ 280,000

Page 5: Production Budget for *Make-Believe*

CATEGORY	Royalty Advance	Fee	Salary	Total	Category Total
ADVERTISING/PUBLICITY (15–20 percent of capitalization)					
Press Agent (preproduction fee)	$ 25,000				
Press Agent (salary 6 weeks)			$ 13,200		
Press expenses incl. video				$ 45,000	
Photos/Signs/Posters				$ 50,000	
Artwork/mechanicals				$ 65,000	
Marquees & Front of House				$100,000	
Television/radio commercial production				$250,000	
Television & radio buys (pre-operating budget)				$650,000	
Print (newspaper/ magazine/outdoor)				$600,000	
Dedicated Social Media expenses (incl. 1 asst @ 8 wks)				$ 65,000	
Marketing Director (preprod. fee includes asst)				$ 25,000	
Marketing and Group sales promotion expenses				$ 24,800	
Programs, printing & miscellaneous costs				$ 35,000	
TOTAL ADVERTISING/PUBLICITY					$1,948,000

Page 6: Production Budget for *Make-Believe*

CATEGORY	# of workers	Salaries	Subtotal	Category Total
PRODUCTION SALARIES				
Load-in crew (4 wks)	150+	$900,000		
Local One heads & assts	15	$180,000		
IATSE Pink heads & assts	6	$ 65,000		
Wardrobe, hair & dressers	10	$ 85,000		
Musical director	1	$ 22,000		
Rehearsal musicians (piano/drums)	4	$ 20,000		
Orchestra musicians (3 rehearsals)	12	$ 30,000		
Orchestra contractor	1	$ 20,000		
Company manager (7 wks)	1	$ 14,000		
Acting & dialect coaches (nonunion)	1	$ 10,000		
SUBTOTAL PRODUCTION SALARIES (to calculate benefits)			$1,346,000	
Production Payroll taxes @ 17% avg (all salaries)			$ 228,820	
Production Pension & Welfare (P&W), Vacation & sick pay (unions only)			$ 400,800	
TOTAL PRODUCTION SALARIES WITH BENEFITS				$1,975,620

Page 7: Production Budget for *Make-Believe*

CATEGORY	# of actors	Base Wkly	Salary Total	Category Total
REHEARSALS: CAST (30 performers @ 5 wks)				
Celebrity lead actors #1 & 2	2	$1,861	$18,610	
Featured actors #1–4	4	$1,861	$37,220	
Actors #1–10	10	$1,861	$93,050	
Chorus members #1–14	14	$1,861	$130,270	
Standbys for celebrities (2 wks)	2	$1,861	$ 7,444	
Swings for chorus (1 male, 1 female, 2 wks)	2	$1,861	$ 7,444	
Extra cast duties: increments			$ 5,000	
Dance Captain increment (5 wks)	1	$ 372	$ 1,860	
Dance Captain assistant increment (5 wks)	1	$ 186	$ 930	
Principal understudies: increments		$ 50	$ 5,000	
Chorus part understudies: increments		$ 20	$ 2,000	
Media fees (2% of contractual salary)	30	$ 37	$ 5,583	
Production Stage Manager (musical 6 wks)	1	$3,058	$18,348	
Stage Manager (musical 6 wks)	1	$2,416	$14,496	

Page 8: Production Budget for *Make-Believe*

CATEGORY	# of actors	Base Wkly	Salary Total	Subtotal	Category Total
First assistant stage manager (5 wks)	1	$2,019	$10,095		
Second assistant stage manager (5 wks)	1	$2,019	$10,095		
Third assistant stage manager (5 wks)	1	$2,019	$10,095		
Per diem & living expenses—1 celebrity (no tax)	1	$2,500	$12,500		
SUBTOTAL REHEARSALS: CAST				$390,040	
Cast Payroll taxes @ 17% avg				$ 57,380	
Cast Pension & Welfare (P&W), Sick & vacation accruals				$113,260	
TOTAL REHEARSALS: CAST WITH BENEFITS					$ 560,680

Page 9: Production Budget for *Make-Believe*

CATEGORY	Total	Category Total
GENERAL AND ADMINISTRATIVE		
Lead producer office fee	$ 35,000	
Office expenses (phone/fax/copying/FedEx)	$ 15,000	
Two cast readings	$ 7,500	
Insurance	$ 75,000	
Payroll service	$ 8,000	
Design studio expenses (blueprints & models)	$100,000	
Casting & audition expenses including pianist	$ 75,000	
Rehearsal hall rentals	$110,000	
Composer & lyricist expenses	$ 15,000	
Crew: NYC housing for late night work	$ 10,000	
Hauling & storage	$200,000	
Truck loaders—take-in	$ 38,000	
Preliminary theatre rent & expenses	$250,000	
Production assistants (2 nonunion @ 6 weeks)	$ 6,000	

Page 10: Production Budget for *Make-Believe*

CATEGORY	Total	Category Total
Preliminary box office/front of house expenses, signage, etc.	$250,000	
Opening night expenses	$ 50,000	
Miscellaneous	$ 20,000	
TOTAL GENERAL & ADMINISTRATIVE		$1,254,500

PRODUCTION BUDGET TOTAL	**without bonds!**	**$12,885,500**
CONTINGENCY (10%)	**$ 1,287,500**	
"2 WEEKS OF ANTICIPATED PREVIEW LOSS (@ 50% of capacity)	**$ 348,000**	
TOTAL PRODUCTION BUDGET	**without bonds!**	**$14,521,000**

"See weekly operating budget below for two preview weeks.

Page 11: Production Budget for *Make-Believe*

CATEGORY	Total	Category Total
RESERVES AND BONDS (approx. 2 weeks of operating salaries, P&W, and admin. fees, refundable at closing)		
Actors' Equity	$101,000	
ATPAM	$ 17,000	
IATSE	$ 46,000	
TWAU	$ 40,000	
AFM (Copyists)	$ 25,000	
Theatre Reserves	$250,000	
TOTAL BONDS		$ 479,000
TOTAL CAPITALIZATION NEEDED (Production Budget plus Bonds)		**$15,000,000**

# # #

WEEKLY OPERATING BUDGET FOR
Make-Believe: A New Imaginary Broadway Musical
(Expenses for One Preview Week of Performances)

ANTICIPATED PREVIEW PERFORMANCE WEEKS: TWO
PROJECTED WEEKLY BOX OFFICE INCOME @ 100% CAPACITY $1,128,000
ANTICIPATED BOX OFFICE INCOME PER WEEK (@ 50% CAPACITY) $ 564,000

CATEGORY	# of people	Salary	Subtotal	Weekly Total
ACTORS' EQUITY WEEKLY SALARIES				
Celebrity lead actor #1	1	$ 15,000	$ 15,000	
Celebrity lead actor #2	1	$ 12,000	$ 12,000	
Featured actor #1–4	4	$ 6,000	$ 24,000	
Actor #1–10	10	$ 2,100	$ 21,000	
15 Chorus members	15	$ 1,861	$ 27,915	
Extra duty increments (total)			$ 7,500	
Understudy increments for onstage cast (total)			$ 7,500	
2 Standbys for celebrities	2	$ 1,861	$ 3,722	

Page 2: Weekly operating budget for *Make-Believe*

CATEGORY	# of people	Salary	Subtotal	Weekly Total
2 Swings (1 male, 1 female)	2	$ 1,861	$ 3,722	
Dance Captain increment	1	$ 372	$ 372	
Production Stage Manager	1	$ 3,058	$ 3,058	
First assistant stage manager	1	$ 2,416	$ 2,416	
Assistant stage managers #2–4	1	$ 2,019	$ 6,057	
TOTAL EQUITY SALARIES				$130,262

CATEGORY	Subtotal	Weekly Total
RENTALS		
Automation	$ 14,500	
Electrics and moving lights	$ 11,500	
Sound	$ 7,500	
Projectors	$ 2,500	
Genie lifts and motors	$ 2,000	
TOTAL RENTALS		$ 38,000

Page 3: Weekly operating budget for *Make-Believe*

CATEGORY		Weekly Total
ADVERTISING/PUBLICITY	$ 119,500	
SPECIAL PROMOTIONAL EVENTS (TONY'S, MACY'S, OTHER)	$ 2,500	
TOTAL ADVERTISING/PUBLICITY (20%)		$ 122,000

CATEGORY	Subtotal	Weekly Total
DEPARTMENTAL EXPENSES		
Carpentry, automation, props	$ 1,000	
Electrics and sound	$ 1,000	
Wardrobe, hair, makeup	$ 3,000	
Understudy costumes	$ 3,000	
Special effects	$ 2,000	
Audition & rehearsal	$ 1,000	
Company & stage management	$ 500	
TOTAL DEPARTMENTALS		$ 11,500

Page 4: Weekly operating budget for *Make-Believe*

CATEGORY	Subtotal	Weekly Total
GENERAL AND ADMINISTRATIVE		
Legal	$ 1,200	
Accounting	$ 1,200	
Insurance	$ 1,000	
Office fee for rent, phone, IT, copies, and postage	$ 2,500	
Payroll service	$ 600	
Miscellaneous travel and local transportation	$ 1,000	
TOTAL GENERAL AND ADMINISTRATIVE		$ 7,500

Page 5: Weekly operating budget for *Make-Believe*

CATEGORY	Subtotal	Weekly Total
THEATRE EXPENSES		
Guaranteed flat rent	$ 10,000	
Percentage rent (in this case: 6% of $564K gross)	$ 33,840	
Theatre operating expenses (utilities, AC, supplies, and $10K flat guarantee)	$ 30,000	
Box office salaries	$ 15,000	
Front of house salaries (including house manager)	$ 15,000	
Local One stagehand salaries (15 running crew)	$ 55,000	
Local 802 musicians' salaries (12)	$ 27,000	
Payroll taxes and benefits	$ 40,000	
TOTAL THEATRE EXPENSES		$225,840

Page 6: Weekly operating budget for *Make-Believe*

CATEGORY	Fee	Salary	Subtotal	Category Total
PRODUCTION SALARIES				
Producer fee	$ 4,000			
General manager	$ 3,750			
Company manager		$ 2,002		
Press agent		$ 2,162		
Marketing director & firm	$ 1,500			
Technical supervisor/production mgr.	$ 2,000			
Casting director	$ 1,750			
Musical supervisor/director		$ 3,500		
IATSE crew (in this case 6 Pinks)		$16,000		
Wardrobe supervisor		$ 2,200		
Dressers & assts. (7)		$10,136		
Hair/make-up supervisor & 2 assts.		$ 4,000		
Payroll taxes, vacation, sick pay and other union benefits		$18,800		
TOTAL PRODUCTION SALARIES				$ 73,300

Page 7: Weekly operating budget for *Make-Believe*

CATEGORY	Weekly Total	Category Total
FLAT WEEKLY ROYALTIES		
Scenic designer	$ 406	
Lighting designer	$ 406	
Costume designer	$ 406	
Sound designer	$ 250	
Orchestrator	$1,000	
Dance music arranger	$ 250	
Vocal arranger	$ 250	
Projections designer	$ 250	
Hair & makeup designer	$ 250	
TOTAL FLAT WEEKLY ROYALTIES		$ 3,318

Page 8: Weekly operating budget for *Make-Believe*

CATEGORY	Weekly Total	Category Total
PERCENTAGE ROYALTIES (based on box office income for 50% of $1,128,000, or $564,000)		
Author (2 percent)	$11,280	
Composer (2 percent)	$11,280	
Lyricist (2 percent)	$11,280	
Director (2 percent)	$11,280	
Choreographer (1.5 percent)	$ 8,460	
Producer/General Partners (2 percent)	$11,280	
TOTAL PERCENTAGE ROYALTIES		$ 64,860
CONTINGENCY (10 percent before percentage royalties)		$ 61,420
TOTAL WEEKLY OPERATING EXPENSES DURING PREVIEWS		$738,000
ANTICIPATED WEEKLY BOX OFFICE INCOME (PREVIEWS @ 50% CAPACITY)		$564,000
ANTICIPATED LOSS FOR EACH WEEK OF PREVIEWS		($174,000)

FINAL NOTE ABOUT BUDGETS

These budgets tell the producer and management of *Make-Believe: The New Broadway Musical,* that $738,000 is needed in box office income to sustain the musical each week. It also says that there is a potential weekly box office earnings of $1,128,000, providing $390,000 in profit. This calculates weekly expenses to be over 65 percent of the box office capacity, just outside the acceptable 50 to 65 percent range. It would be better if weekly expenses are reduced, or if the contingency monies are not needed. But reality tells us that the producer will want to increase the ad budget, or someone's salary demands will require additional funds.

If the show is in demand, then the show can charge premium prices at the box office and raise the $1,128,000 income threshold. Otherwise, it will take about 39 weeks at full capacity for the show to repay the original $15 million investment.

Every show has different budgeting priorities. For example, a show called *Make-Believe* will most likely utilize a lot of special effects and therefore the budget may use funds from the contingency so not to disappoint the audience's expectations. If the musical uses a full orchestra of twenty or more, musicians' salaries will rise dramatically. If the producer likes to bombard the media with ads, then $122,000 per week will not be sufficient. No one has a crystal ball when it comes to budgeting. And every show lives a unique life, subject to the critics, crises, and miscalculations.

PART 6
IN SUMMARY

Chapter 25

How Do I Get Here from There?

No longer do we hear, "Broadway is dying." The past few years have been great in terms of income and attendance. The number of theatres occupied by shows is steady. There is a backlog of shows waiting for theatres. The number of flops remains constant, but the hits are making more money than ever. Of course, this good news can change in a moment's notice.

No two paths to Broadway are the same. Theatre people arrive from every state and nation. Some of them can't even afford a ticket to see a show, but they have hopes that they will work on Broadway. Once in New York City, many start their careers Off Broadway, Off-Off Broadway, and Off-Off-Off Broadway as crew, designers, actors, stage managers, and producers, quickly learning hard knocks and often spending their own money on a production to gain experience.

The old joke, "How do I get to Carnegie Hall? Practice, practice, practice," does not apply to Broadway. The audition process for all jobs on Broadway is a complex combination of what you know, who you know, timing, and luck. Once you get a job, there are no automatic promotions. Shows close and, in most cases, you're looking for your next job all over again.

The mission of this book is to inform those wishing to join the Broadway community about the people, the work, and the methods that somehow come together to produce great theatre, and at a livable wage.

The large available pool of extraordinary talents and experienced professionals gives Broadway the edge for artistic and financial success. It starts with an idea and a script, and then adds layer after layer of money, people, visionaries, and skilled labor. While all theatre aims high, only Broadway offers the possibility of large profits and guaranteed levels of compensation. The more the producers, investors, and talent know about each other, the easier it is to take advantage of the resources afforded each show.

The authors, Mitch Weiss and Perri Gaffney, are well aware that others may have a differing perspective on the value of unions, traditions, and salary levels. To that end, reader's corrections, opinions, and questions are welcome at the book's website where the authors will post updates on this ever-changing industry. Please join the discussion.

www.JustLearnSomething.us

Below are a few of Broadway's veterans. We asked them to tell us why working on Broadway surprises them, and why they stay. We leave you with their thoughts (in alphabetical order).

ISLAH ABDUL-RAHIIM
(Wardrobe/Puppet Department for 16 years on *The Lion King*, Wardrobe on *Rent, Bring in Da Noise/Bring in Da Funk*)

One thing that surprises me after almost twenty years working in wardrobe on Broadway is how often people (both those in attendance and onstage) fail to realize that there are many highly skilled, talented individuals working backstage as necessary components to the complete production. There is a general lack of knowledge of all of the career possibilities in theater and that the Broadway industry, in particular, relies on the efforts of *all* of those varied departments to mount and maintain a seamless show.

What amazes me is how an evening of theater can turn the most jaded adult into a total believer in the world presented onstage. I expect that sense of wonderment from a child, but it delights me when I see an adult release the stress of their day and allow themselves to be taken on a journey. I have experienced days of aggravation and frustration where I'm determined to get a job in any other field, but catching a glimpse of a transfixed adult become a five-year-old watching the elephant walk through the house (in *The Lion King*) can make me fall in love with theater all over again.

PETER BOGYO (General manager: *Love Letters, The Trip to Bountiful, Sly Fox, Time Stands Still, A Moon for the Misbegotten, Fortune's Fool, Voices in the Dark, Stick Fly;* **producer of special events and concerts:** *Anyone Can Whistle, Jubilee* **at Carnegie Hall)**

Even if there are only two actors, there is still an army of people behind the scenes involved in putting on a show. A Broadway show is a big, complex endeavor that requires tremendous coordination and communication. Once the initial capitalization has been raised, it is expensive to keep a show operating, and it is expensive to close one, too!

I had been a company manager, and now I sit in a very different seat as general manager. The longer I do this, the more I try to remind myself that, despite all the crises, all will somehow get solved, all will get done. On Broadway, you realize that you're dealing with the highest level of craftsmanship and professionalism in every department, with the most committed and successful people in the industry. You also learn that no matter how much you budget for advertising, someone will try to persuade you to spend more!

It is a privilege to be able to make one's living on Broadway. I still recall how thrilling it was to walk through a Broadway stage door for the first time, to feel like an insider allowed entrance into this magical world.

ADRIAN BRYAN-BROWN (Public relations and media marketing; Partner at Boneau/Bryan-Brown; ATPAM press representative on more than two hundred shows including *Jersey Boys*, *Monty Python's Spamalot*, *Art*, *Copenhagen*, and *Mamma Mia!*; Recipient of a special 2015 Tony Award)

I studied film at UCLA, but when I began working in New York, I fell into the theatre. My earliest Off Broadway clients as a press assistant, the Phoenix and Chelsea Theatres, are long gone. As a Broadway neophyte (on *A Taste of Honey* starring Amanda Plummer) I recognized that Broadway was the gold standard. No other group of people work so tirelessly and passionately.

Publicity has changed and we have to combat the perception that there are fewer editorial opportunities. I believe there's more with the culture shift to the web, which offers more opportunity to encourage greater dialog between the media, the ticket-buyer, and the production.

Other observations: Every show is different and needs a distinct campaign. The fun part is coming up with and implementing ideas that sell tickets. One of our key roles is to corral everyone connected with the show to be ambassadors through the press and social media. The job is never boring and the good and the bad part is that there is always something more to do.

DAVID CALHOUN (President of the Association of Theatrical Press Agents and Managers; company manager, house manager for nineteen years at Nederlander Theatres)

When I started working on Broadway, it seemed like a mom-and-pop business, with trust among the many players. Over the years the trust has faded a bit, as a somewhat impersonal corporate business model has become the new way of managing.

Early on, I learned to never define myself by the success of the show I was working on, or the theatre I worked in. That being said, I must confess that I did have a dream come true during the revival of *Follies* at the Marquis Theatre, when I got to meet Stephen Sondheim.

During one of my mother's frequent visits, we were talking about my working in the theatre and out of the blue she said, "You're doing what you always wanted to do." She was right. I just can't imagine not doing what I'm doing.

CHOCLATTJARED (Bucket drummer/onstage musician in *Bring in da Noise, Bring in da Funk*; dozens of major TV, movie, and concert credits, and also the Tony Awards)

I love what I do. The work gives me a rush and doing it on Broadway makes it even better because I started on Broadway, as in the street, right there in Times Square. I used to play outside the Ambassador Theatre and peeked inside every now and then when the door was open. Then to be playing *inside* the theatre, *me* on that stage—*that* was *amazing*!

Michael Jackson, Denzel Washington, Janet Jackson, Demi Moore, Luther Vandross—they came to see me backstage, and they thanked me for my work in the show. The support from everyone was surprising.

CHUCK COOPER (Actor: Tony Award winner for *The Life, Chicago, Caroline or Change, Amen Corner, Passion, Someone to Watch Over Me*, and more)

On the positive side, I have been surprised at how generous of heart, time, money, and spirit the Broadway community is in its charitable endeavors. I am amazed at the people I get to work with in the theater. And, I must say, I've been surprised every time I've been hired to do a Broadway show.

Theater people are the most intelligent, engaged, motivated, funny, and obviously entertaining people I have ever come into contact with. I've been equally surprised that talent is not a prerequisite for employment, and that a surprising number of the gatekeepers in the imagination business are woefully devoid of imagination. Very smart people can sometimes make the stupidest mistakes.

I am amazed that after thirty-eight years in show business and twelve Broadway shows on my resume, I still love what I do more than any thing I can think of and cannot begin to express my gratitude and honor in being called upon to do it.

LAWRENCE DARDEN (Shubert Organization Head Security at the Majestic Theatre with *The Phantom of the Opera* for over sixteen years; also *Miss Saigon* and *Cats*)

The longevity of this show is the biggest surprise. People come to NYC to see the Statue of Liberty, the Empire State Building, and *Phantom of the Opera.*

The many people from all over the world I have met over the years is amazing, and I've stayed in contact and developed relationships with many of them. It's a wonderful world and after I soon start collecting [social security], I still intend to work on Broadway.

TINA FABRIQUE (Actress: *Ragtime, Bring in Da Noise/Bring in Da Funk, Truly Blessed, The Gospel at Colonus,* and the revival of *How to Succeed in Business Without Really Trying*)

It is surprising to witness the power the Broadway medium possesses. Many actors have been involved in projects that never made it to the Broadway stage for one reason or another, and it wasn't because those projects weren't good. But there has to be a perfect "marriage" in someone's view of story, music, cast, director, costumes, set, lighting, sound, and relevance. When all of that comes together there is nothing more powerful. The excitement in the theatre is like contained electricity waiting to be unleashed and when audiences leap out of their seats in response—it is sheer joy!

**RICHARD FRANKEL (General manager and producer:
Hairspray, *The Producers*, Patti Lupone revival of *Gypsy*,
John Doyle revivals of *Sweeney Todd* and *Company*)**

My values were set in the Off Broadway nonprofit world, as the particular theatres I worked at (i.e. Circle Rep, Ensemble Studio Theatre) believed that the manager's function is to serve the artist. A big attraction for me has always been the family environment, in working as a unit. I've thought the camaraderie in theatres most akin to fire stations.

In many ways, producing on Broadway was much easier than nonprofits because, among other things, you have more money to solve problems.

When I first got to Broadway, I was prepared in that I knew I didn't know anything. Accumulating knowledge takes a long time. And I was thrilled and intimidated by how great everyone was at their jobs.

ARTHUR FRENCH (Actor: *Dividing the Estate, Ma Rainey's Black Bottom, The River Niger, The Iceman Cometh, All God's Chillun Got Wings, Poison Tree, Design for Living, Ain't Supposed to Die a Natural Death,* the revivals of *The Trip to Bountiful, Death of a Salesman,* and *You Can't Take it With You*)

Broadway is prestigious, it's a great credit, it helps your career, it pays well. People look at you differently. It opens doors. Wherever you go in the world, other countries, people know about Broadway. Working on Broadway legitimizes you. It's the standard.

There are more black characters now. There was a time when if a black person did a role in Shakespeare or Chekhov, they may have burned the theatre down. They may have called security if you didn't leave the audition for Shakespeare, which meant there is no role for you. Now we're allowed to do plays where the roles weren't written for a black character specifically. The opportunities are bigger now.

PERRI GAFFNEY
(Actress, playwright, novelist, co-author of this book)

My first Broadway show—*Timbuktu!*—was everything I thought it would be and more. It titillated all of my senses, captured my heart, and holds me to this day.

As a little girl, I remember planning to move to New York City to be a Broadway actress when I grew up. After watching Shirley Temple on television when I was about three or four years old, I would get up after her scene and do what I thought she should have done. Grownups would look at me and say, "She's a little actress!" I saw numerous productions at the Karamu House, the nation's oldest African American theatre, while growing up in Cleveland, Ohio. Live performances were enchanting. To me it was "real acting." If you're being filmed and you mess up they shoot it again, but if you mess up on stage, you have to fix it right then and there in character and not throw off the rest of the cast.

Most successful long-running Broadway shows are musicals. I can carry a tune, but I'm not a singer. I can move well, but I'm not a dancer. Still, there are always limited run dramas. I have not performed on a Broadway stage yet, and may never, but hope springs eternal like childhood dreams.

DEIDRE GOODWIN (Actor/Dancer/Singer: *Chita Rivera: The Dancer's Life, Never Gonna Dance,* **the revivals of** *Nine, The Boys from Syracuse, The Rocky Horror Show, Chicago* **(and the film),** *A Chorus Line,* **and** *Jesus Christ Superstar***)**

What amazes me about Broadway and theatre in general is how doing a show, just one performance, can touch someone's life. It may even be just one person but that could be the reason they decide to go into theatre, or give them a chance to laugh or cry, and potentially process something they are going through in their own life from a new perspective. Theatre and Art doesn't have to be a "hit" to have an impact.

Nothing about being on Broadway surprised me. It is/was as exciting, hard, magical, challenging, fun, sometimes disappointing, and fulfilling as I thought it would be. I am however interested to see how the process for new shows being developed for Broadway evolves. There will always be great storytellers and stories that need to be told. That being said, with so much competition from other Broadway shows, alternative and more affordable entertainment available, along with the ever rising amount of money that is needed not only to mount but to keep a show running, I am curious to see if and how the current model of producing and marketing Broadway shows changes to stay competitive without compromising the original vision of a show.

THOMAS GRASSO (Local One sound engineer for Radio City Christmas Spectacular (thirteen years), twenty Broadway shows including *Rock of Ages, Rent, Ma Rainey's Black Bottom, Spring Awakening*, recording artist and musician)

When I first arrived on Broadway, I assumed shows lasted as long as the audience kept coming. I was surprised when I first learned that shows sometimes close because the theatre has another show they want to bring in. I've also learned it's not always clear that winning an award or a good review will keep a show running. It's quite bizarre to read a fantastic review of the show you're working on after opening on Sunday, and come to work Tuesday to find a closing notice. It takes a specific type of individual to remain positive and productive in a business that often seems uncertain.

Broadway sound/audio are quite different than sound/audio in the world of recording. In the theatre, the whole creative staff has some input. There have been times when a stage manager has come to me to raise the volume of an instrument or particular voice, and the next day I receive the opposite note from the director. However, Broadway is the melting pot of the theatrical world. People study and hope to get here. It's amazing to see so many creative people in one place. It never gets boring, and it's great to love what you do.

241

© 2011 Lia Chang Photography

**DAVID HENRY HWANG (Tony Award–winning playwright;
M Butterfly, Chinglish, Disney's *Aida, Golden Child,* 2002
revision of *Flower Drum Song*)**

My experience is complicated by having had a personal play become such a
critical and commercial Broadway success (*M Butterfly*). What drives me is the
possibility that it may happen again. I like writing what is personal and having
the chance it will be commercial. Yet I do my best work when I divorce myself
from the notion of commercial success.

I originally thought that working on Broadway would be no different from
opening Off Broadway. My first Broadway show *M Butterfly* had a rough out-
of-town tryout that led to one producer bowing out. The other producer, Stuart
Ostrow, decided to bring the show into New York anyway, mortgaging his
house. There was no money for an opening night party. I quickly learned that
Broadway is a higher pressured situation compared to Off Broadway. Of course,
the rewards are greater and the visibility is huge.

ALBERT KIM (House manager for Jujamcyn Theaters)

A successful house manager needs empathy, not just patience, to provide the best possible guest experience. An effective house manager will invest in ensuring that the front-of-house team creates a consistently positive experience for theatregoers so they leave the theatre on a high, savoring not just the performance but their time in the theatre before the show, during intermission, and after the performance. That positive experience ultimately contributes to the success of the show.

When I first started on Broadway, I did not realize that I would be required to interact with people in so many departments, with, at times, divergent needs. One of the roles of the house manager is to be an effective liaison between the theatre owner and its employees, as well as the theatre makers connected with the show. The house manager must find a way to support all of them while listening to their concerns and finding effective solutions. Communication skills are essential.

For many people, going to a Broadway show often involves extensive planning, saving, and research. To then witness thousands of people each week coming through the doors to experience a live show is amazing and energizing.

**WOODIE KING, JR. (Director *Checkmates, Reggae*,
Co-Producer *For Colored Girls Who Have Considered
Suicide When the Rainbow is Enuf*; Founding producer of Off
Broadway's New Federal Theatre)**

It still amazes me to witness the many different voices writing about the African American experience, from George C. Wolfe and August Wilson to Suzi Lori Parks and Lynn Nottage. These voices are unique and so very different. I would be producing a black play on Broadway every season if money were not the problem.

I am amazed that many white audiences will not attend a play written by a black playwright, thus many theatre owners will not rent their theatres to a black play. However, that is not as true for black musicals. It is somewhat safe to see African Americans singing and dancing.

I am also surprised by our African American businessmen, many of whom collect vast troves of art and support Lincoln Center and Kennedy Center, but will not invest in a commercial play by an African American playwright aimed for Broadway.

What still thrills me about producing is standing at the rear of a theatre and seeing audiences standing, cheering, enjoying a piece of theatre art that I was instrumental in making happen.

HARRISON LEE (Actor: the Yul Brynner and Rudolf Nureyev revivals of _The King and I_, Patti LaBelle's production of _Your Arms Too Short to Box with God_)

As a chorus performer, working on Broadway is very different than performing on the road tour of a Broadway show. The backstage areas and dressing rooms at certain Broadway theatres are more cramped and not as accommodating as regional theatres tend to be. Yet here in NYC, when you walk to work, the energy of the street has no comparison. It's so much easier to find a dance class and that's important to anyone who wants to maintain their technique. A big difference is on tour, you often develop deep and lasting friendships because you hang out with your fellow cast members and crew while exploring strange towns; but in New York, we have our own lives and our own circle of friends, so you might only have a working relationship with your cast and crew.

Although they can't always afford to come, what a great feeling to have your friends see you on Broadway. It's very special for them and you. The producers rarely give the cast comps, but when they do it's usually on short notice, but you can always find two or twenty friends who will sometimes change their schedules to see a Broadway show!

And the audiences! There's nothing like a Broadway audience. They appreciate good theatre and they know who the theatre stars are, not just the TV and film stars. And there's nothing like the opening night party for a Broadway show! It's guaranteed that you'll see and/or meet Broadway royalty and several other celebrities.

JEFF LEE (Associate director/associate producer at Disney Theatrical Productions: *The Lion King, Tarzan, The Little Mermaid International*; **Production Stage Manager/Supervisor:** *Cats, A Chorus Line, The Pirates of Penzance, Joseph and the Amazing Technicolor Dreamcoat, Merlin, Shirley Valentine*; **freelance producer/director)**

No matter how good or how bad social or economic conditions get, Broadway sustains and continues to grow. That alone is amazing! A tribute to the value and resilience of our industry decade after decade.

Nothing about Broadway really tends to surprise me. For example, it's been interesting to note over the years how musicals tend to redefine themselves about every ten years, plus or minus. We've gone from the classic book/song musicals like *The King and I* and *Oklahoma* to concept musicals like *A Chorus Line* and *Chicago*. Broadway then got a bit lazy for a while, not really stepping forward with any new version of the art form we as a nation originated. This left the door open for the British Invasion to take over with pop/rock operas like *Jesus Christ Superstar, Cats,* and *Starlight Express*. Then came the "popsicles" (jukebox-themed) phase, and then the movie phase. I must say it's now terrific to see all of these forms living side by side on Broadway. It offers a healthy opportunity to appeal to a variety of audiences in a variety of ways, serving many distinctly different cultures, thereby lending support to the exploding global market our business has become.

I'm very happy to say that if I ever retire (doubtful), I'll have no regrets whatsoever. It's been a rich career of working alongside and learning from some of the most incredible people in our industry!

PAUL LIBIN (Vice-President of Jujamcyn Theaters; owner of Circle-in-the-Square Theatre; general manager, company manager, assistant stage manager, producer, and almost every other theatre job at one time or another)

The night I saw Arthur Miller's *Death of a Salesman* starring Thomas Mitchell as Willy Lowman was an overwhelming experience and it changed my life. Leaving the theatre, I saw Mitchell walk into the cold wintry night with his coat collar up and the brim of his hat pulled down. I realized that Willy Loman was alive and that is what I must do—act. Later that night, I announced to my mom and dad that I was going to be an actor. Off to New York to study acting at Columbia University. After three years of summer stock, I was drafted into the U.S. Army. During my two years in the Army I started a theatre group, changing my ambitions to producing and directing. With the G.I. bill, I finished Columbia University. My first job on Broadway was as a gofer for $40 a week and then as a stage manager on *Happy Hunting*, starring Ethel Merman. Then to Off Broadway where I met the late Theodore Mann and on a handshake created our partnership that lasted for fifty years: at Circle-in-the-Square, Off Broadway, later moving it to Broadway.

On Broadway, the scale is different. Many say Broadway is not what it used to be. It never was. It's always changing, how it's produced, its artists, playwrights, audiences. That's what makes it exciting. In 1990, I came to Jujamcyn Theaters. Doing different things each day is what energizes my life. Having an array of responsibilities in my career has been a great reward while working on two hundred fifty productions.

KAREN MASON (Actor: *Sunset Boulevard, Wonderland, Hairspray*, original company of *Mamma Mia!, Torch Song Trilogy, Play Me A Country Song*)

My first Broadway show was chaotic. It seems to me that you should make sure that the book of a new musical is the best it can be, even before you raise the money. We did complete rewrites during previews, and that shouldn't be the case. Previews are for adjustments, not overhauls.

The fact that Broadway is always changing is what keeps it fresh. It should never be stagnant. This year's hip-hop and Bollywood musicals are exciting options. Otherwise Broadway is a museum piece and I don't want it to be that.

Broadway is the pinnacle. People move to New York to be close to this pinnacle. Yet producers think they know how to make it better—even when they don't have the experience. They want it to be a business like other businesses, except you are also working with artists. That's what makes it a unique experience and one to be proud of.

One time I was a standby for the lead in a musical. There was no time set aside to rehearse me until four months after the show opened. Yet I was responsible for taking over the lead, so I hired my own coach to work with me at my own expense. It's moments like this that surprise me.

CHRISTOPHER NASS (IATSE and Local One stagehand on *Mamma Mia!, Sweeney Todd, Ballroom, Dreamgirls, A Chorus Line, Sunset Boulevard, Sunday in the Park with George, Into the Woods, The Grapes of Wrath*)

Producers and designers ask a lot. And no matter how many years you prove yourself working with the same production team, you are still blamed for all the overruns. But all of the chaos somehow melds together and the first time the audience goes crazy, it gets to me all over again. You say to yourself, "Maybe it does matter."

My dad was a musician at the Metropolitan Opera. For my early theatre jobs, he would ask Met technicians to help me and let me borrow tools. At one point, they suggested that I take a union test and two weeks later, I had a training job. My dad expected me to be a lawyer! The Broadway show *Working* was my first gig and it was magical. I worked at the Feller Precision shop where we built the automation that I then ran at the theatre.

There were many design changes requiring repainting at the theatre from midnight to 8:00 in the morning. The big Broadway surprise for me was the hours I had to work. The second surprise was seeing the check for all of those worked hours. After that, you get hooked to the job.

NANCY PICCIONE (Director of Casting at Manhattan Theatre Club including *Proof, Time Stands Still, Venus in Fur*, and productions at MTC's Friedman Theatre)

There is no BFA in casting. The Casting Society of America (CSA) is a union for film and television only right now. Hopefully that will change and include theatre casting directors. I like how casting straddles the artistic and the administrative sides of theatre.

I admire the talent I meet and work with. If I can find talented young actors, I want to help them.

Working in both the Off Broadway and Broadway arenas, on Broadway the actors are Tony Award eligible, which is an attractive benefit.

Actors will tell you that the most satisfying kind of work is the stage. And with high production costs, we need to find stars whenever possible. Working on Broadway makes it easier than Off Broadway to find name actors. The limited time commitment of twelve to sixteen weeks in our Broadway theatre is do-able for most stars.

Satisfying a director's vision of the right actor is not always easy. It's even more difficult for new works, like Sisyphus pushing a boulder up the mountain. Luckily, MTC's high level of playwriting attracts stars.

RON RAINES (Actor: Tony nominee for the revival of *Follies*; also seen in *Newsies, Annie, Chicago, Show Boat*; three time Emmy nominee for *Guiding Light*; Grammy nominee for *Follies*)

There is tremendous discipline required for principal actors in a Broadway show. As a singing actor, I have to take care of my voice, which involves periods of vocal silence. Mary Martin said, "Hell is a long Broadway run." She meant that a long period of performing eight shows a week means you never get to catch up with your personal life.

The performer's passion is work that feeds the soul, one's existence, and also pays the bills. What else could I have done? My desire always was to do good work and make a living. There was no other career for me.

CHRISTOPER RECKER
(Company manager: *The Lion King, Spring Awakening*)

What surprises me most about the Broadway community is how interconnected those who work in the industry become. Even when going from job to job, you hear the same names. You see the same faces. I vividly recall my first day as assistant company manager for *Spring Awakening*. I was mortified. It was all new to me. Would people like me? Could I do the job? Could I handle the constant pressures of a new show? But the people surrounding me took me in as one of their own. Immediately. There was an awareness that we all needed each other to make that show happen. We shared pain, and we shared joy. And suddenly my "team" transformed into "family." Some of that family never leaves you. And when you keep having those great (and some not-so-great) experiences, that family grows and morphs. I can happily say that the bloodline of my Broadway family doesn't just exist in one theatre with one company but extends into many theatres down the Great White Way.

I may have occasionally been envious of those onstage, but that was the younger version of me. Now, I'm constantly reminded of my fortunate reality. I regularly have "pinch me" moments as I beeline through Times Square to get to my theatre. I look up at the lights. My show's logo is plastered on billboards and video screens. I smile knowing that my sixteen-year-old farm boy self could never have imagined this.

BOB REILLY (Forty years as stage manager, company manager, house manager, and general manager)

When I first started, I thought the hardest part of my job would be dealing with the unions. By working with them, they will always give you the best solutions easier and cheaper. I've always been able to bring the parties to the table.

I smile going to work every day. Sometimes you see people on the street years later and there's still a wonderful camaraderie.

Each season brings something new. It gladdens my heart to see amazing talents still producing such good work year after year.

JANICE RODRIGUEZ (Head usher at the Al Hirschfeld, August Wilson, and Circle in the Square Theatres)

I have a passion for being around the theatre, and the people who are around theatre. I had no particular expectations about Broadway. My mother was a lady's garment worker and an usher too. One day she brought me to the theatre, gave me $3.00, put a white collar on me and told me to "stand here." The show was *Oh, Calcutta*. I was raised in Catholic school so when the actors dropped their towels, I ran to the bathrooms.

At the theatre, I like to help patrons with wheelchairs, walkers, and crutches. I'm surprised that people can be rude to people with disabilities. There are ushers who are here for the extra dollars, but most never ask about the pay when they are hired.

For most of us, this is a second job. I have a degree in early childhood education and worked at the Hudson Guild for forty years. I play piano and paint.

In this job, I meet people from all over the world. I'm blown away by it.

COUNT STOVALL (Actor: *Cat on a Hot Tin Roof, Streetcar Named Desire, Driving Miss Daisy, Philadelphia Story, Inacent Black*)

Money was never the major reason for working in theatre, any theatre. It's the challenge and the pride you get from doing quality work. Broadway is the penultimate of achievement. There is a prestige that says you're doing the most that your artistry has to offer. It's the top of the mark.

There's also a family feel to it; there's no lack of love. All the other Broadway shows welcome your production, there are discounts at Sardi's, and you can go to the openings of the other Broadway shows. When a show closes, everybody feels bad. And when Audra McDonald wins another Tony, we all win! You are a part of something much, much bigger than yourself. It's Americana. When I was going on for James Earl Jones in *Cat on a Hot Tin Roof*, there was so much anticipation in the wings by everyone, like a baby about to be born. It's that kind of tradition and pride you take in the privilege you have been endowed with to uphold the people that came before, and on whose shoulders we stand: Lena Horne, Bojangles, Sissle and Blake, Paul Robeson, and so many more.

I was used to working with a variety of races in the US Army, at UC Berkeley, and at the American Conservatory Theater, but the racial divisions in American theatre was a surprise and although we have quite a bit of nontraditional casting, black and white shows still exist.

MITCH WEISS (General manager (*Golden Child*), company manager (*A Chorus Line, The Grapes of Wrath*), house manager sub (Nederlander, Shubert, Jujamcyn, Helen Hayes theatres), assistant press rep (*Pacific Overtures*), co-author of this book)

Having worked with stock, Off Broadway, nonprofits, and regional theatres on wonderful productions, I never expected to experience the level of pride I feel being a part of the Broadway community. When creating theatre or any art form, high standards are vital. Those who think their community shows are of high quality have no idea what standards are possible until they see a few Broadway shows.

I also never expected the enormous number of "crises of consequence" that arise every day. If I start a day with three tasks, new demands take over and often none of the original tasks are accomplished. Since the show must go on eight times a week, prioritizing activities becomes essential. There are so many people who need answers and approvals to do their jobs and spend money, that management is truly command central. Each management office has a different personality too. Very exciting and full of stress, much more than I would ever have expected.

The greatest part of being in management is that you know about everyone working on the show—illnesses, pregnancies, family, wardrobe issues, special talents, and impending retirements. The greatest part of doing the job on Broadway is getting to work alongside so many geniuses and hopefuls alike, and learning from the absolute best in theatre. The result is almost always a great production, even if the show is a financial bomb. There is no better experience than entering a Broadway stage door on a daily basis.

STEPHEN TYRONE WILLIAMS (Actor: *Lucky Guy*)

I remember the first day of rehearsals for my Broadway debut, *Lucky Guy*, directed by George C. Wolfe. When I left Alabama after college in 2005 for NYC, it was my goal to one day work with George C. Wolfe, to walk the boards on Broadway.

The first day of rehearsals for my Broadway debut was surreal. My dream was literally coming true, and I was nervous. I remember walking into the rehearsal space. I was the new kid on the first day of school. I made a beeline for the Danishes to eat my feelings. The funny thing about dreaming is I had become accustomed to the space of struggling to make that dream come true. I had not given thought of what I would do, how I would take it, if my dream actually came true; I was unprepared for the challenge of "showing up" once my dream came true.

Then Tom Hanks approaches me and says, "Stephen, I'm so glad you're a part of this cast." "Thanks Mr. Hanks," I say. "Call me Tom," the two-time Oscar winner tells me, "This is going to be great." Courtney B. Vance took me under his wing. He had made his Broadway debut twenty-seven years earlier on the same stage in August Wilson's *Fences*. Courtney told me my obligation was like his: there were people who mentored and guided him and it was his obligation to do the same for me on the condition I pay it forward to the next person.

257

From the beginning of the process, director George C. Wolfe made special efforts to let us all know there were no egos or stars. "It will be the illusion of a democracy," he joked.

After the first show, I got out of costume, said my good-byes, and exited the stage door expecting an empty street. Instead, it was pandemonium: police barricades, mounted officers, all of 45th Street completely congested with fans waiting to meet this cast full of stars, this cast full of people I consider my friends.

Now that you know more about the Broadway community and how it operates, we hope to welcome you on Broadway, backstage, onstage, in marketing, producing, investing, or the audience.

APPENDIX

RESOURCES, MATERIALS, AND WEBSITES

Below are websites, books, organizations, and other resources that work with the Broadway community. If you wish to add valuable resources for the Broadway community, please write to us by joining our online community at www. JustLearnSomething.us. This is a great place to share information among all of us with something to offer each other.

Theatrical Index. Published weekly and sold individually for just under $20 each at the Drama Book Store. It lists what shows are on Broadway and who is working on them. It also tells you shows that are planned and who is producing them. Most Broadway offices have weekly or monthly subscriptions to *Theatrical Index.*

Drama Book Store. Located at 250 West 40th Street between 7th and 8th Avenues, this is the only bookstore remaining in New York dedicated to books, scripts, newspapers, magazines, DVDs, and professional resource materials for theatre professionals and hopefuls.

Playbill Online. www.playbill.com. Up to the minute Broadway gossip and a good source of entry level job openings without any cost.

Backstage **newspaper.** Basically a casting publication with some technical job offers as well. *Backstage* has many interesting articles about theatre and reviews of a wide range of New York shows, but without concentrating on the Broadway community.

Theatre Development Fund (TDF). www.tdf.org. To the public, TDF means discounted tickets to Broadway shows through the famous TKTS booth located in Times Square on West 47th Street and Broadway where unsold tickets for the current day's shows are offered for 40 percent or 50 percent off (plus surcharge). TDF has additional TKTS booths near Wall Street and in Brooklyn. TDF is also a membership organization for audiences willing to take a chance on new shows needing an audience at the beginning of their run. Shows must submit scripts weeks ahead and have a valid reason to receive this support. For example, a serious play without a celebrity in the cast may need a larger audience while making changes during previews. For these shows, TDF sells a limited number of very low-cost tickets and provides financial support to counter the inevitable weekly box office losses before the glowing reviews turn the show into a hit. TDF's education projects include the Commercial Theatre Institute (co-sponsored with The Broadway League): commercialtheatreinstitute.com.

Theatre Communications Group (TCG). www.tcg.org. TCG is an association of nonprofit theatres across America and has almost nothing to do with Broadway. Their ArtSearch job listings are perhaps the most comprehensive listings for regional and stock theatres and their *American Theatre Magazine* has wonderful articles about these theatre companies.

The New York Times. Still the most influential listing of Broadway shows, along with some interesting articles and gossip every now and then. Online and in printed form. www.nytimes.com

On Stage. On NY1-TV, Time-Warner Cable's twenty-four-hour news station only seen in NYC. This is a half-hour weekend television show dedicated to the New York theatre. *On Stage* airs at five different times from Saturday morning to Monday evening.

The Broadway League. www.broadwayleague.com. The association of Broadway producers and theatre owners from which union contracts are negotiated and theatre services, research, and marketing are sponsored.

The Broadway League Resource Guide. An online searchable source of theatrical booking agencies, production supervisors, press agents, trucking companies, etc. An annual subscription is available at http://www.broadwayleague.com/resource-guide/.

American Theatre Wing. Mostly known as the producer of the Tony Awards, but a wonderful educational organization sponsoring programs that contribute to the theatre community. ATW-related websites include:

broadwayfanclub.com   stagespecs.org
kidsnightonbroadway.com   tonyawards.com
broadway.org

Lincoln Center Library for the Performing Arts, West 66th Street between Broadway and Amsterdam Avenue (10th Avenue). Exhibits and an amazingly large collection of books, music, scripts, posters, costumes, and more preserve the rich history of Broadway and the professional theatre world.

Lincoln Center Theater on Film and Tape Archives, in the Library for the Performing Arts, 40 Lincoln Center Plaza, 3rd Floor, 212-870-1642. One-camera shoots of many Broadway shows since 1970 are housed here, available for viewing by theatre students, researchers, and other professionals with a specific purpose, and a Library access card.

IBDB.com (Internet Broadway Database). Official database for Broadway information including box office grosses, theatre history, etc.

Miscellaneous Broadway news, chats, gossip and jobs: the titles tell it all:

BroadwayWorld.com
Broadway.com
backstagejobs.com
allthatchat.com
theatremania.com
broadwaystars.com

livebroadway.com
talkinbroadway.com
americantheaterweb.com
artsjournal.com
broadwaybriefing.com

Broadway theatre history:
www.newyork.com/resources/broadway-and-theater-history/

Theatre Management written by David M. Conte and Stephen Langley, a comprehensive look at producing and managing theatre in America.

Theatre World Books is the only annual pictorial and statistical record of American theatre in print publication and includes comprehensive Broadway data since 1945. It includes Off Broadway and regional theatres as well as obituaries.

Casting for professional actors:
actorsequity.org/CastingCall/castingcallhome.asp
Chiff.com
Call Sheet by Backstage (formerly Ross Report):
http://www.dramabookshop.com/call-sheet-formerly-ross-report

Diversity on Broadway: Minority shows, actors and participation
Actors' Equity Association's Diversity Program: actorsequity.org, go to contact page
    or call 212-869-8530
Hispanic Organization of Latino Actors: hellohola.org
Alliance for Inclusion in the Arts: inclusioninthearts.org
Asian American Arts Alliance: aaartsalliance.org
Association of Hispanic Arts: latinoarts.org
Black Theatre Network: blacktheatrenetwork.org
Asian American Performers Action Coalition (AAPAC): aapacnyc.org

Charity and Assistance:
Broadway Cares / Equity Fights AIDS, 165 W. 46 St. #1300, NYC 10036, 212-840-
    0770, info@broadwaycares.org
The Actors Fund, 729 Seventh Ave. 10th Floor, New York, N.Y. 10019, 800-221-
    7303, info@actorsfund.org, (in Los Angeles: 888-825-0911)
Career Transitions for Dancers, 165 West 46th St. #701, New York, N.Y. 10036,
    212-764-0172, info@careertransition.org

Support for Broadway and Beyond:
International Theatre Institute: iti-worldwide.org
League of Resident Theatres: lort.org
National Endowment for the Arts: nea.gov
New York City Arts and Education Roundtable: nycaieroundtable.org
New York City Department of Cultural Affairs: nyc.gov/html/dcla/home.html
New York City Mayors Office of Film, TV and Theatre: nyc.gov/film
New York Foundation for the Arts: nyfa.org
Volunteer Lawyers for the Arts: vlany.org
Alliance of Resident Theatres/New York (ART/NY): offbroadwayonline.com
Americans for the Arts: artsusa.org
New York Foundation for the Arts: nyfa.org
Broadway Green Alliance: BroadwayGreen.com

Location for all forty Broadway theatres (block by block from south to north):
West 41th Street between 7th & 8th Avenues: Nederlander Theatre
West 42nd Street between 7th & 8th Avenues: New Amsterdam Theatre, American
    Airlines Theatre, Lyric Theatre (Lyric is also accessible from West 43rd Street)
West 43rd Street between 6th & 7th Avenues: Stephen Sondheim Theatre
West 44th Street between 6th & 7th Avenues: Belasco Theatre
West 44th Street between 7th & 8th Avenues: Shubert Theatre, Broadhurst Theatre,
    Majestic Theatre, St. James Theatre, Helen Hayes Theatre
West 45th Street between 6th & 7th Avenues: Lyceum Theatre
West 45th Street between 7th & 8th Avenues: Booth Theatre, Gerald Schoenfeld
    Theatre, Bernard B. Jacobs Theatre, John Golden Theatre, Imperial Theatre, Music
    Box Theatre, Minskoff Theatre (Minskoff is also accessible from West 44th Street)
West 45th Street between 8th & 9th Avenues: Al Hirschfeld Theatre
West 46th Street between 7th & 8th Avenues: Lunt-Fontanne Theatre, Marquis
    Theatre, Richard Rodgers Theatre
West 47th Street on Seventh Avenue: Palace Theatre
West 47th Street between 7th & 8th Avenues: Ethel Barrymore Theatre, Samuel J.
    Friedman Theatre, Brooks Atkinson Theatre
West 48th Street between 6th & 7th Avenues: Cort Theatre
West 48th Street between 7th & 8th Avenues: Longacre Theatre, Walter Kerr
    Theatre
West 49th Street between 7th & 8th Avenues: Eugene O'Neill Theatre, Ambassador
    Theatre
West 50th Street between 7th & 8th Avenues: Circle in the Square Theatre,
    Gershwin Theatre (Gershwin is also accessible from West 51st Street)
Broadway between West 50th & 51st Streets: Winter Garden Theatre
West 52nd Street between 8th & 9th Avenues: Neil Simon Theatre, August Wilson
    Theatre
West 53rd Street at Broadway: Broadway Theatre
West 54th Street between 8th & 9th Avenues: Studio 54 Theatre
West 65th Street within the Lincoln Center complex between Broadway &
    Amsterdam Avenue (10th Avenue): Vivian Beaumont Theater

AUTHORS' BIOGRAPHIES

Mitch Weiss has thirty-five years of management experience in theatre and music. He has managed over 180 Broadway and Off Broadway shows including Tony Award–winners *A Chorus Line*, *The Grapes of Wrath*, and *Beauty and the Beast*, and has also held senior management positions at Disney Theatricals International, New York Shakespeare Festival, Barrington Stage Company, and Big Apple Circus.

Mr. Weiss has served on the Board of Broadway's Association of Theatrical Press Agents and Managers and has been a certified ATPAM manager since 1985. He has been an adjunct professor at NYU's School of Professional Studies for over a decade and mentors future arts administrators and creative artists through his classes at www.JustLearnSomething.us.

Additionally, he is the co-author of *Managing Artists in Pop Music* with Ms. Gaffney (Allworth Press), now in its second edition, based on his years of management for music, sports, and Broadway artists. A graduate of Oberlin College, Mr. Weiss has been a consultant, speaker, director, musical director, composer/lyricist, and producer of a wide variety of shows and events through his New York–based production and management company MW Entertainment Group.

Perri Gaffney adapted her debut novel, *The Resurrection of Alice*, into a one-woman play that won the 2014 African American Arts Alliance of Chicago Outstanding Actress Award and the 2014 Black Theater Alliance's Best Lead Actress Award (Chicago). *The Resurrection of Alice* has received many nominations including the 2014 Black Theater Alliance's Best Play and Best Playwright Award categories, a 2014 Helen Hayes Award for Outstanding Lead Actress, Visiting Production (Washington, DC), and Best Solo Performance by the Audelco Awards in 2010 and 2012 (New York City). Perri wrote and performs *Josephine*, a multimedia monodrama based on the life of Josephine Baker. She wrote and narrates *C2EA: The Campaign to End AIDS*, a feature-length documentary.

Ms. Gaffney is a freelance contributor to *Routes: A Guide to African American Art and Culture*, an online publication (routes-mag.com). She wrote *The Substitute*, a compilation of short stories, has written numerous other plays, and has been commissioned to write several poems including *Something Marvtastic* (a memorial poem for Larry Leon Hamlin, founder of the National Black Theatre Festival) and *Kickin' It With My Girl Friends* (a celebration for the Ohio Chapter of Girl Friends, Inc.). Ms. Gaffney lives in New York City.

INDEX